OTHER BOOKS FROM MOOSEWOOD RESTAURANT:

New Recipes from Moosewood Restaurant
Sundays at Moosewood Restaurant
The Moosewood Restaurant Kitchen Garden

MOOSEWOOD RESTAURANT
COOKS at HOME
Fast and Easy Recipes for Any Day

THE MOOSEWOOD
COLLECTIVE

A FIRESIDE BOOK

PUBLISHED BY SIMON & SCHUSTER

NEW YORK LONDON TORONTO SYDNEY TOKYO SINGAPORE

Contributors to this book include Laura Ward Branca, Linda Dickinson, Susan Harville, David Hirsch, Nancy Lazarus, Eliana Parra, Sara Wade Robbins, Wynelle Stein, Maureen Vivino, Tommy Walls, and Kip Wilcox.

SIMON & SCHUSTER / FIRESIDE
Rockefeller Center
1230 Avenue of the Americas
New York, New York 10020

ART DIRECTION BY BONNI LEON

DESIGNED BY CAROL HARALSON

ILLUSTRATIONS BY GIL ADAMS

Manufactured in the United States of America
10 9 8 7 6 5 4 3 2 1
10 9 8 7 6 5 4 3 2 1 PBK
Library of Congress Cataloging-in-Publication Data
Moosewood Restaurant cooks at home : fast and easy recipes for any day / the Moosewood Collective.
p   cm.
"A Fireside book."
1. Vegetarian cookery.   2. Cookery (Natural foods)   3. Moosewood Restaurant.   I. Moosewood Restaurant.
II. Moosewood Collective.
TX837.M674   1994

641.5'636—dc20   93-39126

CIP
ISBN 0-671-87954-5
0-671-67992-9 PBK

This book is dedicated to our hardworking parents,
who somehow found the time.

ACKNOWLEDGMENTS

As always, we give our fondest acknowledgments to our literary agents, Elise and Arnold Goodman, for their long-term encouragement and enduring support.

The Moosewood Collective is grateful to Sydny Weinberg Miner, our enthusiastic editor, for her professionalism, leadership, and intelligent good humor.

We praise Bonni Leon and Carol Haralson for their inspired artistry, impeccable craftwork, and constant patience.

We give well-deserved thanks to John E. Alexander, President of the CBORD Group, Inc., Ithaca, New York, for his generous assistance. He made his company's services available to us, to provide the nutritional analyses for this book. This is just one application out of hundreds provided by their software, which specializes in the management of food and nutrition services. The analyses were performed by CBORD's Department of Database Services, managed by Laura B. Winter, R.D., and assisted by Katherine Isacks. We appreciate their expertise and guidance. Special thanks to Jude Tulla for getting us together.

Contents

Introduction

From the customers in Moosewood Restaurant, the students in our cooking classes, the readers of our previous cookbooks, our friends, and our own experiences, we know that most of us face two strong and seemingly contradictory needs: a longing for relaxed, interesting, and meaningful dining and the necessity of slapping dinner on the table in short order.

Like everyone else, each of us at Moosewood juggles work, home, family, social life, and other interests. We hustle all day, trying to accomplish the things we must do, hoping to create a spare moment for what we'd like to do, arranging our schedules to connect with the people we'd like to do them with. However, we do have a certain edge at suppertime because we have learned to cook "under fire" at the restaurant. Making a good dinner quickly at home on Tuesday is small potatoes compared to preparing entrées on a busy Saturday night in Moosewood's small action-packed, pressure-cooker kitchen. Also, we are constantly sharing our ideas and experiences and combining and compiling our knowledge so that it can be of use to everyone. Eighteen heads *are* better than one for some tasks.

But even with experience and numbers on our side, we haven't been able to discover any single solution or magical technique for a workweek cuisine. Frankly, we don't think there is one. However (drumroll, please), we have been able to collectively figure out a lot of little solutions. The combination of carefully honed and tested recipes, tasty ingredients, time-saving tricks, and planning suggestions can all add up to a delightful whole-foods cuisine that is quick and easy.

There is empowerment and satisfaction in providing this basic need. You could buy the kids a so-so pizza for dinner and then complain about the price and wonder about the nutritional value. But you might realize that rather than saving time and energy, you actually spent a frazzled half hour arguing about how many video games your children could play while you waited in line. Wouldn't you prefer the kids to remember that *you* made great pizza (10 or 15 minutes preparation time, see pages 274–81), that your kitchen smelled wonderful, and that you somehow found the time to provide this gift?

We usually consider it time well spent, even if a dinner entrée requires 45 minutes to prepare (the longest time in this book—most take 30 minutes or less). The hands-on preparation time is often much less than the total time. (You get an extra 15 or 20 minutes to play with the dog.) Spend 10 or 15 minutes after dinner or in the morning putting together a dish that needs to chill or that can be popped into the oven the next evening. When you can't wait 30 or 40 minutes to eat, look for the many very quick last-minute recipes in this book. The truth is that the best reason to prepare meals faster is so that there is more time to spend lingering at the table, enjoying life.

The food at Moosewood has always derived from an ethnic home-style tradition—"peasant food," created by hardworking people who cooked for themselves using minimal equipment, fresh foods, and simple cooking methods. We have found many dishes among these classics that serve our own needs.

We've been careful not to sacrifice quality as we've sought out the fastest and most versatile dishes. We've sometimes simplified traditional dishes by using fewer ingredients or have substituted ingredients that were more readily available or faster-cooking. Often we've experimented with quicker or more healthful cooking methods. We've researched and given our advice on some convenience products (there *are* some we can recommend), and we've provided plenty of other shopping tips.

You'll find suggestions in this book for organizing your work, preparing food ahead of time, double-purpose cooking, and the creative use of leftovers. We indicate appropriate substitutions for ingredients and often give variations of a recipe, so that you can have more flexibility. We offer a host of menu-planning ideas that can save you a tremendous amount of time and effort. We discuss the aesthetics and logistics of combining dishes, and give a step-by-step walk-through of some sample menus. We'll show you how a well-stocked pantry can be your most valuable asset when you need to throw together a last-minute meal, and we've included shopping tips and information on storing food.

All of this extra advice adds more text to the simple procedure for the recipe, so we arranged the information on the page to make each recipe easy to read and follow. We've tested and retested the recipes, and we believe that our instructions will direct you toward maximum efficiency and minimum cleanup.

At Moosewood we continue to place an ever greater importance on the healthful value of foods. The new USDA Food Guide Pyramid validates the health benefits of a low-fat vegetarian diet. The broad base of the pyramid is composed of a balance of grains, vegetables, and fruits with only the small tip formed by dairy foods, eggs, fish, fats, and sweets. This rather accurately describes most of the world's ancient starch-based ethnic cuisines, which have been our inspiration all along.

We know that many of you are concerned with the nutritional aspect of cooking, so we've included a nutritional analysis at the end of each recipe. On pages 17–18, you'll find more detailed information on the food pyramid, nutritional analysis, and some easy-to-use formulas for culinary computations, particularly for determining recommended percentages of dietary fat.

Healthful eating has become a fashionable choice, and so the goals of a nutritious vegetarian diet and gourmet dining have drawn much closer. In many ways, maintaining a meatless diet is much easier now than it once seemed. For one thing, it's no longer considered weird to eat this way. Supermarkets are exploding with previously unfamiliar vegetables, exotic fruits, fresh herbs, and a large variety of recently rediscovered grains and beans. It's not hard to find whole-grain breads and good Italian pastas. Pestos and salsas, fresh mozzarella and goat cheeses, are no longer found only in "gourmet" or ethnic markets. All of this bounty is an inspiration to honor the fresh and simple.

We admit that years ago we overcompensated for the lack of meat on the menu at Moosewood Restaurant by using cheese and other rich dairy products in almost every casserole, but no longer. Our tastes have evolved toward a simpler, lighter, and more vital style of food. Now we prefer a bold, fresh salsa, to a rich, complex sauce. We try to use fewer ingredients in order to highlight the natural flavors of the good basic foodstuffs. We enjoy our foods served closer to their natural state—we do less to them. Of course, this type of cooking demands that the ingredients be in peak condition, and we find it worthwhile to shop for local organically grown produce and other food products with little or no preservatives.

Our ideas about what can constitute a meal have changed, too. Although it's certainly important that foods served together be in harmony and balance, we find that we're easing away from a strict adherence to the model of a series of courses or a central main dish complemented by "sides." We might mix-and-match several side dishes served all at once for a more relaxed spread. Sometimes we like the appetizer so much that we make a meal of it. Almost anything goes.

The recipes in this book can be incorporated into your routine with very little effort. A recent study revealed that the average American home cook has a repertoire of only ten dishes. If you were using only ten recipes regularly and you find another ten here to add to your repertoire, you'll have doubled your enjoyment and added variety to an important daily event.

A thoughtfully planned, carefully prepared meal is not only a pleasure to consume, it forges a bond between those who share it, connects us to the earth, and enriches our experience. We need the communion, the home-place rituals, where one is nourished and given a sense of place in the world.

The rewards of cooking wholesome, delicious food at home are self-evident. There is great potential for pleasure in creatively nurturing oneself and others. Even the humblest foods are capable of providing transcendent moments of beauty and well-being. In the kitchen, stepping out of the busy fray, one has the sense of being truly home.

About Time

To help you plan ahead, we indicate the preparation and/or total time required for each recipe. Preparation time is actual hands-on time—the time when you probably can't do anything else. Total time is figured from the moment you stand in your kitchen tying your apron, ready to begin, until the dish is ready to eat.

These times can be only approximate guides, of course. There will be variations in stovetops, in oven temperature, in knife sharpness, and in how well equipped you are with time-saving gadgets. Even the temperature of the raw ingredients can make a significant difference. Then there is the matter of how well you've organized your kitchen. How quickly can you find your nutmeg grater? Are you sure you have chili oil? Is the sink still full of last night's dirty dishes? Where *is* that colander? We can't begin to account for all the differences in personal style.

We did not include extra time for phone calls, refreshing your makeup before dinner, checking the sump pump, or chasing your toddler. But we did test and retest and test again each recipe in our own homes, which we suspect are fairly typical in terms of dinner-hour distractions. Despite these limitations, we hope that the times given will serve as a useful guide.

As you become familiar with the recipes, you'll probably feel no need to measure each ¼ teaspoon of thyme or cup of chopped onions. Experience begets a more relaxed attitude. Cooking will become looser, easier, more creative, and as an extra bonus, faster.

About Nutritional Analysis

Things have changed in the twenty years that Moosewood Restaurant has been around—and not just us growing older and wiser. For one thing, we are increasingly concerned about the nutritional values of foods, and we know that many of you are paying attention to this also. Although the science of nutrition is constantly evolving, the body of knowledge on this topic has grown enormously.

In this book, each recipe is analyzed for calories, proteins, fats, carbohydrates, sodium, and cholesterol. The number of servings given at the top of each recipe is based on our own honest, but often generous, assessment. In the nutritional analysis at the bottom of the page, the portions are given in clearly specified amounts based on industry standards.

Calories are units for measuring the energy produced by food when oxidized in the body. All foods have calories, but not all calories are created equal. Calories are found in three primary sources: proteins, carbohydrates, and fats. It is best to consume more calories from carbohydrates and fewer from fats, which contain a greater concentration of calories in much less bulk and are much harder for the body to metabolize.

Proteins are found not only in animal products like eggs and cheese but also in grains, beans and bean products, and nuts. We need protein each day because our bodies can store only small amounts, but most Americans routinely take in at least 1½ times as much as their bodies need. Creating complete proteins by combining proteins from vegetable sources alone, such as rice and tofu, or corn and beans, can occur over the course of several days rather than in each dish.

Fats have recently been the focus of our nutritional concerns, which is legitimate because while fat is a naturally occurring substance that is necessary for life, reducing fat in the diet can help reduce the risk of many life-threatening diseases. Most experts recommend limiting dietary fat intake to 30 percent of calories. This may be decreased further in the future as an increasing number of health professionals today suggest a fat intake of 20 percent or even lower as optimum.

All fats contain about 9 calories per gram (approximately 120 calories per tablespoon), which is more than twice as many calories as contained in equal amounts of proteins or carbohydrates. To figure the percent of fats in a food, multiply the number of grams of fat by 9 (number of calories in the fat) and then divide that number by the total number of calories.

To figure approximately how many grams of fat consumption per day is right for you, just divide your ideal weight in half. In other words, a moderately active person who wishes to maintain a weight of 140 pounds should limit fat consumption to 70 grams.

Carbohydrates contain 4 calories per gram, the same as proteins. However, our bodies derive energy from the starches and sugars of carbohydrates in a more efficient way. As seen in the Food Pyramid on the following page, the complex carbohydrates found in grains, fruits, and vegetables are the basis of a healthful diet—not just side dishes anymore. Hurrah for pasta!

Sodium is found naturally in many foods, particularly in animal products, in ample quantities. Sodium is added to many processed foods in excessive proportions. Experts recommend that we maintain sodium consumption below 4,000 milligrams per day. Sodium is an important electrolyte in our bodies, but some people have problems with too much salt in their diet. We recommend you use salt only in moderation. Added salt is usually optional in our recipes.

The USDA's Eating Right Pyramid offers an easily understood and graphic guideline for promoting more healthful eating patterns:

Food Guide Pyramid

A Guide to Daily Food Choices

KEY   **F** = Fat (naturally occurring and added)   **S** = Sugars (added)

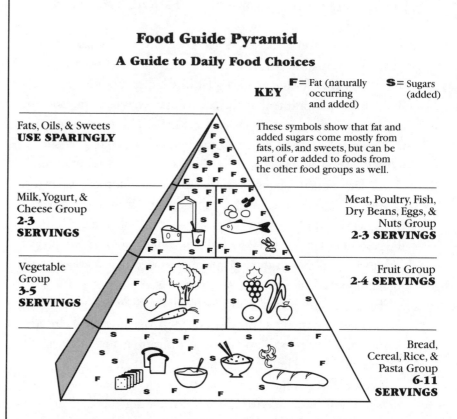

Fats, Oils, & Sweets
USE SPARINGLY

These symbols show that fat and added sugars come mostly from fats, oils, and sweets, but can be part of or added to foods from the other food groups as well.

Milk, Yogurt, & Cheese Group
2-3 SERVINGS

Meat, Poultry, Fish, Dry Beans, Eggs, & Nuts Group
2-3 SERVINGS

Vegetable Group
3-5 SERVINGS

Fruit Group
2-4 SERVINGS

Bread, Cereal, Rice, & Pasta Group
6-11 SERVINGS

SOURCE: U.S. Department of Agriculture / U.S. Department of Health and Human Services

Use the Food Guide Pyramid to help you eat better every day . . . the Dietary Guidelines way. Start with plenty of Breads, Cereals, Rice, and Pasta; Vegetable, and Fruits. Add two to three servings from the Milk group and two to three servings from the Meat group. Each of these food groups provides some, but not all, of the nutrients you need. No one food group is more important than the other—for good health you need them all. Go easy on fats, oils, and sweets, the foods in the small tip of the Pyramid.

SOUPS

I T SEEMS EVERYONE likes soup. At Moosewood Restaurant, each day we serve four or five different soups from an always growing repertoire. We renew the selection constantly because soup is so popular — some of our customers order soup every day. Whether the soup is an old favorite, newly invented, or wildly exotic, it makes a comforting, nourishing meal. Perhaps more than any other category of foods, soup is a symbol of hearth and home.

Nearly instant convenience soups have been around for a long time now. Your supermarket may have a whole aisle of them. But no commercial canned or freeze-dried soup can compare to the genuine homemade article for taste and nutrition (not to mention economy and originality). Although none of the soups in this chapter can be made in as little time as it takes to open a can, they have much to recommend them.

Green Jade Soup, Red Lentil Soup, and Portuguese White Bean Soup make highly nutritious and appealing meals. With a well-stocked pantry, Noodles with Mirin or Black Bean Soup can be made at a moment's notice. Golden Cheddar Cheese Soup and Tomato Garlic Soup with Tortellini are certain to please children (and their parents). Some of these soups are perfectly suited for a fancy dinner party: we suggest North African Cauliflower Soup, Pumpkin and Porcini Soup, Shrimp Bisque, or Mexican Tomato Lime Soup when company's coming. Some, such as Chilled Moroccan Tomato Soup and Simple Garlic Broth, clock in at only 15 or 20 minutes' preparation time. Not bad for a great pot of soup! Any of the soups here can be the main dish of a meal, and all of them can be made ahead, at your convenience.

Stock is usually our first choice of liquid for a soup, although it's not essential to any recipe. In anticipation of making soup often, you can easily prepare vegetable stock while you perform other kitchen chores (see page 359 for homemade, page 330 for information on packaged bouillon). Vegetable stock freezes well, so it's smart to make double or triple batches.

There are many good ways to thicken a soup. You can use puréed cooked vegetables or beans, bread crumbs, cornmeal, farina, oats, or powdered rice. (Powdered rice is made by finely grinding raw rice kernels in a blender or spice grinder. Use 2 or 3 tablespoons per quart of liquid to thicken a soup.)

Having mastered a few soup recipes, the novice cook can begin to experiment with relative ease — soup is a forgiving medium. Leftover cooked beans, sauces, grains, sautés, vegetables, and even some salads might be incorporated into a soup. Here's a procedure for making soup out of almost anything: Sauté onions and/or garlic until tender in just enough oil or butter to coat the pan. Add any other vegetables, along with the herbs and spices of your choice. Sauté until tender, then add liquid (water, juice, milk, canned tomatoes, or vegetable stock) and cook until hot. That's it!

Black Bean Soup

10 sun-dried tomatoes (not packed in oil)
1 cup boiling water

≈

1½ cups finely chopped onions
3 garlic cloves, minced or pressed
1 jalapeño chile, minced, or ¼ teaspoon cayenne
2 tablespoons vegetable oil
1 teaspoon ground cumin
⅓ cup water
3 cups undrained canned tomatoes (28-ounce can)
4 cups undrained cooked black beans (two 16-ounce cans)
¼ cup chopped fresh cilantro
additional water or tomato juice

≈

yogurt or sour cream

In a small bowl, cover the sun-dried tomatoes with the boiling water and set aside.

In a soup pot, sauté the onions, garlic, and chile or cayenne in the oil for about 5 minutes, stirring frequently, until the onions are translucent. Add the cumin, ⅓ cup water, and the juice from the tomatoes. Break up the tomatoes by squeezing them into the soup pot, or chop them coarsely right in the can and add them to the pot. Cover and bring to a boil. Lower the heat and simmer, covered, for 5 minutes. Add the black beans and their liquid, and continue to simmer, stirring occasionally to prevent sticking.

Drain and chop the softened sun-dried tomatoes. Add them to the soup and cook for 5 to 10 minutes longer, until the onions are tender. Stir in the cilantro and remove the soup from the heat. Purée half of the soup in a blender or food processor and return it to the pot. If the soup is too thick, add some water or tomato juice. Reheat gently.

Serve each bowl of soup with a dollop of yogurt or sour cream.

PER 8-OZ SERVING: 204 CALORIES, 10.8 G PROTEIN, 4.1 G FAT, 33.6 G, CARBOHYDRATE, 337 MG SODIUM, 1 MG CHOLESTEROL.

Serve with Corn Scones (see page 53) and a tossed salad with Orange Mustard Dressing (see page 125).

Full-flavored and fortifying.

BROCCOLI EGG-LEMON SOUP

TOTAL TIME

35 minutes

SERVINGS

4

MENU

Serve with Easiest
Artichokes (see page 77)
and pita or another crusty
bread for a complete
meal.

*A*n inspired
*variation on
the traditional
Greek soup* avgole-
mono. *If you have no
leftover rice or orzo,
begin to cook some
when you start the soup.
Orzo or white rice will
cook in about 20
minutes, brown rice in
about 45 minutes.*

2 cups finely chopped onions
3 garlic cloves, minced or pressed
2 tablespoons olive oil
2½ cups finely chopped broccoli florets
1 small red bell pepper, diced
1 tablespoon minced fresh dill (1 teaspoon dried)
½ teaspoon salt
¼ teaspoon ground black pepper
4 cups vegetable stock, or 1 bouillon cube dissolved
    in 4 cups water

≈

2 large eggs
¼–⅓ cup fresh lemon juice
1 cup cooked orzo or rice

≈

chopped fresh parsley (optional)

In a soup pot, sauté the onions and garlic in the oil for about 5 minutes, until the onions are translucent. Add the broccoli, bell pepper, dill, salt, and black pepper, and sauté for several minutes, until the broccoli turns bright green. Add 3 cups of the stock and bring the soup to a boil. Reduce the heat and simmer, covered, until the vegetables are tender. Remove the soup from the heat.

In a bowl, whisk together the eggs and ¼ cup of the lemon juice. Whisk in the remaining cup of stock, and then add about a cup of the hot soup broth. Gradually pour the egg mixture into the soup pot while stirring the soup. Stir in the orzo or rice. Gently reheat the soup, but don't let it boil or it might curdle. Add more salt and lemon juice to taste.

Broccoli Egg-Lemon Soup can be served immediately, but it tastes even better gently reheated after sitting awhile. Garnish with fresh parsley, if desired.

PER 8-OZ SERVING: 149 CALORIES, 4.8 G PROTEIN, 6 G FAT, 20.1 G CARBOHYDRATE, 184 MG SODIUM, 53 MG CHOLESTEROL.

CANTONESE FISH AND VEGETABLE SOUP

5 dried shiitake mushrooms
1½ cups boiling water

≈

1 large onion, quartered and thinly sliced (about 2 cups)
3 garlic cloves, minced or pressed
1 tablespoon grated fresh ginger root
2 tablespoons vegetable oil
1 large carrot, cut into matchsticks
4 cups water
1½ pounds cod fillets, cut into 1-inch chunks

≈

¼ cup soy sauce
1 tablespoon dark sesame oil
3 tablespoons cornstarch dissolved in 3 tablespoons
    cold water
1 red bell pepper, diced

≈

chopped scallions

TOTAL TIME
25 minutes
SERVINGS
Serves 4 as main course,
6 as a first course
MENU
Accompanied by a bowl
of rice, this soup makes a
substantial meal. Finish
with ice cream or frozen
yogurt topped with
Gingered Plum Sauce
(see page 312).

Place the shiitake mushrooms in a heatproof bowl, cover with the boiling water, and set aside for about 10 minutes.

In a soup pot, sauté the onions, garlic, and ginger in the oil until the onions are translucent. Stir in the carrots. Drain the shiitake, reserving the soaking liquid. Remove and discard the stems, and slice the softened caps. Add the shiitake caps, their soaking liquid, and the 4 cups of water to the pot and cover it. When the broth begins to boil, add the fish and cover the pot again.

In a small bowl, mix together the soy sauce, sesame oil, and dissolved cornstarch. When the soup returns to a boil, stir in the cornstarch mixture and the bell pepper. Simmer for 2 or 3 minutes, until the soup thickens. Serve immediately, topped with scallions.

PER 8-OZ SERVING: 147 CALORIES, 15.2 G PROTEIN, 4.5 G FAT, 11 G CARBOHYDRATE, 400 MG SODIUM, 34 MG CHOLESTEROL.

CHILLED MOROCCAN TOMATO SOUP

TOTAL TIME
15 minutes

SERVINGS
4 to 6

MENU
For a delicious outdoor summer meal, serve this soup with Roasted Vegetable Salad with Garlic and Rosemary (see page 84), Crostini with Olivada and Fresh Mozzarella (see pages 262–63), and chilled sliced melon for dessert.

This flavorful soup is best made ahead of time; the flavors meld after sitting for a few hours or a day.

2 medium tomatoes, diced
1 stalk celery, minced
1 scallion, finely chopped
1 quart chilled tomato juice
¼ cup chilled orange juice

≈

1 tablespoon olive oil
1 garlic clove, minced or pressed
1 teaspoon ground cumin
½ teaspoon paprika
¼ teaspoon cinnamon

≈

2–3 tablespoons fresh lemon juice
Tabasco or other hot pepper sauce to taste

In a saucepan or a large refrigerator container, combine the tomatoes, celery, scallions, tomato juice, and orange juice.

In a small skillet on low heat, warm the olive oil. Sauté the garlic, cumin, paprika, and cinnamon for just a minute, being careful not to scorch them. Stir the spice mixture into the soup, and add lemon juice and Tabasco to taste. Serve immediately or refrigerate until ready to serve.

PER 8-OZ SERVING: 71 CALORIES, 1.9 G PROTEIN, 2.8 G FAT, 12.1 G CARBOHYDRATE, 562 MG SODIUM, 0 MG CHOLESTEROL.

GOLDEN CHEDDAR CHEESE SOUP

1 cup chopped onions
2 tablespoons vegetable oil
2 medium potatoes, thinly sliced
1 medium carrot, thinly sliced
1 medium yellow summer squash, thinly sliced
½ teaspoon ground black pepper (or to taste)
pinch of turmeric
2 cups vegetable stock or water
1 cup buttermilk or milk
1 cup grated sharp cheddar cheese
salt to taste

≈

minced fresh scallions, chives, or parsley

Sauté the onions in the oil for about 5 minutes or until the onions begin to soften. Stir in the potatoes, carrots, squash, black pepper, and turmeric. Add the stock or water and simmer for 15 to 20 minutes, until the vegetables are soft. Stir in the buttermilk or milk and the cheese. Purée the soup in a blender or food processor. Gently reheat. Add salt to taste, and serve topped with minced scallions, chives, or parsley.

PER 8-OZ SERVING: 192 CALORIES, 7 G PROTEIN, 9.9 G FAT, 19.8 G CARBOHYDRATE, 227 MG SODIUM, 18 MG CHOLESTEROL.

TOTAL TIME
35 minutes

SERVINGS
4 to 6

MENU
Serve with muffins (see pages 54, 56) or Corn Scones (see page 53).

A gorgeously colored soup with a rich, smooth texture. Mildly flavored, yet very tasty—a great soup for kids!

GREEN JADE SOUP

TOTAL TIME
35 minutes

SERVINGS
4 to 6

MENU
Serve with rice or noodles
with Miso Sauce
(see page 113).

*This gingery,
warming,
nutritious soup is
particularly welcome in
the fall or winter, but
it's enjoyable at any
time. It is delicately
flavored, satisfying, and
almost fat-free. Green
Jade Soup looks best
when it's just cooked. If
you're preparing the
soup ahead of time
don't add the spinach
until just before serving.*

4 dried shiitake mushrooms
1 cup boiling water

≈

6 cups vegetable stock, or 2 cubes vegetable bouillon
    dissolved in 6 cups water
1½ tablespoons grated fresh ginger root
1½ cups thinly sliced carrot rounds
1½ cups thinly sliced leeks or onions
2 cups chopped Chinese cabbage, bok choy, or kale
4 cups firmly packed rinsed, chopped fresh spinach
1 cake tofu, cut into ½-inch cubes (¾ pound)
salt to taste

≈

chopped scallions
several drops dark sesame oil (optional)

Place the shiitake mushrooms in a heatproof bowl, cover with the
boiling water, and set aside for about 10 minutes.

Heat the stock or bouillon in a large soup pot. When it comes to a
boil, add the ginger, carrots, leeks or onions, and Chinese cabbage or
other greens. Lower the heat and simmer for about 10 minutes, until
the vegetables are tender.

Drain the shiitake and add the soaking liquid to the soup. Thinly
slice the shiitake caps and stir them into the soup along with the
spinach and tofu. Cook for 5 minutes. Add salt to taste.

Serve garnished with scallions and sesame oil, if desired.

PER 8-OZ SERVING: 89 CALORIES, 4.7 G PROTEIN, 2.6 G FAT, 13.1 G CARBOHYDRATE, 61 MG SODIUM,
0 MG CHOLESTEROL.

HERBED GREEN PEA SOUP

4 scallions, chopped
2 tablespoons vegetable oil
1 tablespoon fresh thyme (1 teaspoon dried)
2 tablespoons fresh tarragon (2 teaspoons dried)
1 pound frozen green peas (about 3 cups)
¼ teaspoon nutmeg
1 teaspoon salt
½ teaspoon ground black pepper
3 cups hot water
1 cup milk

≈

chopped scallions
croutons (optional)

In a soup pot, sauté the scallions in the oil for a minute. Add the thyme and tarragon, and sauté for another minute. Stir in the peas, nutmeg, salt, pepper, and hot water. Cover and bring to a boil. Boil for 2 minutes, until the peas are tender but still bright green.

Using a slotted spoon, remove about a cup of the peas and set them aside. In a blender or food processor, purée the rest of the soup. Return the puréed soup to the pot, and stir in the milk and the reserved peas. Gently reheat, or chill for about 1½ hours.

Garnish with scallions, and with croutons if you like.

PER 8-OZ SERVING: 118 CALORIES, 4.7 G PROTEIN, 5.4 G FAT, 13.3 G CARBOHYDRATE, 400 MG SODIUM, 4 MG CHOLESTEROL.

TOTAL TIME
30 minutes

SERVINGS
4

MENU
Accompany with Asparagus with Fried Eggs and Cheese (see page 287), Greek Spinach Frittata (see page 291), or Apple-Celery en Bleu (see page 63) for a substantial meal.

A comforting soup that's good hot or cold.

MEXICAN TOMATO LIME SOUP

TOTAL TIME

15 minutes

SERVINGS

6

MENU

Serve as the first course of
a Mexican meal, or with
Polenta with Endive
(see page 151), Bulghur
Burgers (see page 144), or
simply a tossed green or
fruit salad.

*A n almost-
instant and
refreshing soup.*

3 garlic cloves, minced or pressed
2 teaspoons ground cumin
1 tablespoon vegetable oil
6 cups tomato juice (46-ounce can)
2 cups chopped fresh tomatoes
juice of 1 large lime (about ¼ cup)
3 tablespoons chopped fresh cilantro
Tabasco or other hot pepper sauce to taste

≈

2 cups coarsely crushed tortilla chips
1 cup grated Monterey Jack cheese
cilantro leaves, whole or chopped

In a soup pot on low heat, sauté the garlic and cumin in the oil for
a minute. Be careful not to brown the garlic. Stir in the tomato juice,
fresh tomatoes, lime juice, and cilantro. Bring to a simmer and continue to cook for several minutes. Add Tabasco to taste.

Place the tortilla chips in large, shallow soup bowls, and ladle the
soup over them. Top with the grated cheese and cilantro.

PER 8-OZ SERVING: 225 CALORIES, 6.2 G PROTEIN, 10.9 G FAT, 25.9 G CARBOHYDRATE, 672 MG SODIUM,
10 MG CHOLESTEROL.

VARIATION: This soup is also delicious chilled. Sauté the garlic and
cumin as described. Add the tomato juice, tomatoes, lime juice, cilantro,
and Tabasco, and refrigerate for about 1½ hours or until ready to serve.
Omit the tortilla chips and cheese and top with cubes of fresh avocado.

Miso Soup

Good

4 dried shiitake mushrooms
1½ cups boiling water

≈

2 medium carrots, sliced diagonally into ¼-inch-thick
    rounds (about 1 cup)
4 cups vegetable stock or water
1½ cups shredded greens, such as bok choy, endive,
    Chinese cabbage, or spinach
2 tablespoons red miso (see page 336)
2 tablespoons light miso
1 cake tofu

≈

chopped scallions
crumbled toasted nori (see page 337) (optional)

TOTAL TIME
25 minutes

SERVINGS
4

MENU
Serve with Fried Rice
(see page 230), Asian Fish
in a Packet (see page 244),
or Udon Noodles and
Vegetables (see page 136).

We wouldn't even consider writing a cookbook without including miso soup. This is a basic recipe for a soup that could have a thousand variations. We like using both red and white miso; the heartier flavor of the red is offset by the lighter, sweet flavor of the white; however, you can make this soup using only one type if you prefer. We recommend Onozaki brand.

Place the shiitake mushrooms in a heatproof bowl, cover with the boiling water, and set aside for about 10 minutes.

In a soup pot, cover the carrots with 3½ cups of the stock or water and bring to a boil. Lower the heat and simmer for about 10 minutes, until the carrots are crisp-tender.

Drain the shiitake and add their soaking liquid to the carrots and stock. Slice the shiitake caps into thin strips and add them to the soup. Stir in the greens and continue to simmer for about 5 minutes, until they are just tender or wilted.

In a small bowl, blend both misos with the remaining ½ cup of stock. Cut the tofu into ½-inch cubes. Stir the miso mixture into the soup, add the tofu, and heat gently. Be careful not to let the soup boil.

Garnish the soup with scallions, and with nori flakes if you wish.

PER 8-OZ SERVING: 90 CALORIES, 5.5 G PROTEIN, 3.2 G FAT, 11.3 G CARBOHYDRATE, 164 MG SODIUM, 0 MG CHOLESTEROL.

NOODLES WITH MIRIN

TOTAL TIME
20 minutes

SERVINGS
4

MENU
Accompany with Stir-
Fried Bok Choy and
Hijiki (see page 89), or
Teriyaki Broiled or Grilled
Fish (see page 256).

*S*imple and light,
this soup is
equally inviting
served cold in hot
weather or warm in
cool weather.

8 ounces noodles (somen, linguini, or whole wheat
spaghetti)

≈

½ cup mirin*
2 cups water
1½ tablespoons vegetable bouillon powder (1½ cubes)
¼ cup soy sauce
⅔ cup fresh or frozen snow peas or green peas
2 teaspoons powdered wasabi mixed with 2 teaspoons
water (see page 344)

≈

chopped scallions

If mirin is unavailable, sweet sherry is an acceptable substitute.

Bring a large covered pot of water to a rapid boil, and add the
pasta.

While the pasta cooks, bring the mirin, 2 cups of water, bouillon
powder, and soy sauce to a simmer in a small saucepan. Add the peas
and cook briefly, until they are tender but still bright green. Stir in the
wasabi paste.

When the pasta is al dente, drain it and transfer it to a serving
bowl. Pour the peas and sauce over the pasta, and toss well.

Top with chopped scallions and serve warm, at room temperature,
or chilled. (To serve at room temperature, allow the finished dish to
sit for 15 to 20 minutes. To serve chilled, refrigerate for at least an
hour.)

PER 8-OZ SERVING: 173 CALORIES, 6.6 G PROTEIN, 1.6 G FAT, 29.7 G CARBOHYDRATE, 994 MG SODIUM,
33 MG CHOLESTEROL.

North African Cauliflower Soup

2½ cups chopped onions
2 tablespoons vegetable oil
2 potatoes (about 2 cups diced)
1 medium head cauliflower (about 5 cups chopped)
2 teaspoons ground cumin
1½ teaspoons ground fennel
4 cups hot water
1 tablespoon vegetable bouillon powder
    or 1 bouillon cube (optional)

≈

2 tablespoons fresh lemon juice
salt and ground black pepper to taste

≈

chopped fresh tomatoes
chopped chives or scallions

TOTAL TIME
30 minutes

SERVINGS
4 to 6

MENU
This soup makes a satisfying meal with a crisp green salad and pita wedges or a dark rye or sourdough bread. Or for a more exotic taste treat, serve it with Apricot Bulghur Pilaf (see page 143) or vegetable crudités with Spicy Peanut Dip (see page 50).

This soup is thick, smooth, and creamy without any cream at all.

In a soup pot on medium heat, sauté the onions in the oil for 5 to 10 minutes, until translucent. While the onions sauté, dice the potatoes and chop the cauliflower.

Stir the cumin, fennel, and potatoes into the pot, and cook for a minute. Then add the hot water. Cover, turn up the heat, and bring to a boil. Add the cauliflower and optional bouillon, and return to a boil. Then lower the heat and simmer, covered, for about 10 minutes, until the vegetables are tender.

In a blender or food processor, purée the vegetables and broth until smooth. Add the lemon juice, and salt and pepper. Reheat the soup if necessary, taking care not to scorch it.

Serve garnished with the chopped tomatoes and chives or scallions.

PER 8-OZ SERVING: 92 CALORIES, 2.5 G PROTEIN, 3.2 G FAT, 14.5 G CARBOHYDRATE, 272 MG SODIUM, 0 MG CHOLESTEROL.

Portuguese White Bean Soup

TOTAL TIME

35 minutes

SERVINGS

4

MENU

Serve with Lemon
Tomato Salad
(see page 70) and
Savory Scallion Biscuits
(see page 58) or
Multigrain Muffins
(see page 56).

A rustic, hearty soup that's quick and delicious. It tastes even better after sitting for a few hours or overnight and can be enhanced by the addition of Seasoned Tempeh (see page 85).

1 cup chopped onions
1 garlic clove, minced or pressed
2 tablespoons olive oil
1 medium red or yellow bell pepper
1 bay leaf
pinch of salt
½ teaspoon ground fennel
1 medium potato
2 tablespoons dry sherry
1 tablespoon fresh lemon juice
2 cups vegetable stock or water
2 cups undrained canned white beans (16-ounce can)
ground black pepper to taste

≈

chopped fresh parsley

In a soup pot, sauté the onions and garlic in the olive oil, stirring often, for about 5 minutes or until the onions soften. While the onions sauté, chop the bell pepper. Add the bay leaf, salt, fennel, and bell peppers to the pot, and continue to cook for about 5 minutes, stirring regularly.

Cube the potato and add to the pot along with the sherry, lemon juice, and stock or water. Cover and simmer for 10 to 15 minutes, until the potatoes are tender. Stir in the beans and gently reheat. Add black pepper to taste.

Garnish with parsley and serve immediately.

PER 8-OZ SERVING: 176 CALORIES, 6.6 G PROTEIN, 5.1 G FAT, 26.5 G CARBOHYDRATE, 104 MG SODIUM, 0 MG CHOLESTEROL.

PUMPKIN AND PORCINI SOUP

½ cup broken pieces dried porcini mushrooms
    (about ¾ ounce)
2 cups boiling water
≈
2 large onions, minced (about 3 cups)
2 tablespoons vegetable oil, olive oil, or butter
2 garlic cloves, minced or pressed
2 cups chopped fresh mushrooms
1 teaspoon fresh thyme (½ teaspoon dried)
1½ tablespoons fresh sage (2 teaspoons dried)
dash of nutmeg
¼ cup Marsala or dry sherry
1 tablespoon soy sauce
1 cup unsweetened apple juice and 1 cup water,
    or 2 cups vegetable stock
4 cups puréed cooked pumpkin (29-ounce can)
salt and ground black pepper to taste
1 cup milk or half-and-half (optional)

TOTAL TIME

30 minutes

SERVINGS

4 to 6

MENU

Serve with cornbread and Easiest Artichokes (see page 77), or with crisp Crostini (see page 263) topped with quickly sautéed slightly bitter greens, such as endive.

Break up any large pieces of porcini. Place the porcini in a heat-proof bowl, cover with the boiling water, and set aside to soak.

In a soup pot on medium heat, sauté the onions in the oil for 5 to 10 minutes, until softened. Add the garlic, fresh mushrooms, thyme, and sage, and sauté until the mushrooms are soft, about 5 to 10 minutes. Stir in the nutmeg, Marsala or sherry, and soy sauce. Add the apple juice and water, or vegetable stock, and heat almost to a boil. Stir in the pumpkin.

Remove the porcini from the soaking water with a slotted spoon and add them to the soup. Pour the soaking water through a coffee filter or a paper towel into another bowl to remove any grit, and add it to the soup. Add salt and pepper to taste. If you prefer a creamier soup, add the milk or half-and-half. Serve hot.

PER 8-OZ SERVING: 90 CALORIES, 1.9 G PROTEIN, 3 G FAT, 14.9 G CARBOHYDRATE, 144 MG SODIUM, 0 MG CHOLESTEROL.

This thick, rich-tasting soup, which features the intense woodsy flavor of dried porcini, is a good choice for a chilly fall or winter day. Try topping the soup with crisp garlicky croutons. It's a good choice for the first course in a festive holiday meal, because it's light and colorful as well as delicious.

Frozen puréed winter squash may be substituted for the pumpkin.

RED LENTIL SOUP

TOTAL TIME

35 minutes

SERVINGS

4 to 6

MENU

This soup is good served with toasted pita wedges and topped with yogurt, minced onion, or sprigs of fresh mint, parsley, or cilantro. Serve with Vegetables in Mint Vinaigrette (see page 72) or Curried Cauliflower (see page 75), or for a simple meal, accompany with a tossed green salad and bread.

A golden soup with flecks of red and orange. Variations of this soup are found in cuisines from Egypt to India.

This soup tastes even better as a leftover, when the flavors have fully mingled.

1½ cups red lentils
6 cups water
3 bay leaves
4 garlic cloves, chopped
2 slices fresh ginger root, each about the size of a quarter
≈
2 medium carrots (1 cup grated)
1 cup canned tomatoes, or 1 medium fresh tomato, chopped (undrained)
1 small red or green bell pepper (½ cup finely chopped)
≈
1½ cups chopped onions
2 tablespoons olive oil
1½ teaspoons ground cumin
1½ teaspoons ground coriander
pinch of cayenne
2 tablespoons fresh lemon juice
salt and ground black pepper to taste

Sort and rinse the lentils. Put them into a soup pot with the water, bay leaves, garlic, and ginger. Cover and place on high heat.

Prepare the carrots, tomatoes, and bell peppers, and add them to the pot. Bring to a boil, stir, reduce the heat, and simmer, covered, for 15 to 20 minutes, until the lentils are tender.

While the vegetables simmer, sauté the onions on medium heat in the olive oil in a heavy skillet for about 10 minutes or until browned. Add the cumin, coriander, and cayenne, and sauté for another minute, stirring to prevent sticking. Remove from the heat. When the lentils are tender, remove the bay leaves, and ginger from the soup pot. Stir in the sautéed onions and the lemon juice. Add salt and pepper to taste.

PER 8-OZ SERVING: 82 CALORIES, 3.3 G PROTEIN, 3.2 G FAT, 11.2 G CARBOHYDRATE, 74 MG SODIUM, 0 MG CHOLESTEROL.

SHRIMP BISQUE *Very good*

1 pound fresh or frozen small shelled shrimp

≈

1 cup finely diced onions
1 cup shredded peeled apple
2 tablespoons butter or vegetable oil
1 rounded tablespoon unbleached white flour
1½ cups water or vegetable stock
1 teaspoon fresh lemon juice
1 2-inch-long piece lemon peel
⅛–¼ teaspoon curry powder *
1 teaspoon chopped fresh dill (⅓ teaspoon dried)
¼ teaspoon salt
¼ teaspoon ground white pepper
2 tablespoons dry white wine
1 cup half-and-half

≈

thin lemon slices

Rinse the shrimp and set them aside.

In a covered saucepan, sauté the onions and apples in the butter or oil for about 10 minutes, until the onions are translucent. Sprinkle in the flour and cook, stirring, for a minute or two. Then stir in the water or stock, lemon juice, lemon peel, curry powder, dill, salt, white pepper, and wine. Simmer, covered, for about 5 minutes, until the mixture thickens slightly. Add the shrimp and the half-and-half, and simmer gently just until the shrimp turn pink. Be careful not to overcook the shrimp or they will become tough.

Remove the lemon peel. In a blender or food processor, purée about one third of the soup and then return it to the pot. Serve immediately, garnished with thin slices of lemon.

PER 8-OZ SERVING: 191 CALORIES, 17.7 G. PROTEIN, 9.2 G FAT, 11.2 G CARBOHYDRATE, 323 MG SODIUM, 172 MG CHOLESTEROL.

SERVINGS
6 as first course
4 as main dish

MENU
Delicious for dinner served with a green salad and Corn Scones (see page 53).

Lemon and curry add subtle fragrance to this elegant dish.

*If your curry powder is strongly flavored, even ¼ teaspoon may overpower the other delicate flavors in this soup. Start by adding ⅛ teaspoon; then add more to taste.

SIMPLE GARLIC BROTH

Simple garlic soups are found in peasant cuisines all over the world and are often considered a cure for a variety of ills. This rustic broth is subtle, mellow, and versatile. Try one of the variations we suggest, or allow your own creativity to inspire you.

Simple Garlic Broth makes a wonderful liquid in which to cook rice or potatoes. It will keep, covered, in the refrigerator for one week. It also freezes well.

8 cups vegetable stock, or 8 cups water and 2 cubes
    vegetable bouillon
3 tablespoons minced garlic (1 large or 2 small heads)
2 tablespoons olive oil
½ teaspoon paprika
1 sprig fresh sage
1 sprig fresh thyme
several sprigs fresh parsley
salt and ground black pepper to taste

In a covered pot, bring the stock or water to a boil. In a soup pot on low heat, gently sauté the garlic in the olive oil until golden, taking care not to let it brown. Add the boiling stock, or the boiling water and the bouillon cubes. Stir in the paprika. Tie the sage, thyme, and parsley into a little bundle with string, and add the "bouquet" to the pot. Bring the broth to a boil and simmer for 10 to 15 minutes, or up to 30 minutes for a more intense flavor. Remove the bouquet and season with salt and pepper.

VARIATIONS

GARLIC BROTH WITH PASTA AND PEAS: Add pastina or other tiny pasta and lots of fresh or frozen green peas to the garlic broth. Serve topped with Parmesan cheese.

SAFFRON GARLIC SOUP: Add a generous pinch of saffron to the simmering broth. For a delicious traditional Mediterranean meal, place toast or croutons and a fried or poached egg in each serving bowl, and ladle some saffron garlic broth over them. Sprinkle with grated cheese, if desired.

VEGETABLE SOUP: Add about 2 cups of shredded vegetables — such as carrots, green beans, zucchini, kale, turnips, or sweet potatoes — to the simmering broth and cook until the vegetables are tender but still brightly colored. Stir in about 2 cups of cooked orzo (see page 149) or other small pasta and serve topped with grated cheese.

POTATO AND PEPPER SOUP: Cook about a cup each of cubed potatoes and diced red bell peppers in the simmering broth until tender. Just before serving, add a cup of chopped fresh greens, such as spinach, chard, or kale, and cook until the greens wilt. Serve topped with grated feta or other cheese.

SPANISH POTATO ONION SOUP

For a hearty cold-weather meal, serve with Bruschetta (see page 262) or other crusty bread and White Bean and Tomato Salad (see page 137).

An aromatically seasoned, substantial soup.

4 medium onions, halved and thinly sliced (about 4 cups)
2 tablespoons olive oil
4 cups water
2 or 3 medium potatoes (about 4 cups sliced)
2 teaspoons paprika
1 teaspoon fresh thyme (½ teaspoon dried)
2 large bay leaves
¼ cup dry sherry
1 teaspoon salt
¼ teaspoon ground black pepper
pinch of saffron

≈

sprigs of fresh parsley
strips of pimiento
dash of Tabasco or other hot pepper sauce,
        or pinch of cayenne (optional)

In a soup pot on medium heat, sauté the onions in the oil, stirring occasionally to prevent sticking. While they sauté, bring the water to a boil in a separate pan. Cut the potatoes in half lengthwise, and then slice each half crosswise into ¼-inch-thick slices. Keeping the slices together, cut them in half lengthwise again to form wedge-shaped pieces.

When the onions are translucent, add the paprika, thyme, and bay leaves. Sauté for a minute. Pour the boiling water into the onion mixture and add the potatoes, sherry, salt, and pepper. Return to a boil. Then lower the heat and simmer, covered, for about 10 minutes. Crumble in the saffron and continue to cook until the potatoes are tender. Remove the bay leaves.

Garnish each bowl of soup with a sprig of parsley and a strip of pimiento, and add a dash of Tabasco or cayenne if you wish.

PER 8-OZ SERVING: 113 CALORIES, 1.8 G PROTEIN, 4.3 G FAT, 16.7 G CARBOHYDRATE, 332 MG SODIUM, 0 MG CHOLESTEROL.

SWEET PEPPERS SOUP

2 cups chopped onions
1 tablespoon butter or vegetable oil
6 cups chopped red and green bell peppers
    (about 6 peppers)
2 cups water or vegetable stock
1 cup sour cream*
⅓ cup chopped fresh dill
2 tablespoons fresh lemon juice
salt and ground black pepper to taste
≈
seasoned croutons (optional)

We prefer sour cream, but light sour cream or plain yogurt could be substituted.

In a covered soup pot, sauté the onions on medium heat in the butter or oil for about 3 minutes, until barely softened. Add the bell peppers and cook, covered, until just soft, stirring occasionally. In a blender or food processor, whirl the cooked onions and peppers with the water or stock, sour cream, dill, and lemon juice. Don't over-process; small pieces of peppers should remain. Return the soup to the pot and gently reheat, adding salt and pepper to taste. Serve topped with croutons, if you wish.

PER 8-OZ SERVING: 116 CALORIES, 2.6 G PROTEIN, 6.9 G FAT, 13.4 G CARBOHYDRATE, 99 MG SODIUM, 0 MG CHOLESTEROL.

MEXICAN VARIATION: Omit the dill and croutons. Sauté 1 teaspoon of ground cumin, 1 teaspoon of ground coriander, and ¼ teaspoon of cayenne with the onions and peppers. Serve topped with chopped fresh cilantro and crumbled tortilla chips.

TOTAL TIME
30 minutes

SERVINGS
4 to 6

MENU
This soup makes an elegant first course or a light meal supported by bread and salad.

This creamy dill-and-lemon-flavored bell pepper soup should be as colorful as you can make it. Use red and green peppers — yellow or orange too, if they are available.

TOMATO GARLIC SOUP
WITH TORTELLINI

TOTAL TIME
25 minutes

SERVINGS
6 to 8

This is a very
satisfying meal
in itself, served
with crudités or a green
salad.

6 cups Simple Garlic Broth (see page 38)
2 cups undrained canned tomatoes, or 4 medium fresh
tomatoes (about 3 cups chopped)
9 ounces fresh or frozen cheese-filled tortellini *

≈

grated Pecorino or Parmesan cheese
chopped fresh parsley

*Fresh tortellini are available in Italian markets and in the dairy case or
frozen-foods section of many supermarkets.*

In a saucepan, bring the garlic broth to a simmer. While the broth
heats, chop the tomatoes. Add the tomatoes to the broth, return it to
a boil, and simmer for 10 to 15 minutes.

In a separate pot, cook the tortellini in boiling water until al dente,
4 or 5 minutes. Drain.

When ready to serve, place the tortellini in individual serving
bowls and ladle the soup over them. Serve topped with grated cheese
and chopped parsley.

PER 8-OZ SERVING: 193 CALORIES, 8.1 G PROTEIN, 8.9 G FAT, 21 G CARBOHYDRATE, 304 MG SODIUM,
2 MG CHOLESTEROL.

VARIATION: Omit the tortellini. Add chopped greens—such as
endive, chard, escarole, spinach, kale, or watercress—to the broth and
simmer for 2 to 3 minutes, until wilted.

DIPS, SPREADS, AND QUICK BREADS

THE DIPS AND SPREADS in this chapter are flavorful, distinctive, and very easy to prepare. As leftovers, many are useful as side dishes, toppings, or sandwich spreads. For each recipe we suggest ways of serving—with fresh vegetable sticks, for example, or with crackers, pita, or a specific bread.

Breads, muffins, and biscuits fresh from the oven fill the kitchen with a special homey fragrance and have traditionally signified family warmth. All you need to make one of life's nicest gestures is a heart full of love and an extra half hour.

Whip up a batch of fruit-filled or multigrain muffins before going to bed, and then surprise someone special with a basket of them the next morning. You might also make some Yogurt Cheese, which prepares itself overnight in the refrigerator, as a healthful alternative to butter or cream cheese.

For an easy afternoon or evening meal, bake some light and flavorful Corn Scones. While they're in the oven, it takes only minutes to make Mockamole to serve alongside.

Savory Scallion Biscuits are delicious any time of day, served perhaps with an omelet or a frittata, or with one of our satisfying stews.

Try rich and flaky Pesto Palmiers, made from a few convenient store-bought ingredients. You'll have a quick appetizer or snack that looks and tastes as though you spent hours making it.

DIPS AND SPREADS

BLACK BEAN DIP

TOTAL TIME

15 minutes

SERVINGS

2 cups

MENU

For a handsome, quickly prepared meal, serve Black Bean Dip with Avocado Corn Salad (see page 119) and warm tortillas.

*S*erve Black Bean Dip either hot or cold. It is delicious as a dip with raw vegetables and tortilla chips, in a pita with lettuce and tomato, or as a quesadilla filling. The walnuts and olives are optional, but do try them — they add texture along with their distinctive flavors.

2 cups cooked drained black beans (16-ounce can)
1 teaspoon ground toasted cumin seeds (see page 354)
½ teaspoon ground coriander
pinch of cayenne
1 garlic clove, minced or pressed
⅔ cup chopped fresh parsley
1 teaspoon olive oil
2 teaspoons fresh lemon juice
salt to taste

≈

⅓ cup chopped toasted walnuts (see page 354) (optional)
2 tablespoons minced Spanish olives (optional)

Drain the beans, place them in a shallow bowl, and mash them well with a fork. Stir in the cumin, coriander, cayenne, garlic, parsley, olive oil, and lemon juice. Mix thoroughly. Add salt to taste. If you add the walnuts and/or olives, either stir them into the dip or sprinkle them on top as a garnish.

PER 2-OZ SERVING: 73 CALORIES, 4.6 G PROTEIN, 0.7 G FAT, 12.5 G CARBOHYDRATE, 171 MG SODIUM, 0 MG CHOLESTEROL.

BORANI

10 ounces fresh spinach, well rinsed, stemmed
    and chopped
1 cup chopped onions
3 scallions, chopped
1 garlic clove, minced or pressed
¼ cup olive oil
1 tablespoon minced fresh dill or mint (1 teaspoon dried)
⅓ cup grated feta cheese
2 tablespoons plain yogurt
salt and ground black pepper to taste

In a covered saucepan, cook the still-damp spinach for a few minutes on medium heat, stirring a couple of times, until it is limp but
still bright green. In a colander or sieve, gently press the cooked
spinach to squeeze out the excess moisture. Set it aside.

Sauté the onions, scallions, and garlic in the olive oil. When the
onions are translucent, stir in the spinach and the dill, and heat for
about 2 minutes. Using a slotted spoon and pressing out any excess
liquid, transfer the spinach mixture to a bowl. Stir in the feta and yogurt. Add salt and pepper to taste. Refrigerate for 1 hour.

Serve well chilled.

PER 2-OZ SERVING: 87 CALORIES, 2 G PROTEIN, 7.4 G FAT, 4.2 G CARBOHYDRATE, 133 MG SODIUM, 4 MG
CHOLESTEROL.

PREPARATION TIME
20 minutes

CHILLING TIME
1 hour

SERVINGS
about 2 cups

MENU
Serve as a dip for French
bread rounds, crackers,
wedges of pita bread, or
vegetable sticks. Use it as
a tangy spread for
Crostini (see page 263),
or serve it with Chilled
Moroccan Tomato Soup
(see page 26) and Broiled
Eggplant (see page 74).

A timeless
combination
of flavors in a
delicious, healthful dip,
spread, or side dish.

MOCKAMOLE

TOTAL TIME
10 minutes

SERVINGS
about 2 cups

MENU
Tasty as a dip for crudités, a side dish for a Mexican meal, a stuffing for pita, or a topping for burritos.

Mockamole is a lower-fat, higher-protein version of guacamole.

1 ripe Haas avocado
1 block silken tofu (about 10 ounces)
5 tablespoons fresh lemon juice
2 small garlic cloves
½ teaspoon salt
Tabasco or other hot pepper sauce to taste
2 tablespoons fresh parsley leaves (optional)

Cut the avocado in half, remove the pit, and scoop out the flesh, placing it in a blender or a food processor bowl. Crumble in the tofu. Add the rest of the ingredients, and process until smooth and creamy. You may need to scrape the sides of the container and/or add a tablespoon or two of water. Taste, and add more salt or hot pepper sauce if needed. Serve chilled or at room temperature.

Mockamole will keep in the refrigerator, covered, for 2 or 3 days. To prevent discoloration, make an airtight seal with plastic wrap lightly pressed onto the top of the mockamole.

PER 2-OZ SERVING: 56 CALORIES, 2.8 G PROTEIN, 4.4 G FAT, 2.8 G CARBOHYDRATE, 119 MG SODIUM, 0 MG CHOLESTEROL.

OLIVADA

2½ cups drained pitted black olives (two 6-ounce cans) *
1 garlic clove, minced or pressed
2 tablespoons pine nuts
1–2 tablespoons extra-virgin olive oil

We like Olivada just fine when it's made with mild-flavored canned, pitted California ripe olives, but for an intense essence-of-the-Mediterranean Olivada, take the time to pit the strongly flavored Greek or Italian olives found in specialty stores and delis.

Coarsely chop half of the olives and set them aside. In a food processor or blender, whirl the remaining olives with the garlic, pine nuts, and 1 tablespoon of the olive oil until the mixture is somewhat smooth (it's okay if some of the pine nuts remain whole). If the mixture is too stiff, add the remaining tablespoon of olive oil. Stir in the chopped olives.

Covered and refrigerated, Olivada will keep for about a week. It is best served at room temperature.

PER 2-OZ SERVING: 217 CALORIES, 1.5 G PROTEIN, 23.1 G FAT, 5.4 G CARBOHYDRATE, 1,901 MG SODIUM, 0 MG CHOLESTEROL.

TOTAL TIME
10 minutes

SERVINGS
2 cups

MENU
Olivada is at its best as a topping spread on crisp toasted bread with fresh tomato slices and/or fresh mozzarella. It's also good as a pasta topping, especially combined with mushroom paste, which can also be purchased in specialty stores. Or try it as a pizza topping, stuffed vegetable filling, dip for chips, or topping on baked potatoes.

Glossy and dramatic-looking, pungent and potent, olive paste can be purchased in (expensive) tiny jars, but why bother when it's so easy to make yourself?

Spicy Peanut Dip

TOTAL TIME
10 minutes

SERVINGS
1½ cups

MENU

Use Spicy Peanut Dip to coat linguini, soba, or buckwheat noodles for an Asian-style noodle salad, and serve it with steamed broccoli and / or chunks of cucumber and tofu. Or use it as a sauce for steamed vegetables and rice, Indonesian style. Spicy Peanut Dip combined with puréed pumpkin can also be a flavorful base for a soup.

*E*veryone likes this versatile dip. Serve it with sticks of raw carrots, celery, peppers, and / or cucumbers, with toasted pita wedges, or with crisp blanched vegetables such as cauliflower florets, zucchini sticks, and chunks of waxy potatoes.

⅔ cup peanut butter
1 tablespoon brown sugar
¼ cup fresh lemon juice
⅔ cup prepared spicy hot salsa (Mexican tomato-chile type)
½ teaspoon ground cumin
salt to taste

≈

2 teaspoons Worcestershire sauce (see page 344) (optional)
Tabasco or hot pepper sauce to taste (optional)

Mash all of the ingredients together in a bowl, adding the Worcestershire sauce if you like more zing. Taste, and add more lemon juice and / or a few drops of Tabasco to reach the tartness and hotness you like. Stir well.

PER 2-OZ SERVING: 174 CALORIES, 6.8 G PROTEIN, 12.5 G FAT, 13.4 G CARBOHYDRATE, 375 MG SODIUM, 0 MG CHOLESTEROL.

NOTE: This dip keeps very well—about 2 weeks covered and refrigerated—so you may want to double the recipe to make sure there's always some around for a quick snack or meal.

TOFU TAHINI SPREAD

1 cake firm tofu (¾ pound)
2 tablespoons tahini
1 tablespoon miso (see page 336)
1–2 teaspoons soy sauce
2 scallions, minced
1 carrot, grated
ground black pepper to taste

Using a potato masher or food processor, mix the tofu with the tahini, miso, and 1 teaspoon of the soy sauce until well blended. Stir the scallions and carrots into the tofu mixture. Add black pepper and more soy sauce to taste.

PER 2-OZ SERVING: 38 CALORIES, 3.5 MG PROTEIN, 2 G FAT, 2.3 G CARBOHYDRATE, 71 MG SODIUM, 0 MG CHOLESTEROL.

TOTAL TIME
10 minutes

SERVINGS
2 cups

MENU
A simple yet delicious spread. We like this on sesame crackers, rice cakes, and pita, rye, or even pumpernickel bread.

A dish that combines four pillars of New Age East-West cuisine—tofu, tahini, miso, and soy sauce.

YOGURT CHEESE

PREPARATION TIME
5 minutes

DRAINING TIME
10 – 24 hours

SERVINGS
about 2 cups

MENU

Try Yogurt Cheese with a baked potato (a sweet potato would be especially nice) and Peperonata (see page 83) for a light meal. It's also a tasty spread for Savory Scallion Biscuits (see page 58) or Corn Scones (see page 53). With any of the suggested additions, Yogurt Cheese makes a good vegetable dip.

Yogurt Cheese is a versatile condiment. Plain, it can be used interchangeably with sour cream.

1 quart fresh low-fat plain yogurt (without gelatin)
salt to taste

Line a colander or large sieve with overlapping paper coffee filters or several layers of cheesecloth. Place the colander or sieve in a large bowl. Spoon in the yogurt and cover with a plate or plastic wrap. Refrigerate for at least 10 hours. After 3 or 4 hours or overnight, pour out the liquid collected in the bowl to ensure that it doesn't reach the bottom of the colander. The yogurt will thicken to a consistency similar to that of soft cream cheese. Discard the drippings. Taste the yogurt cheese and add salt to your liking.

Yogurt Cheese, if covered well, will keep refrigerated for 1 week.

PER 2-OZ SERVING: 36 CALORIES, 3 G PROTEIN, 0.9 G FAT, 4 G CARBOHYDRATE, 112 MG SODIUM, 3 MG CHOLESTEROL.

VARIATIONS

To vary the flavor of Yogurt Cheese, add any of the following:

• chopped fresh herbs — basil, dill, marjoram, tarragon, thyme, or chives
• minced capers or sun-dried tomatoes
• curry powder, currants, and chopped walnuts
• freshly ground black pepper
• chopped nuts

I like these a lot,

QUICK BREADS

Corn Scones

¼ cup butter or margarine
½ cup low-fat or whole milk
2 tablespoons brown sugar
½ cup cornmeal
1½ cups unbleached white flour
¼ teaspoon salt
1 teaspoon baking powder
¼ cup currants

TOTAL TIME

30 minutes

SERVINGS

8 scones

MENU

Serve with soup and salad, or at high tea with butter and honey or jam.

Preheat the oven to 375°.

Melt the butter or margarine in a small heavy saucepan. While the butter melts, pour the milk into a medium bowl and mix in the brown sugar. Add the melted butter to the milk mixture. In a separate mixing bowl, combine the cornmeal and flour. Sprinkle in the salt and the baking powder, and mix thoroughly. Stir in the currants. Add the liquid ingredients to the flour mixture and stir until just combined.

On a floured board or countertop, press the dough into an 8-inch circle about ½ inch thick. Slice the circle into eighths. Separate the eight wedges and place them on an oiled baking sheet. Bake for 15 to 20 minutes, until puffed and golden.

Cornmeal adds crunch and color to this classic scone recipe. We use low-fat milk and less butter to reduce the calories without sacrificing flavor.

PER SCONE: 195 CALORIES, 3.7 G PROTEIN, 6.6 G FAT, 30.4 G CARBOHYDRATE, 239 MG SODIUM, 17 MG CHOLESTEROL.

Excellent

MUFFIN MADNESS

PREPARATION TIME
15 minutes

BAKING TIME
20–25 minutes (10–15 minutes for mini-muffins)

SERVINGS
12 muffins

Popular at Moosewood brunches, muffins are an almost instantly gratifying, fresh-from-the-oven quick bread. These are sweet enough to serve as dessert.

BASIC WET INGREDIENTS
2 large eggs
½ cup vegetable oil
¾–1 cup brown sugar
½ teaspoon pure vanilla extract

≈

BASIC DRY INGREDIENTS
2 cups unbleached white flour
1 teaspoon baking powder
½ teaspoon salt

≈

ADDITIONAL INGREDIENTS
Choose a variation from the next page.*

The basic wet and dry ingredients are not intended to be a recipe for plain muffins; always choose one of the variations from the next page.

Preheat the oven to 350°.

In a large bowl, mix together the eggs, oil, brown sugar, and vanilla. Stir in the fruit or vegetable ingredients of your choice and mix well. In a separate bowl, sift together the flour, baking powder, and salt, and any spices your variation calls for. Stir the dry ingredients into the wet ingredients until just combined, being careful not to overmix the batter. Fold in the additional ingredients called for in your variation.

Spoon the batter into oiled standard muffin tins and bake for 20 to 25 minutes, until puffed and golden brown. (If you are using mini-muffin tins, bake for 10 to 15 minutes.) A knife inserted into the center of a muffin should come out clean.

These muffins will keep in a sealed container for 3 or 4 days, if they escape being devoured hot from the oven.

PER PLAIN MUFFIN: 219 CALORIES, 3 G PROTEIN, 10.5 G FAT, 28.3 G CARBOHYDRATE, 176 MG SODIUM, 35 MG CHOLESTEROL.

APPLE MUFFINS: Add 2 cups of grated tart apples and 1 teaspoon of freshly grated lemon peel to the wet ingredients. Add ½ teaspoon of cinnamon to the dry ingredients. If you like, fold ½ cup of chopped walnuts or pecans into the batter.

BANANA MUFFINS: Add 1½ cups of mashed ripe bananas to the wet ingredients. If you like, fold 1 cup of chopped nuts and/or ½ cup of chocolate chips into the batter.

BLUEBERRY-LEMON MUFFINS: Add 1½ cups of fresh or frozen blueberries and 1 tablespoon of freshly grated lemon peel to the wet ingredients.

ZUCCHINI MUFFINS: Add 2 cups of grated *small* zucchini to the wet ingredients, and 1 teaspoon of cinnamon and ½ teaspoon of ground cardamom to the dry ingredients. Fold ½ cup of raisins or currants, and ¾ cup of chopped nuts if you like, into the batter.

ok need to be sweeter

MULTIGRAIN MUFFINS

TOTAL TIME
30 minutes

SERVINGS
12 muffins

These muffins have a crisp crust and an unexpectedly delicate, light interior, despite being made with oats and wheat bran. Because Multigrain Muffins are not too sweet, they're welcome anytime from breakfast to dinner, or even as a midnight snack with hot cider or tea. They stay fresh and moist for 2 to 3 days and freeze well.

1 large egg or 2 egg whites, lightly beaten
¼ cup vegetable oil
1 cup buttermilk
⅓ cup packed brown sugar
½ cup quick-cooking oats

≈

1 cup unbleached white flour
1 cup whole wheat pastry flour (up to ½ cup may be replaced by wheat bran)
¼ teaspoon salt
1 teaspoon baking soda
1 teaspoon baking powder

Preheat the oven to 400°.

In a bowl, stir together the egg or egg whites, oil, buttermilk, brown sugar, and oats. In another bowl, combine the flours, optional wheat bran, and salt. Sprinkle in the baking soda and baking powder, and mix well. Add the liquid mixture to the dry ingredients, and stir just until a smooth batter is formed.

Spoon the batter into oiled muffin tins and bake for 20 minutes, until puffed and golden. A knife inserted in the center of a muffin should come out clean. Cool for 5 minutes and remove the muffins from the pan.

PER MUFFIN: 146 CALORIES, 5.8 G PROTEIN, 5.8 G FAT, 18 G CARBOHYDRATE, 171 MG SODIUM, 18 MG CHOLESTEROL.

VARIATIONS
• Add ½ teaspoon of cinnamon to the dry ingredients, and fold 1½ cups of chopped peeled apples into the finished batter.
• Add 1 tablespoon of freshly grated lemon peel to the dry ingredients, and fold 1½ cups of fresh or frozen blueberries into the finished batter.

PESTO PALMIERS

1 sheet commercially prepared puff pastry, defrosted
    (about ½ pound) (see page 339)
3 tablespoons pesto, homemade (see pages 362–63)
    or commercially prepared
3 tablespoons grated Parmesan or Pecorino cheese

Preheat the oven to 400°.

Working gently but quickly, unfold the puff pastry sheet. If you don't handle it too much and your counter is dry, you can ignore the recommendations on the back of the box and dispense with the floured board and the rolling pin. Spread the pesto and sprinkle the cheese evenly onto the sheet of pastry.

Curl the two longer edges up and roll them inward to meet in the middle. Dip your fingers in water and lightly dampen the pastry between the two rolls, then press them together along the seam. The pastry will now be a long rectangle. Cut it into ½-inch-thick slices, and place them flat on an ungreased baking sheet (the slices will be heart-shaped). Bake for about 20 minutes, or until the pastries are puffed and golden.

Serve immediately.

PER PASTRY: 80 CALORIES, 1.1 G PROTEIN, 6 G FAT, 5.2 G CARBOHYDRATE, 62 MG SODIUM, 1 MG CHOLESTEROL.

VARIATION

For different but equally tasty palmiers, substitute Salsa Verde (see page 105) or Olivada (see page 49) for the pesto in this recipe.

TOTAL TIME

30 minutes

SERVINGS

18 pastries

MENU

Serve as an appetizer, or make a light meal of them with Herbed Green Pea Soup (see page 29).

These savory palm-leaf-shaped pastries are quickly and easily made using the ingredients in a well-stocked pantry.

Excellent

SAVORY SCALLION BISCUITS

TOTAL TIME
30 minutes

SERVINGS
8 large wedges

This dependable quick bread is delicious with soups, stews, or salads, or on its own for brunch or breakfast.

1½ cups unbleached white flour
½ cup whole wheat pastry flour
2 teaspoons baking powder
½ teaspoon salt
2 tablespoons vegetable oil
1 cup low-fat plain yogurt
½ cup minced scallions
1 tablespoon chopped fresh dill
¼ teaspoon ground black pepper

Preheat the oven to 400°.

In a medium bowl, combine the white and whole wheat flours. Sprinkle in the baking powder and salt, and stir well. In a separate bowl, combine the oil, yogurt, scallions, dill, and pepper. Blend the yogurt mixture into the flour mixture quickly and thoroughly to form a soft dough.

On a floured board or countertop, pat the dough into a ¾-inch-thick circle and cut it into eight wedges. Separate the wedges and place them on an oiled baking sheet. Bake for 20 minutes, until a knife inserted in the center of a biscuit comes out clean. Serve warm.

PER BISCUIT: 141 CALORIES, 6 G PROTEIN, 4.2 G FAT, 19.5 G CARBOHYDRATE, 363 MG SODIUM, 2 MG CHOLESTEROL.

SALADS
AND SIDES

S UPPOSE YOU DON'T REALLY FEEL like doing much cooking, but the green beans or sugar snap peas in your garden are at their peak. What if the bok choy or kale at the market looks especially appealing, or you spot artichokes or red peppers at a price you can't resist, but you don't have a big production in mind? Look here for quick and simple dishes that can give a big boost to a meal.

Spicy Kale is a perfect side dish for Cajun Skillet Beans (see page 167). Apple-Celery en Bleu wonderfully complements Kasha with Mushrooms (page 148). Not Your Mother's Green Beans or Easy Elegant Asparagus can elevate a simple omelet to a *très chic* supper. Gigondes take only 5 minutes but can add substance to a meal of Spaghetti with Zucchini and Lemon (see page 195). Seasoned Tempeh is just the right side dish to pair with Curried Fried Rice (see page 226).

We find that the addition of one or two of these small dishes can speedily put a whole new slant on a meal of leftovers. No matter how good that soup or stew was yesterday, it may seem dreary to face it again today. But prospects will start to look up when a colorful Fresh Mozzarella and Tomato Salad or a crisp, bright Carrot and Parsley Salad appears on the table alongside it.

These versatile dishes are also ideal for mixing and matching with each other. Serving several of them together makes an interesting and satisfying casual meal that truly reflects the way most of us eat at home. Here and on the next page are some combinations out of the many possibilities:

Fresh Mozzarella and Tomato
Salad
Broiled Eggplant
Not Your Mother's Green Beans

Seasoned Tempeh
Asian Cabbage Slaw
Curried Cauliflower

Roasted Vegetable Salad with
Garlic and Rosemary
Lemon Tomato Salad

SALADS

APPLE-CELERY EN BLEU

1 Empire or Mutsu apple
2–3 celery stalks
⅓ cup crumbled blue or Roquefort cheese
enough of your favorite leafy salad greens for 2 servings
1 tablespoon balsamic vinegar or fresh lemon juice
1 tablespoon olive oil
1 teaspoon honey
salt and ground black pepper to taste

Core the apple and cut it into ½-inch pieces. Thinly slice the celery. Combine the apples, celery, and crumbled cheese in a serving bowl. Rinse the greens, shake them dry, tear them into bite-sized pieces, and add them to the bowl. In a cup, use a fork to whisk together the vinegar or lemon juice, oil, and honey. Pour the dressing over the salad, toss well, and add salt and pepper to taste. Serve immediately.

PER 4-OZ SERVING: 118 CALORIES, 5 G PROTEIN, 7.7 G FAT, 9.1 G CARBOHYDRATE, 368 MG SODIUM, 14 MG CHOLESTEROL.

TOTAL TIME
10 minutes
SERVINGS
2

A crisp and refreshing side dish or dessert salad. If you can't get Empire or Mutsu apples, any sweet variety with a nice crunch will do.

ASIAN CABBAGE SLAW

PREPARATION TIME

15 minutes

SITTING TIME

10 – 15 minutes

TOTAL TIME

25 – 30 minutes

SERVINGS

4

MENU

Serve with Broiled
Eggplant (see page 74),
Teriyaki Broiled or Grilled
Fish (see page 256), or a
simple tofu dish such
as Broiled Tofu
(see page 261).

A delicious and refreshing change from the usual coleslaw. This salad will keep, covered and refrigerated, for 3 or 4 days.

2½ cups finely shredded cabbage
1 cup grated carrots
½ cup diced or julienned red or green bell pepper

DRESSING
2 tablespoons vegetable oil
2 tablespoons rice vinegar
1 tablespoon soy sauce
2 teaspoons brown sugar
½ teaspoon grated fresh ginger root
dash of chili oil, Tabasco, or
       other hot pepper sauce (optional)

≈

⅓ cup chopped peanuts, or 1 tablespoon toasted sesame
       seeds (see page 354) (optional)

Combine the cabbage, carrots, and bell peppers in a serving bowl and set aside. In a separate bowl, whisk together the oil, vinegar, soy sauce, brown sugar, ginger, and optional chili oil. Pour the dressing over the vegetables and toss well. Set aside to marinate for 10 to 15 minutes.

Just before serving, mix the slaw well and add the chopped nuts or toasted seeds, if you like.

PER 4-OZ SERVING, WITH DRESSING: 154 CALORIES, 1.5 G PROTEIN, 11.6 G FAT, 13 G CARBOHYDRATE, 408 MG SODIUM, 0 MG CHOLESTEROL.

DRESSING ALONE PER 2-OZ: 152 CALORIES, 0.5 G PROTEIN, 14.2 G FAT, 6.8 G CARBOHYDRATE, 470 MG SODIUM, 0 MG CHOLESTEROL.

CARROT AND PARSLEY SALAD

3½ cups grated carrots
1 bunch parsley, finely chopped (about 2 cups)
1 garlic clove, minced or pressed
3 tablespoons fresh lemon juice
¼ cup vegetable oil *
½ teaspoon salt
plenty of freshly ground black pepper to taste

Extra-virgin olive oil, canola oil, peanut oil, or any combination of these is fine.

Combine the carrots, parsley, garlic, lemon juice, oil, salt, and pepper in a serving bowl and toss well.

Carrot and Parsley Salad can be made ahead and refrigerated, covered, until serving time. It will keep nicely for 2 or 3 days.

PER 4-OZ SERVING: 122 CALORIES, 1.4 G PROTEIN, 8.9 G FAT, 10.5 G CARBOHYDRATE, 237 MG SODIUM, 0 MG CHOLESTEROL.

VARIATIONS

• Add 1 tablespoon of chopped fresh mint.
• Add 1 tablespoon of chopped fresh chives.
• Add 1 teaspoon of ground cumin.

TOTAL TIME
15 minutes

SERVINGS
6

MENU
Colorful, crisp, tangy, and sweet, this light and refreshing salad provides a bright counterpoint to a smoother, softer, substantial entrée such as Pasta with Beans and Endive (see page 185) or North African Cauliflower Soup (see page 33).

If your main dish already contains plenty of greenery, you might choose this to accompany it instead of a green salad. It can be made in no time with a food processor and takes only a little longer if you're grating the carrots by hand.

DILLY BEANS

TOTAL TIME

15 minutes

SERVINGS

4 to 6

MENU

Serve as a garnish for green salads or as a side dish with sandwiches or frittatas.

Many of us at Moosewood Restaurant "put up" Dilly Beans during the summer and then conjure up fond memories of the vegetable garden as we eat them during the winter. These intensely flavored beans can be prepared on the spot anytime.

1½ cups water
2 cups stemmed green beans (about ¾ pound)
2 tablespoons chopped fresh dill

≈

2 large garlic cloves, pressed
¼ teaspoon red pepper flakes
⅓ cup cider vinegar
½ teaspoon sugar or honey
1 teaspoon vegetable oil (optional)

Bring the water to a boil in a small pot. Cook the beans, covered, for 3 to 5 minutes. Drain the beans when they are still bright green and just tender, and place them in a bowl. Stir the dill into the warm beans.

Combine the garlic, red pepper flakes, vinegar, and sugar or honey in a saucepan and quickly bring to a boil. Simmer for 2 minutes. Pour the dressing over the green beans and mix well. Add the oil if you like. Serve immediately, or chill for about 20 minutes and serve later.

Covered and refrigerated, Dilly Beans will keep for 4 days.

PER 4-OZ SERVING: 38 CALORIES, 1.7 G PROTEIN, 0.3 G FAT, 9 G CARBOHYDRATE, 3 MG SODIUM, 0 MG CHOLESTEROL.

FENNEL AND ORANGE SALAD

2 fennel bulbs (also called finocchio or fresh anise)
4 oranges
juice of 1 lemon
2 tablespoons extra-virgin olive oil
salt and freshly ground black pepper to taste

Remove the feathery leaves and stalks of the fennel. Slice off the root end and discard it. Discard any discolored or damaged outer layers. Slice each fennel bulb crosswise into thin slices. If the slices are too wide to be bite-sized, cut them in half. Place the fennel slices in a bowl. Section the oranges into the bowl, squeezing in the extra juice as well. Stir in the lemon juice and olive oil, and add salt and pepper to taste. Cover and refrigerate for at least 20 minutes or until ready to serve.

PER 4-OZ SERVING: 70 CALORIES, 1.9 G PROTEIN, 7.4 G FAT, 24.8 G CARBOHYDRATE, 48 MG SODIUM, 0 MG CHOLESTEROL.

PREPARATION TIME
15 minutes

CHILLING TIME
20 minutes

TOTAL TIME
35 minutes

SERVINGS
4 to 6

MENU
Its mild anise flavor, celery-like crispness, and visual appeal make this a refreshing salad to follow a rich pasta meal or a hearty stew.

A newcomer to many American tables, fennel, or finocchio, has been a staple in Italy for as long as anyone can remember.

FRESH MOZZARELLA AND TOMATO SALAD

TOTAL TIME
10 minutes

SERVINGS
4 to 6

MENU
Serve with Spaghetti with Zucchini and Lemon (see page 195), or Chick Pea and Artichoke Heart Stew (see page 204), or as a side dish with Bruschetta and Crostini (see pages 262–63).

This dish is an inspired juxtaposition of flavors, textures, and colors — mild, creamy fresh mozzarella and sweet but acidic juicy tomatoes, held together by a thread of olive oil. It should be served only when tomatoes are in season.

¾ **pound fresh mozzarella, sliced into ¼-inch-thick rounds**
2 – 3 ripe tomatoes, cut into ¼-inch-thick slices
1 tablespoon chopped fresh basil
salt and ground black pepper to taste
extra-virgin olive oil to taste

On a large serving platter, arrange rows or rings of alternating and slightly overlapping slices of mozzarella and tomatoes. Sprinkle the basil over them, and add salt and pepper to taste. Drizzle a thin line of oil down the center of each row of slices, and serve.

If you make the salad ahead of time, don't salt it. Store it, covered, in the refrigerator. Before serving, allow it to warm to room temperature and add the salt at the last minute.

PER 4 OZ SERVING: 190 CALORIES, 17.2 G PROTEIN, 11.2 G FAT, 5.5 G CARBOHYDRATE, 357 MG SODIUM, 39 MG CHOLESTEROL.

VARIATIONS

• Instead of the basil, use chopped fresh thyme, oregano, parsley, or chives.
• Top each slice of tomato and cheese with a tiny dollop of Salsa Verde (see page 105) or Cilantro Pesto (see page 363).
• Instead of mozzarella, sprinkle the tomato slices with a piquant cheese such as feta, ricotta salata, or chèvre.
• Add any of the following to the basic recipe: thinly sliced red onion, sliced olives, capers, chopped watercress or arugula, minced sun-dried tomatoes.

GIGONDES

1½ cups drained canned gigondes, butter beans,
 or giant lima beans (14-ounce can)
1 tablespoon olive oil
juice of ½ lemon
1 tablespoon minced fresh parsley or basil

≈

½ cup Creamy Garlic Dressing (see page 95) (optional)

Gently rinse the beans and drain again. Place the drained beans in a serving bowl. Sprinkle with the olive oil, lemon juice, and parsley or basil. Mix gently with a wooden spoon. Store refrigerated up to 3 days. Serve at room temperature.

PER 4-OZ SERVING: 173 CALORIES, 9.8 G PROTEIN, 3.9 G FAT, 26 G CARBOHYDRATE, 6 MG SODIUM, 0 MG CHOLESTEROL.

TOTAL TIME
5 minutes

SERVINGS
4 as an appetizer

MENU
Gigondes are perfect as part of a meal composed of a few other small dishes, such as Pesto Palmiers (see page 57) or Peperonata (see page 83) with a few olives, either on the side or added to the peperonata.

Prepared in a matter of minutes, this uncomplicated first course is full of flavor. The big buttery beans are good simply marinated in olive oil, lemon, and parsley, or really jazzed up with a drizzling of Creamy Garlic Dressing. You could also serve the dressing in a separate bowl for dipping.

Lemon Tomato Salad

TOTAL TIME
5 minutes

SERVINGS
2 to 4

MENU
Serve this with
Mushroom and
Smoked-Cheese Pizza
(see page 280), Pasta with
Greens and Ricotta
(see page 188), or Greek
Spinach Frittata
(see page 291).

For serious lemon lovers, a salad to complement a cheese-rich entrée or merely to highlight fresh, ripe tomatoes.

2 tomatoes, chopped or thinly sliced
juice of 1 lemon
1 tablespoon vegetable oil or olive oil
salt and ground black pepper to taste

OPTIONAL
½ cucumber, sliced
½ avocado, pitted, peeled, and cubed
2 thin slices red onion, separated into rings

In a serving bowl, combine the tomatoes, lemon juice, oil, and salt and pepper. If you choose to add the cucumber, avocado, and/or red onion, stir them into the tomatoes. Serve immediately.

PER 4-OZ SERVING: 63 CALORIES, 0.9 G PROTEIN, 5.1 G FAT, 5.2 G CARBOHYDRATE, 66 MG SODIUM, 0 MG CHOLESTEROL.

MARINATED ZUCCHINI

Good

2–3 medium-small zucchini (about 1 pound)
2 tablespoons olive oil
4 garlic cloves, minced or pressed
1 tablespoon chopped fresh mint, basil, or thyme
1 tablespoon red wine vinegar
dash of salt

Wash and dry the zucchini. Cut them diagonally into long, oval-shaped ⅓-inch-thick slices. In a large heavy skillet, heat just enough oil to coat the bottom of the skillet. Quickly fry the zucchini slices in a couple of batches (add more oil if necessary) until golden-speckled on both sides and tender in the center. Drain the fried zucchini slices on paper towels. Lower the heat and sauté the garlic, stirring it constantly until just golden but not brown. Arrange the zucchini on a platter or in a bowl, and sprinkle with the chopped mint, vinegar, salt, and garlic. Cover and set aside to serve at room temperature.

This marinated zucchini may be kept, refrigerated, for a week or so, but bring it to room temperature before serving.

PER 4-OZ SERVING: 85 CALORIES, 0.9 G PROTEIN, 7.2 G FAT, 5.5 G CARBOHYDRATE, 48 MG SODIUM, 0 MG CHOLESTEROL.

VARIATIONS

• Use balsamic vinegar or lemon juice instead of the red wine vinegar.
• Use very small or Japanese eggplants instead of the zucchini.

TIME-SAVING TIP: If you want to double or triple this recipe, it will be faster and easier to broil the zucchini: Sauté the garlic in the oil in a small saucepan until golden but not brown. Remove the garlic pieces with a slotted spoon, and set them aside. Using a pastry brush, coat the zucchini slices on both sides with the garlic-flavored oil. Place them on a broiler pan and broil close to the heat for 3 to 4 minutes on each side, until golden-speckled. Arrange and season as described.

TOTAL TIME
25 minutes

SERVINGS
4

MENU
Serve as an accompaniment to grilled fish or on an antipasto platter with olives, tomatoes, and celery. You might eat Marinated Zucchini with bread and cheese and call it lunch. Tuck a few slices into a grilled cheese sandwich, put some in an omelet, or mix a few into a tossed salad.

Sautéing vegetables quickly in oil and then marinating them in vinegar is an age-old Mediterranean cooking method. It's best to use small, firm, young zucchini that have no large seeds.

Vegetables in Mint Vinaigrette

TOTAL TIME

15 minutes

SERVINGS

4

*H*ere crisp
*vegetables are
graced with a
subtle and refreshing
dressing.*

1 cup water
2½ cups fresh or frozen cut corn (10 ounces)
1 medium zucchini, diced
¼ cup diced red bell pepper

≈

2 tablespoons vegetable oil
2 tablespoons cider vinegar (or more to taste)
4 leaves fresh mint, minced
¼ cup chopped fresh parsley
½ teaspoon sugar or honey
salt and ground black pepper to taste

≈

minced scallions (optional)

In a covered saucepan, bring the water, corn, and zucchini to a boil. Add the bell pepper and simmer for about a minute. Drain the vegetables and set them aside in a serving bowl.

In a separate bowl, mix together the oil, vinegar, mint, parsley, and sugar or honey. Pour the vinaigrette over the hot vegetables and mix well. Add salt and pepper to taste. Serve at room temperature, topped with minced scallions if you like.

PER 4-OZ SERVING: 95 CALORIES, 2 G PROTEIN, 4.6 G FAT, 13.8 G CARBOHYDRATE, 38 MG SODIUM, 0 MG CHOLESTEROL.

NOTE: To chill the salad, refrigerate it for at least 15 minutes. The vegetables will absorb some of the flavor while chilling, so you may want to add a dash of vinegar or black pepper just before serving.

SIDES

BROCCOLI AND CARROTS WITH LIME DRESSING

2 carrots, thinly sliced on the diagonal
3 stalks broccoli, heads cut into florets, stalks peeled and
    sliced on the diagonal

DRESSING
1 tablespoon dark sesame oil
1 tablespoon soy sauce
2 teaspoons honey
3 tablespoons fresh lime juice (about 1 lime)
salt and ground black pepper to taste
dash of chili oil, Tabasco, or other hot pepper sauce
    (optional)

Bring about 2 inches of water to a rapid boil in a covered pot. When the water boils, add the vegetables, cover, and simmer for about 5 minutes, until tender but firm. While the vegetables cook, mix together all of the dressing ingredients. Drain the vegetables, plunge them into cold water, drain again, and chill until ready to serve or serve at room temperature.

Just before serving, toss the vegetables with the dressing.

PER 4-OZ SERVING: 166 CALORIES, 5.4 G PROTEIN, 10.1 G FAT, 17.7 G CARBOHYDRATE, 797 MG SODIUM, 0 MG CHOLESTEROL.

DRESSING PER 2-OZ SERVING: 120 CALORIES, 0.7 G PROTEIN, 9.9 G FAT, 8.5 G CARBOHYDRATE, 777 MG SODIUM, 0 MG CHOLESTEROL.

TOTAL TIME
20 minutes

SERVINGS
4 to 6

MENU
Serve with Noodles with Mirin (see page 32) or Fried Rice (see page 230) for a light meal.

Contrasting tastes and colors make this a brightly flavored dish.

BROILED EGGPLANT

This recipe has infinite variations. Broiled Eggplant can be served hot or at room temperature. Leftovers are good in sandwiches or chopped for a pasta sauce or pizza topping.

Broiled Eggplant is the kind of dish that slips up and down menus, as an antipasto, an entrée, or a side dish, rounding out any number of meals with little effort. Here are some possibilities:

• Broiled Eggplant sprinkled with olive oil and vinegar as an antipasto before Spaghetti with Pecorino and Black Pepper (see page 194) or Pasta Fresca (see page 184).

• Broiled Eggplant topped with sesame oil and lemon, followed by Udon Noodles and Vegetables (see page 136) and spinach or green beans.

• Broiled Eggplant sprinkled with feta cheese, served with Mediterranean Lentil Salad (see page 131) and imported olives.

• Broiled Eggplant served with chunks of boiled potatoes, a steamed green vegetable, and Aioli (see page 107).

**oil (olive oil, vegetable oil, sesame oil, or hot sesame oil)
eggplants (1 Japanese eggplant serves 2,
　　1 medium eggplant serves 4)
salt and ground black pepper**

Using a pastry brush, coat a baking sheet with oil. If you're using a large eggplant, cut it into ½-inch-thick rounds. If you're using Japanese or small eggplants, cut them lengthwise into ½-inch-thick slices. Arrange the slices in a single layer on the baking sheet. Brush the tops of the slices with oil.

Broil a few inches from the heat for 7 to 12 minutes, until the slices are golden brown. Turn the baking sheet once if your broiler heat is uneven. If the interior is still too firm when the outside is browned, bake the eggplant at 400° for a few minutes until soft. Sprinkle with salt and pepper to taste.

PER 4-OZ SERVING: 34 CALORIES, 1 G PROTEIN, 0.3 G FAT, 7.8 G CARBOHYDRATE, 86 MG SODIUM, 0 MG CHOLESTEROL.

CURRIED CAULIFLOWER

1 medium head cauliflower
2 tablespoons vegetable oil
1 teaspoon black or brown mustard seeds *
2 teaspoons grated fresh ginger root
1 teaspoon ground coriander
½ teaspoon turmeric
¼ teaspoon ground cardamom
⅛ teaspoon cayenne (or to taste)
½ cup unsweetened apple juice
2 tablespoons fresh lemon juice
dash of salt

Yellow mustard seeds can be used in a pinch if black or brown seeds are not available.

Wash the cauliflower and cut it into florets of nearly equal size. Heat the oil on high heat in a skillet or saucepan large enough to hold the cauliflower in a single layer. Add the mustard seeds and cook them until they begin to pop. Stir in the ginger, coriander, turmeric, cardamom, cayenne, and the cauliflower florets, and toss them together. Pour in the apple and lemon juices, sprinkle with salt, cover, and simmer, stirring a couple of times, until the cauliflower is just tender, about 5 minutes.

Serve hot or at room temperature.

PER 4-OZ SERVING: 73 CALORIES, 1.9 G PROTEIN, 4.4 G FAT, 7.8 G CARBOHYDRATE, 31 MG SODIUM, 0 MG CHOLESTEROL.

VARIATIONS

• Toss Curried Cauliflower with a cup of plain yogurt.
• Chill Curried Cauliflower for 30 minutes, and then serve it topped with a dollop of plain yogurt and 2 tablespoons of currants.

TOTAL TIME
20 minutes

SERVINGS
4

MENU
Serve with a sweet chutney, Seitan – Green Bean Curry (see page 238), and Coconut Basmati Rice (see page 155) for an Indian feast. For a quick soup, blend leftovers with cooked potatoes, sautéed onions, and plain yogurt or unsweetened apple juice.

A very attractive low-calorie dish of tangy golden florets sprinkled with black mustard seeds, Curried Cauliflower looks especially pretty when it's garnished with tomato wedges and cilantro sprigs.

CURRIED CORN AND PEPPERS

TOTAL TIME

15 minutes

SERVINGS

4

MENU

Serve as a filling for an omelet or burrito, as an accompaniment to Coconut Basmati Rice (see page 155) or Saffron Orzo (see page 149), or as a stuffing for pita bread along with some Monterey Jack cheese.

A simple dish that can play many roles.

1 cup chopped scallions
1 red or green bell pepper, diced
1 tablespoon butter
1 teaspoon curry powder
2½ cups fresh or frozen cut corn (10-ounce box)
2 tomatoes
salt and ground black pepper to taste

Sauté the scallions and bell pepper in the butter on medium heat for about 2 minutes. Stir in the curry powder and the corn. Chop the tomatoes and add them to the skillet. Continue to cook for about 5 minutes, stirring frequently, until the vegetables are thoroughly heated. Add salt and pepper to taste.

PER 4-OZ SERVING: 74 CALORIES, 2.2 G PROTEIN, 1.3 G FAT, 16 G CARBOHYDRATE, 38 MG SODIUM, 1 MG CHOLESTEROL.

EASIEST ARTICHOKES

4 whole artichokes
juice of 2 lemons (about 1½ tablespoons per artichoke)
4 teaspoons extra-virgin olive oil (or more to taste)

TO FLAVOR THE COOKING WATER
(OPTIONAL)
bay leaves, peppercorns, lemon juice, vinegar, garlic,
   capers, or fennel seeds

Bring about 4 inches of water to a rapid boil in a large covered nonreactive pot. Add any of the optional flavorings you choose. While the water heats, place each artichoke on its side and remove the stem with a vertical cut to create a flat base. Slice ½ to ¾ inch from the top of the artichoke cone to produce a neat flat top.

For a gourmet touch, you can trim off the barbed top of each of the outer leaves with scissors. This is not necessary, however, since the barbs will soften with cooking. When trimming many artichokes at once, or if trimming them an hour or so ahead of time, rub the cut surfaces with a piece of fresh lemon, or dip the trimmed artichokes into lemon water, to prevent discoloration.

When the water boils, ease the trimmed artichokes, stem end down, into the pot. Cover, lower the heat, and simmer for 25 to 40 minutes, until the bottoms of the artichokes are easily pierced with a fork and the leaves are easy to pull off. The cooking time will vary depending upon the variety, maturity, size, and tenderness of the particular artichokes.

Drain the artichokes, place them upright on a serving plate, and drizzle the lemon juice and olive oil over them. Serve immediately, or allow to cool to room temperature, or chill for at least 30 minutes. Cooked artichokes will keep in a tightly sealed container in the refrigerator for several days.

PER 4-OZ SERVING: 98 CALORIES, 3.7 G PROTEIN, 4.9 G FAT, 13.1 G CARBOHYDRATE, 95 MG SODIUM, 0 MG CHOLESTEROL.

TOTAL TIME
30–45 minutes

SERVINGS
4

MENU
Hot, room temperature, or chilled, artichokes are delicious plain, stuffed, or served with any number of sauces or dips. We've enjoyed them with Aioli (see page 107), Roasted Garlic Dressing (see page 99), Honey Mustard Vinaigrette (see page 97), Orange Mustard Dressing (see page 125), and Salsa Verde (see page 105).

This is the fastest, simplest way to prepare artichokes. They make a perfect first course for a last-minute pasta meal, yet they also serve well as a slow-down course in the middle of a more elaborate meal.

EASY ELEGANT ASPARAGUS

TOTAL TIME

15 minutes

SERVINGS

3 to 4

MENU

Serve as an accompaniment to an omelet or frittata, fish, or a pasta dish.

*T*his dish is a harmonious combination of four delicious flavors.

1 **pound fresh asparagus**
1½ **tablespoons pine nuts**
2 **tablespoons melted butter**
2 **teaspoons balsamic vinegar**

Wash the asparagus and snap off the tough ends. Steam the asparagus or cook them in a small amount of boiling water for 3 to 6 minutes, until bright green and just tender. The cooking time will vary depending on the age and thickness of the spears. While the asparagus cook, toast the pine nuts (see page 354). In a small bowl, stir together the melted butter and the vinegar.

When the asparagus are ready, drain them and arrange them on a serving platter. Drizzle the butter sauce on top and sprinkle with the toasted pine nuts. Serve immediately, and offer salt and pepper at the table.

PER 4-OZ SERVING: 93 CALORIES, 3.5 G PROTEIN, 7.6 G FAT, 5.3 G CARBOHYDRATE, 63 MG SODIUM, 16 MG CHOLESTEROL.

EASY REFRITOS

⅔ cup chopped onions
2 garlic cloves, minced or pressed
1½ tablespoons olive oil
2 teaspoons ground cumin
¼ cup diced green or red bell pepper (optional)
2 cups cooked black beans or pinto beans (16-ounce can)
ground black pepper to taste

In a heavy skillet, sauté the onions and garlic in the oil on medium heat for 3 to 4 minutes, until the onions begin to soften. Add the cumin and the optional bell pepper, and continue to sauté for 5 minutes, until the onions begin to brown. While the vegetables sauté, drain the beans, reserving their liquid. Add the drained beans to the skillet and continue to cook for 2 minutes, stirring constantly, until the beans are hot. Remove the skillet from the heat. Using a potato masher, thoroughly mash the beans while adding as much of the reserved bean liquid as necessary to reach a soft, spreadable consistency. Add black pepper to taste. Serve hot.

PER 4-OZ SERVING: 176 CALORIES, 8.2 G PROTEIN, 4.6 G FAT, 26.6 G CARBOHYDRATE, 4 MG SODIUM, 0 MG CHOLESTEROL.

VARIATION

Add 1 or 2 tablespoons of chopped fresh cilantro to the sautéing vegetables just before you add the beans.

TOTAL TIME
15 minutes

SERVINGS
4

MENU
This is wonderful as a topping for crisp tortillas, a filling for quesadillas, or a side dish for a Mexican meal.

Try tossing Easy Refritos with chunks of Monterey Jack cheese, cubes of fresh avocado, and chopped tomatoes or salsa. Black beans work just as well as the more traditional pinto beans, so you may like to try them for a change. Olives are a nice garnish — black olives with pinto beans, Spanish olives with black beans.

MEXICAN SEITAN

TOTAL TIME
20 minutes

SERVINGS
2 to 4

MENU
Serve with rice,
cornbread, warmed
tortillas, or tortilla chips.
At Moosewood
Restaurant we often use
Mexican Seitan to fill
burritos, or to top pizzas
and tostadas.

*S*eitan, or wheat
gluten, is a
low fat,
pleasantly chewy high-
protein food available
in health food stores.

1 cup chopped onions
3 garlic cloves, minced or pressed
2 tablespoons olive oil
½ medium green bell pepper
½ pound seitan (wheat gluten)
1 tablespoon chili powder
½ teaspoon dried oregano
½ teaspoon dried basil
1 teaspoon soy sauce
1 teaspoon Tabasco or other hot pepper sauce (or to taste)
1 cup chopped tomatoes
salt or soy sauce to taste

Sauté the onions and garlic in the oil for about 4 minutes, until softened. Chop the pepper and add it to the pan. Coarsely grate or finely chop the seitan. Mix it into the vegetables along with the chili powder, oregano, basil, soy sauce, and Tabasco. Sauté for a minute, stirring constantly to prevent sticking. Stir in the tomatoes, reduce the heat, and simmer, uncovered, for about 5 minutes. Mexican Seitan should be moist but not too juicy.

Add salt or soy sauce to taste, and serve.

PER 4-OZ SERVING: 82 CALORIES, 8.5 G PROTEIN, 3.8 G FAT, 4.3 G CARBOHYDRATE, 44 MG SODIUM, 0 MG CHOLESTEROL.

MUSHROOMS IN LEMON MARINADE

1 pound small mushrooms
3 tablespoons olive oil
3 garlic cloves, minced or pressed
1 tablespoon minced fresh basil or marjoram (1 teaspoon
    dried)
2 tablespoons minced fresh parsley
juice of 1 lemon (about ¼ to ⅓ cup)
salt and ground black pepper to taste

Wash the mushrooms, and slice off and discard the stems. In a heavy nonreactive skillet, heat the olive oil. Sauté the garlic for just a moment, taking care not to scorch it. Add the mushrooms and herbs, and sauté on medium heat, stirring occasionally, for 4 minutes. Add the lemon juice, toss it well with the mushrooms, and cook for another minute. Pour the mushrooms and juice into a serving bowl, and add salt and pepper to taste.

Serve hot or at room temperature.

PER 4-OZ SERVING: 128 CALORIES, 2.4 G PROTEIN, 11.2 G FAT, 7.4 G CARBOHYDRATE, 47 MG SODIUM, 0 MG CHOLESTEROL.

TOTAL TIME
15 minutes

SERVINGS
6 to 8

MENU
This tasty dish is good as an appetizer, a garnish for green salad, an addition to an antipasto platter, or a side dish for pasta, such as Pasta with Beans and Endive (see page 185) or Spaghetti with Pecorino and Black Pepper (see page 194). It is an excellent dish to add to a buffet table.

very good

NOT YOUR MOTHER'S GREEN BEANS

MENU
Serve these beans with a simple fish dish, such as Fish Otis (see page 251), or with Broiled Polenta with Mushrooms and Cheese (see page 152).

Green beans step out! Their elegant companions here are pine nuts and a shallot vinaigrette. The bright flavor of this dressing is also delicious on steamed asparagus and other vegetables.

½ cup pine nuts
3–4 cups water
1 pound green beans

≈

1 large shallot, peeled and minced, or ¼ cup chopped scallions
¼ cup raspberry or balsamic vinegar
¼ cup olive oil
2 tablespoons chopped fresh parsley, chervil, or basil
salt and ground black pepper to taste

Toast the pine nuts (see page 354) for about 10 minutes or until golden brown. While the nuts are toasting, bring the water to a boil in a small saucepan, and remove and discard the ends of the green beans. Ease the beans into the boiling water and cook them for about 3 to 6 minutes, or until just tender.

Combine the shallots or scallions, vinegar, oil, and herb of your choice in a medium bowl. Drain the beans thoroughly and immediately add them to the bowl, tossing them with the dressing. Stir in the toasted pine nuts. Add salt and pepper to taste. Serve warm, or chill for 20 minutes and then serve.

PER 4-OZ SERVING: 163 CALORIES, 3.8 G PROTEIN, 14.5 G FAT, 9 G CARBOHYDRATE, 41 MG SODIUM, 0 MG CHOLESTEROL.

PEPERONATA

3 red bell peppers
3 green or yellow bell peppers
2–3 red or white onions (about 3 cups sliced)
2 tablespoons olive oil

≈

1 cup undrained canned plum tomatoes, or
    2 fresh tomatoes (optional)
2 tablespoons red wine vinegar (optional)
salt and ground black pepper to taste
1 teaspoon sugar (optional)

Slice the peppers and onions lengthwise into strips. Heat the oil in a large skillet or saucepan. Add the peppers and onions and sauté on medium heat, stirring frequently, for 10 to 15 minutes, until tender and lightly browned.

While the vegetables sauté, chop the tomatoes if you'll be using them. Stir the tomatoes and optional vinegar into the peppers and cook for about 5 minutes more, until the liquid has evaporated. Add salt and pepper to taste. Add sugar if desired.

Serve hot or at room temperature.

Covered in the refrigerator, Peperonata will keep for about 1 week. Allow it to come to room temperature before serving.

PER 4-OZ SERVING: 58 CALORIES, 1.1 G PROTEIN, 3.1 G FAT, 7.7 G CARBOHYDRATE, 62 MG SODIUM, 0 MG CHOLESTEROL.

VARIATION

• Add capers or chopped black or green olives at the same time as the tomatoes.

TOTAL TIME
30 minutes

SERVINGS
about 6 cups

MENU
Serve on toasted bread or grilled polenta, over pasta with a piquant cheese such as ricotta salata, as a vegetable side dish or relish, mixed with steamed green beans, on a baked potato, with hard-boiled eggs as a salad, or as a quesadilla filling. It's wonderful in frittatas; and then you can use the frittata leftovers in a sandwich!

This colorful classic Italian pepper and onion sauté is extremely versatile.

ROASTED VEGETABLE SALAD WITH GARLIC AND ROSEMARY

TOTAL TIME
35 minutes

SERVINGS
4

MENU
A nice main course with bread, cherry tomatoes, and cheese. An excellent side salad for a simple fish or bean dish. This salad can be served warm or at room temperature and is perfect for picnics, trips, and covered-dish suppers.

The pungent flavors of rosemary, wine vinegar, and olives balance the sweetness of the vegetables in this good-looking salad.

4 cups water
6 red potatoes (2–3 inches in diameter), cut into
    1-inch cubes
1 red bell pepper, cut into bite-sized chunks
1 green bell pepper, cut into bite-sized chunks
3 cups mushrooms, cleaned, stemmed, and halved if large
10 garlic cloves, coarsely chopped
¼ cup olive oil
2 teaspoons chopped fresh or dried rosemary
salt and freshly ground black pepper

     ≈

2 tablespoons wine vinegar or balsamic vinegar

Bring the water to a rapid boil in a large saucepan. Boil the potato cubes for 5 minutes. Drain the potatoes thoroughly, and in a bowl, toss the cooked potatoes with the bell peppers, mushrooms, garlic, olive oil, and rosemary until the vegetables are well coated with the rosemary and oil. Spread the vegetables on a broiler pan, sprinkle generously with salt and pepper, and broil for 10 to 12 minutes, until slightly crisped and browned at the edges. Stir once or twice to ensure even cooking.

Return the roasted vegetables to the bowl and toss with the vinegar. Serve hot or at room temperature.

HINT: If you line your broiler pan with aluminum foil, it will hold all the savory juices and speed the cleanup process.

PER 4-OZ SERVING: 111 CALORIES, 1.9 G PROTEIN, 4.6 G FAT, 16.7 G CARBOHYDRATE, 17 MG SODIUM, 0 MG CHOLESTEROL.

SEASONED TEMPEH

8 ounces tempeh (fresh or defrosted)

MARINADE
2 tablespoons white or cider vinegar
2 tablespoons soy sauce
1 tablespoon water
½ teaspoon ground fennel seeds
1 garlic clove, minced or pressed (optional)
≈
2 tablespoons vegetable oil
salt and ground black pepper to taste

TOTAL TIME
15 minutes
SERVINGS
4
MENU
Serve as a side dish for Curried Fried Rice (see page 226) or Couscous with Sun-Dried Tomatoes (see page 145).

This tasty dish can also be added to soups, stews, salads, or filled tortillas. Tailor the seasoning to suit your meal.

Cut the tempeh into small cubes or strips and set aside. In a non-reactive shallow bowl, stir together the marinade ingredients. Add the tempeh pieces and toss until the marinade is absorbed.

In a heavy skillet, sauté the tempeh in the oil on medium-high heat for 7 to 10 minutes, until golden and crisp. If necessary, add more oil to prevent sticking. Add salt and pepper to taste, and serve immediately.

PER 4-OZ SERVING: 239 CALORIES, 14.5 G PROTEIN, 15.3 G FAT, 13.6 G CARBOHYDRATE, 220 MG SODIUM, 0 MG CHOLESTEROL.

VARIATIONS

• For Mexican-style tempeh, add ½ teaspoon of ground cumin and ½ teaspoon of dried oregano to the basic marinade.
• For Italian-style tempeh, add ½ teaspoon of dried basil to the marinade.
• For Greek-style tempeh, add ½ teaspoon of dried oregano and ½ teaspoon of dried mint to the marinade.

SESAME SPINACH

TOTAL TIME
15 minutes

SERVINGS
2 to 4

MENU
Serve with rice and
Seasoned Tempeh
(see page 85), with
Broiled Tofu
(see page 261), with
Teriyaki Grilled Fish
(see page 256), or with
Broiled Eggplant with
Miso Sauce (see page 74).

*T*his is an
unusual way to
prepare
spinach — with the
zing of ginger and the
nutty flavor of sesame.

10 ounces fresh spinach, well rinsed and stemmed
1 teaspoon sesame seeds
2 – 3 tablespoons Asian Marinade (see page 108)*
1 tablespoon dark sesame oil (optional)

** If you don't have Asian Marinade on hand and you want only enough
for this dish, use the following quantities: 1 tablespoon soy sauce, 1
tablespoon dry sherry, 1½ teaspoons rice vinegar, a rounded ½ teaspoon
brown sugar, and a ¼-inch-thick slice of ginger root. Bring to a boil in a
tiny saucepan. Let cool while the spinach cooks. Remove the ginger before
tossing with the spinach.*

In a covered saucepan, cook the still-damp spinach on medium
heat for about 4 minutes, until limp but still bright green (the water
clinging to the leaves will provide enough moisture). While the
spinach is cooking, toast the sesame seeds (see page 354).

In a colander or sieve, drain the spinach, pressing it to remove excess moisture. Toss the drained spinach with the toasted sesame seeds,
marinade, and sesame oil if you like. Serve hot or chilled. This can be
made up to 3 hours ahead if chilled.

PER 4-OZ SERVING: 36 CALORIES, 3.6 G PROTEIN, 1 G FAT, 4.9 G CARBOHYDRATE, 154 MG SODIUM, 0 MG
CHOLESTEROL.

SHREDDED ZUCCHINI
good

2 – 3 small zucchini (about 2 cups shredded)
1 tablespoon olive oil
2 – 3 garlic cloves, minced or pressed
salt and ground black pepper to taste

≈

lemon wedges

Scrub the zucchini and slice off the ends. Shred them on the coarsest side of a hand grater or on the equivalent blade in a food processor. Heat the oil in a large skillet and add the zucchini and garlic. Sauté on medium heat, tossing often, for about 5 minutes, until the excess moisture has evaporated. The zucchini should be bright green and firm-tender. Add salt and pepper, and serve garnished with lemon wedges.

PER 4-OZ SERVING: 32 CALORIES, 0.7 G PROTEIN, 1.6 G FAT, 4.5 G CARBOHYDRATE, 23 MG SODIUM, 0 MG CHOLESTEROL.

VARIATIONS
The flavor of this dish may be varied by adding herbs or spices of your choice during the last minute or two of cooking.

• For an Italian version, add 1 teaspoon of chopped fresh basil and a sprinkling of Parmesan or Romano cheese.
• For a Greek version, add 2 teaspoons of chopped fresh dill and a sprinkling of grated feta cheese, or stir in ¼ cup of plain yogurt and 1 teaspoon of chopped fresh mint.
• For an Indian version, substitute vegetable oil for the olive oil and add ½ teaspoon of curry powder (or more to taste).
• For a Mexican version, add ½ teaspoon of ground cumin, a dash of cayenne, and 2 tablespoons of chopped fresh cilantro; and/or serve topped with a prepared salsa.

NOTE: This recipe is easily increased to serve more people. Simply add about 1 cup of shredded zucchini and 1 garlic clove per serving.

TOTAL TIME
15 minutes

SERVINGS
2

MENU
Besides serving as a side dish, Shredded Zucchini can be a pizza topping or a filling for a quesadilla or omelet. Or you can dress it up with Pesto (see page 362), Salsa Verde (see page 105), or Chimichurri Sauce (see page 109).

Here is a very simple preparation that is light, delicious, and adaptable. This recipe is good for any season, but especially during late summer when the garden is overflowing with zucchini or other summer squash.

SPICY KALE

TOTAL TIME
20 minutes

SERVINGS
4

We keep hearing about the high nutrient value of healthful greens. Luckily for us, one green or another is available all year round, and they are at their best when quickly cooked. Kale is a favorite, especially in fall or winter, but this sprightly dish can also be made with collard, beet, or mustard greens, or with escarole, chard, or spinach.

1 large onion, diced (about 1½ cups)
1 tablespoon olive oil
1 bunch kale (about 2 pounds)
2 teaspoons vinegar (or to taste)
¼ teaspoon crushed red pepper flakes (or more to taste)
salt and ground black pepper to taste

Sauté the onion in the oil in a large skillet or saucepan on low heat for about 10 minutes, until translucent. While the onion sautés, thoroughly rinse the kale. Remove and discard the large stem ends, and coarsely chop the leaves.

Add the moist kale to the onions and cook, covered, for about 5 minutes, stirring occasionally, until the leaves are wilted but still bright green. Stir in the vinegar and red pepper flakes. Add salt and pepper to taste, and serve immediately or at room temperature.

PER 4-OZ SERVING: 55 CALORIES, 2 G PROTEIN, 2.2 G FAT, 7.5 G CARBOHYDRATE, 43 MG SODIUM, 0 MG CHOLESTEROL.

VARIATIONS

• Replace the vinegar and crushed red pepper flakes with Tabasco or other hot pepper sauce to taste.
• Add a cup of canned crushed tomatoes and/or 2 cups of cooked potato cubes.
• Omit the vinegar and add up to ½ cup of prepared sauerkraut.
• Add about 2 cups of cooked field peas or lima beans.
• Top with chopped black olives and chopped hard-boiled eggs.

NOTE: Kale is best stored unwashed in a plastic bag in the refrigerator.

STIR-FRIED BOK CHOY AND HIJIKI

½ cup dried hijiki seaweed (see page 335)
½ cup hot water

≈

1 medium onion
2 garlic cloves
2 small bunches bok choy (7 – 8 cups sliced)
1 tablespoon vegetable oil
1 tablespoon dark sesame oil
2 – 3 tablespoons soy sauce *
toasted sesame seeds (see page 354) (optional)

If you are concerned about saltiness, try using 1½ tablespoons of soy sauce and a tablespoon of water, and then adjust to taste just before serving.

Soak the hijiki in the hot water for 6 to 8 minutes. In the meantime, thinly slice the onion, mince or press the garlic, and slice the stalks and leaves of the bok choy on the diagonal. Drain the soaked hijiki, reserving the liquid.

Have all the ingredients assembled nearby before beginning to stir-fry. Combine the oils in a wok and place it on high heat. Just before it begins to smoke, add the onions and garlic and stir-fry. When the onions are translucent and turning golden, add the bok choy and the drained hijiki, and continue to stir-fry. When the bok choy leaves have turned a darker bright green and wilted slightly, add the soy sauce. When the stem pieces are hot and tender but still firm, add the hijiki soaking liquid. Serve immediately, garnished with the toasted sesame seeds if desired.

PER 4-OZ SERVING: 58 CALORIES, 2.2 G PROTEIN, 2.7 G FAT, 8 G CARBOHYDRATE, 127 MG SODIUM, 0 MG CHOLESTEROL.

TOTAL TIME
20 minutes
SERVINGS
4
MENU
Serve with rice and Broiled Tofu (see page 261). Leftovers can be refrigerated for 2 or 3 days and served as a chilled salad.

A refreshing, healthful dish accented by the briny flavor of seaweed.

SUGAR SNAPS IN LEMON BUTTER

Very good

TOTAL TIME
10 minutes

SERVINGS
4

MENU
Serve with Spanish Potato
Onion Soup (see page 40)
and Couscous with
Sun-Dried Tomatoes
(see page 145).

Sugar snap peas
have a brief
season in New
York State, so we
appreciate them while
they are available.
Their edible pods have
a sweet, delicate flavor
and a wonderful
crispness when quickly
blanched. When sugar
snaps are not available,
green beans, snow peas,
asparagus, or broccoli,
blanched until tender, is
an acceptable substitute.

2 cups water
2 cups sugar snap peas
1 tablespoon butter
2 – 3 tablespoons fresh lemon juice
¼ teaspoon minced fresh tarragon (pinch of dried)
1 teaspoon minced fresh chives (optional)
¼ cup toasted unsalted whole almonds (see page 354)
salt and ground black pepper to taste

Bring the water to a boil in a saucepan. While the water heats,
stem the snap peas and remove the strings. Blanch the snap peas in
the boiling water for 2 minutes, and drain them well. In a serving
bowl, combine the hot snap peas, butter, lemon juice, tarragon, and
optional chives. Mix in the toasted almonds, and add salt and pepper
to taste. Serve hot.

PER 4-OZ SERVING: 105 CALORIES, 5 G PROTEIN, 3.8 G FAT, 13.7 G CARBOHYDRATE, 151 MG SODIUM, 8
MG CHOLESTEROL.

VARIATION
Eliminate the lemon juice and sauté 1 minced garlic clove in the butter.

DRESSINGS, SALSAS, AND SAUCES

AT MOOSEWOOD RESTAURANT we are continually developing new dressings, salsas, and sauces to give special flavor to a recently invented dish or to enliven an old favorite. Fresh, lively salsas add interest to all kinds of dishes, without being overly rich or calorie-laden. A tantalizing topping for vegetables, pasta, or fish, or the final touch on a beautiful salad, a dressing, salsa, or sauce enhances the flavor and lends visual appeal.

Although most of these recipes take only minutes, we encourage you to prepare some ahead and store them in your refrigerator so that you'll be ready the moment inspiration strikes. The serving suggestions with each recipe will help you plan delicious, easy-to-prepare meals—sometimes the topping itself sparks an inspired combination!

DRESSINGS

CAESAR SALAD DRESSING

TOTAL TIME

5 minutes

SERVINGS

1 cup

MENU

There's no need to limit this dressing to Caesar Salad (see page 122) — it's also a wonderful sauce for any steamed or raw vegetables, particularly asparagus, artichokes, and new potatoes. We transform it into a dip for crudités by adding 1 cup of low-fat yogurt.

Our version of this dressing is rich, creamy, and garlicky. The traditional recipe uses raw eggs, but when we tried hard-boiling the eggs as a health precaution, we found that we preferred both the flavor and texture of the dressing.

2 hard-boiled eggs
⅓ cup olive oil (preferably extra-virgin)
3 tablespoons fresh lemon juice
½ teaspoon salt
1 teaspoon Dijon mustard
1 garlic clove, minced or pressed
ground black pepper to taste

Peel and chop the hard-boiled eggs. Place all of the ingredients in a blender and purée until smooth. Covered and refrigerated, this dressing will keep for about 5 days.

PER 2-OZ SERVING: 217 CALORIES, 3.8 G PROTEIN, 22 G FAT, 1.7 G CARBOHYDRATE, 336 MG SODIUM, 120 MG CHOLESTEROL.

CREAMY GARLIC DRESSING

3 garlic cloves, minced or pressed
¾ cup vegetable oil
¼ cup red wine vinegar
1 tablespoon chopped fresh basil (1 teaspoon dried)
1 teaspoon salt
1 tablespoon grated Parmesan cheese
½ teaspoon coarsely ground black pepper

≈

½ cup milk (whole, 2%, or skim)

Put the garlic, oil, vinegar, basil, salt, Parmesan, and pepper into a blender, and whirl for a couple of seconds. With the blender still running, slowly add the milk, whirling until the dressing is thick and smooth. Covered and refrigerated, this dressing will keep for a week.

PER 2-OZ SERVING: 268 CALORIES, 1.4 G PROTEIN, 28.8 G FAT, 2.4 G CARBOHYDRATE, 416 MG SODIUM, 1 MG CHOLESTEROL.

VARIATIONS

• Add ½ teaspoon of honey or sugar to offset the tartness of the vinegar.
• Add 1 teaspoon of fresh lemon juice for extra tartness.
• Add 1 tablespoon of minced fresh parsley for flecks of color without altering the flavor.

TOTAL TIME
5 minutes

SERVINGS
1½ cups

MENU
Serve over fresh greens, steamed asparagus or cauliflower, or boiled potatoes. This dressing is so thick and flavorful that it can be used as a dip for artichokes or Gigondes (see page 69).

The piquant flavors of fresh garlic, black pepper, and Parmesan combine to make this an assertive dressing.

CREAMY PINE NUT VINAIGRETTE

TOTAL TIME
10 minutes

SERVINGS
1¼ cups

MENU
Serve over crisp greens, spinach, asparagus, sliced tomatoes, steamed vegetables, or broiled fish.

Prized for their rich flavor, pine nuts add a distinctive taste to this dressing.

⅔ cup olive oil

2½ tablespoons red wine vinegar

1 large garlic clove, minced or pressed

1½ teaspoons freshly grated orange peel

¼ cup pine nuts

⅓–½ cup milk (whole, 2%, or skim)

¼ teaspoon salt (or to taste)

⅛ teaspoon ground black pepper (or to taste)

≈

1 tablespoon minced fresh tarragon, chives, basil, dill, or thyme (optional)

In a blender or food processor, combine the olive oil, vinegar, garlic, orange peel, pine nuts, ⅓ cup milk, salt, and pepper. Purée until thick and creamy, adding more milk if the dressing is too thick. Taste for salt and pepper, and stir in any of the optional fresh herbs suggested.

Creamy Pine Nut Vinaigrette will keep, tightly covered and refrigerated, for up to 2 weeks.

PER 2-OZ SERVING: 264 CALORIES, 1.3 G PROTEIN, 28.8 G FAT, 2.4 G CARBOHYDRATE, 110 MG SODIUM, 3 MG CHOLESTEROL.

HONEY MUSTARD VINAIGRETTE

⅓ cup cider vinegar
⅓ cup Dijon mustard
⅓ cup honey
1 cup vegetable oil
salt to taste

In a small mixing bowl, whisk together the vinegar and mustard. Continue to whisk while drizzling in first the honey and then the oil, until well blended. Add salt to taste. Stored covered and refrigerated, this dressing will keep for at least 2 weeks.

PER 2-OZ SERVING: 280 CALORIES, 0.5 G PROTEIN, 28.8 G FAT, 6.9 G CARBOHYDRATE, 190 MG SODIUM, 0 MG CHOLESTEROL.

TOTAL TIME
5 minutes

SERVINGS
about 2 cups

MENU
A creamy golden dressing that can also be used as a dip for crudités or as a sauce for fish or steamed vegetables.

LEMON SESAME DRESSING

This dressing is superb on tossed salad and on spinach and mushroom salads. It's also good over steamed broccoli, carrots, green beans, or other vegetables.

3 tablespoons sesame seeds

≈

¾ cup vegetable oil
⅓ cup fresh lemon juice
1 tablespoon soy sauce
½ teaspoon salt
¼ teaspoon ground black pepper
several dashes of Tabasco or other
  hot pepper sauce (optional)

Toast the sesame seeds (see page 354) until just golden and fragrant. Pour them onto a plate and set aside to cool.

Whisk together the oil, lemon juice, soy sauce, salt, pepper, and optional Tabasco until smooth. Stir in the cooled sesame seeds. Tightly covered and refrigerated, this dressing will keep for 2 weeks.

PER 2-OZ SERVING: 330 CALORIES, 1 G PROTEIN, 36 G FAT, 2.7 G CARBOHYDRATE, 417 MG SODIUM, 0 MG CHOLESTEROL.

ROASTED GARLIC DRESSING

10 – 12 garlic cloves, unpeeled
1 cup olive oil (not extra-virgin)
⅓ cup balsamic vinegar
⅓ cup water
1 teaspoon salt
¼ teaspoon ground black pepper
1 tablespoon Dijon mustard

In an unoiled small, heavy skillet, roast the unpeeled garlic cloves on medium heat, turning them occasionally. Cook the garlic for about 10 to 15 minutes, until it is soft and covered with dark spots. To test for doneness, press a garlic clove with a spoon. When you see small bubbles of juice bursting through the skin, remove the garlic from the skillet. When the cloves are cool enough to handle, peel the garlic.

In a blender or food processor, purée the garlic with the oil, vinegar, water, salt, pepper, and mustard until smooth. Covered and refrigerated, this dressing will keep for several weeks.

PER 2-OZ SERVING: 260 CALORIES, 0.3 G PROTEIN, 28.4 G FAT, 2.2 G CARBOHYDRATE, 309 MG SODIUM, 0 MG CHOLESTEROL.

TOTAL TIME
20 minutes

SERVINGS
1⅔ cups

MENU
Serve on your favorite salads, steamed asparagus, broccoli spears, or boiled new potatoes.

*D*o not be intimidated by the amount of garlic used in this recipe. Roasting gives the garlic a sweet and mellow flavor, which is enhanced by the balsamic vinegar.

TOFU-BASIL DRESSING

TOTAL TIME

5 minutes

SERVINGS

about ¾ cup

MENU

Use to dress tossed salads, chopped tomatoes, steamed green beans, asparagus, or little new potatoes.

This healthful dressing is a lovely green color. Use the remaining half block of silken tofu to make Tofu Mayonnaise (see page 101).

½ block silken tofu (about 5 ounces) (see page 343)
2 tablespoons cider vinegar
2 tablespoons unsweetened apple or orange juice
½ teaspoon Dijon mustard
1 small garlic clove, minced or pressed
2 tablespoons chopped fresh basil
¼ teaspoon salt

Place all of the ingredients in a blender or food processor and purée until smooth. Covered and refrigerated, Tofu-Basil Dressing will keep for about a week.

PER 2-OZ SERVING: 46 CALORIES, 3.7 G PROTEIN, 1.9 G FAT, 5.4 G CARBOHYDRATE, 157 MG SODIUM, 0 MG CHOLESTEROL.

TOFU MAYONNAISE

½ block silken tofu (about 5 ounces) (see page 343)

2 tablespoons olive oil (may be part extra-virgin)

2 tablespoons fresh lemon juice

¼ teaspoon Dijon mustard

¼ teaspoon salt

dash of ground black pepper, or several splashes of Tabasco
or other hot pepper sauce

1 tablespoon chopped scallion bulbs, or 1 small
garlic clove (optional)

Place all of the ingredients in a blender or food processor and whirl until smooth. Add a tablespoon of water if the mayonnaise seems too thick.

Covered and refrigerated, Tofu Mayonnaise will keep for about a week.

2-OZ SERVING: 92 CALORIES, 3 G PROTEIN, 8.8 G FAT, 1.4 G CARBOHYDRATE, 151 MG SODIUM, 0 MG CHOLESTEROL.

TOTAL TIME

10 minutes

SERVINGS

about ¾ cup

Using tofu rather than eggs creates this more healthful, cholesterol-free alternative to traditional mayonnaise. Use the remaining half block of silken tofu in Tofu-Basil Dressing (see page 100).

You can use Tofu Mayonnaise anytime regular mayonnaise is called for.

SALSAS

Brazilian Onion Salsa

TOTAL TIME
10 minutes

SERVINGS
about 1 cup

MENU
Serve with beans, enchiladas, quesadillas, or any food that needs a little extra zip.

I nspired by the sauce traditionally served with the Brazilian dish feijoada, this sauce can range from merely spicy to knock-your-socks-off, depending upon how many chiles you add.

½ cup coarsely chopped onions
1 or 2 fresh chiles (or more to taste), stemmed and seeded
⅓ cup fresh lemon and/or lime juice
2 garlic cloves, minced or pressed
¼ cup fresh cilantro or parsley
½ cup chopped fresh tomatoes
1 tablespoon olive oil
¼ teaspoon salt or to taste

Whirl all of the ingredients together in a blender until smooth. This salsa keeps, refrigerated, for 3 or 4 days.

PER 2-OZ SERVING: 40 CALORIES, 0.7 G PROTEIN, 2.7 G FAT, 4.5 G CARBOHYDRATE, 107 MG SODIUM, 0 MG CHOLESTEROL.

Mango Salsa

2 medium ripe mangoes
1 small cucumber, peeled, seeded, and diced
1 ripe tomato, chopped
juice of 1 lime
pinch of salt
½ – 1 small fresh chile pepper, minced, or Tabasco or other
    hot pepper sauce to taste
1 tablespoon chopped fresh cilantro (optional)

Peel and chop the mangoes (see page 351). In a large bowl, mix together the mangoes, cucumber, tomato, lime juice, salt, chile or Tabasco, and optional cilantro. Let the salsa sit for 10 minutes to allow the flavors to blend before serving. Mango Salsa keeps, refrigerated, for 2 or 3 days.

PER 2-OZ SERVING: 19 CALORIES, 0.3 G PROTEIN, 0.1 G FAT, 4.7 G CARBOHYDRATE, 14 MG SODIUM, 0 MG CHOLESTEROL.

PREPARATION TIME
10 minutes

SITTING TIME
10 minutes

TOTAL TIME
20 minutes

SERVINGS
2½ cups

MENU
Serve with Caribbean Black Beans (see page 168), grilled or broiled fish, burritos, or Caribbean Yellow Rice and Pigeon Peas (see page 154).

Luscious, smooth mangoes are the base for a sauce that manages to tantalize all the taste buds; sweet, sour, spicy, and pungent.

QUESO BLANCO SALSA

TOTAL TIME

15 minutes (45 minutes
if served cold)

SERVINGS

2 cups

A creamy, spicy topping for enchiladas, quesadillas, beans, and burritos that also does well as a dip for chips and raw vegetable sticks. Combine it with leftover rice and beans to make a hearty casserole.

½ cup commercial Mexican-style red salsa
2 scallions, chopped
1 tablespoon chopped fresh cilantro
½ cup canned roasted red peppers, chopped
8 ounces low-fat cream cheese (Neufchâtel)

Mix all of the ingredients together in a saucepan. Gently heat, stirring occasionally, until hot. Serve hot on warm dishes, or chill for 30 minutes to use as a dip for chips or crudités. Refrigerated and tightly sealed, Queso Blanco Salsa will keep for about 2 weeks.

PER 2-OZ SERVING: 78 CALORIES, 2.8 G PROTEIN, 5.4 G FAT, 5.2 G CARBOHYDRATE, 249 MG SODIUM, 17 MG CHOLESTEROL.

SALSA VERDE

½ cup olive oil
1 cup fresh parsley leaves, packed
3 garlic cloves
⅓ cup fresh lemon juice
2 tablespoons capers, rinsed and drained
¼ cup chopped scallions or onions
¼ teaspoon salt
ground black pepper to taste

TOTAL TIME
10 minutes

SERVINGS
1 cup

A vividly green sauce that adds piquancy to steamed or raw vegetables, Broiled Tofu (see page 261), frittatas, and fish dishes.

Combine the oil, parsley, garlic, lemon juice, capers, scallions or onions, and salt in a blender or food processor and whirl until smooth. Add black pepper to taste. Tightly covered and refrigerated, Salsa Verde will keep for about 5 days.

PER 2-OZ SERVING: 211 CALORIES, 0.5 G PROTEIN, 22.8 G FAT, 2.9 G CARBOHYDRATE, 240 MG SODIUM, 0 MG CHOLESTEROL.

VARIATION

Add 1 or 2 tablespoons of fresh chopped basil, tarragon, or dill. Or try ½ teaspoon of rosemary or sage, or a teaspoon of Dijon mustard.

Tomato-Orange Salsa

TOTAL TIME
15 minutes

SERVINGS
2½ cups

With the fresh, surprising bite of orange, this salsa gives an almost instant flavor boost to black beans, chili, and broiled or grilled fish.

3 ripe tomatoes, diced

4 scallions, chopped

½ – 1 fresh green chile, seeded and minced, or
    ¼ teaspoon cayenne

2 teaspoons freshly grated orange peel

1 orange, sectioned and seeded, each section cut in half

2 tablespoons fresh lemon juice

½ teaspoon ground cumin

½ teaspoon ground coriander

salt to taste

Combine all of the ingredients in a bowl, and let sit for 10 to 15 minutes to allow the flavors to blend. Covered and refrigerated, this salsa will keep for 2 to 3 days.

PER 2-OZ SERVING: 18 CALORIES, 0.5 G PROTEIN, 0.2 G FAT, 4.1 G CARBOHYDRATE, 57 MG SODIUM, 0 MG CHOLESTEROL.

SAUCES

AIOLI

1 cup commercial mayonnaise
3 tablespoons fresh lemon juice (or 1 tablespoon cider
    vinegar and 2 tablespoons lemon juice)
2 tablespoons olive oil (preferably extra-virgin)
3 – 4 garlic cloves, minced or pressed
ground black pepper to taste

In a small mixing bowl, combine the mayonnaise, lemon juice, olive oil, and garlic. Add pepper to taste. Refrigerate until ready to serve. Aioli should keep for about a week, covered, in the refrigerator.

PER 2-OZ SERVING: 232 CALORIES, 0.6 G PROTEIN, 20.9 G FAT, 12.3 G CARBOHYDRATE, 323 MG SODIUM, 12 MG CHOLESTEROL.

TOTAL TIME
5 minutes

SERVINGS
1 cup

MENU
Serve on broiled fish, steamed vegetables, baked potatoes, or crudités.

This addictive garlic-studded sauce comes from the Provençal region of southern France. If you prefer your garlic cooked rather than raw, swirl it gently in the olive oil on low heat and then add it to the mayonnaise.

ASIAN MARINADE

*Y*ou might want to double the quantity of this versatile sauce and keep it on hand to season steamed or sautéed vegetables and baked, broiled, or grilled fish, or to marinate tofu, tempeh, or seitan.

1-inch piece fresh ginger root, cut into thin slices
½ cup soy sauce
½ cup dry sherry
2 tablespoons brown sugar or honey
¼ cup rice vinegar

Combine all of the ingredients in a small nonreactive saucepan and bring to a boil. Reduce the heat and simmer for a minute. Set aside to cool. Strain the cooled marinade to remove the ginger root, unless you prefer a strong ginger flavor. Covered and refrigerated, this marinade keeps indefinitely.

PER 2-OZ SERVING: 41 CALORIES, 1.1 G PROTEIN, 0 G FAT, 7 G CARBOHYDRATE, 1,159 MG SODIUM, 0 MG CHOLESTEROL.

VARIATIONS

Add dark sesame oil, chili paste, chili oil, or ground anise seeds to vary the flavor.

CHIMICHURRI SAUCE

⅓ cup olive oil

¼ cup cider vinegar

½ cup fresh parsley leaves, packed

⅓ cup fresh cilantro leaves, packed

3 garlic cloves, minced or pressed

¼ teaspoon cayenne (or to taste), or 1 fresh chile, stemmed (seeds removed for a milder "hot")

1 tablespoon fresh oregano (1 teaspoon dried)

1½ teaspoons fresh thyme (½ teaspoon dried)

¼ teaspoon salt

Combine all of the ingredients in a blender or food processor and whirl until smooth. Serve immediately, or allow to sit for about an hour for the flavors to mellow and marry. Chimichurri Sauce will keep, refrigerated and tightly covered, for about a week.

PER 2-OZ SERVING: 235 CALORIES, 0.4 G PROTEIN, 25.3 G FAT, 3.2 G CARBOHYDRATE, 197 MG SODIUM, 0 MG CHOLESTEROL.

This tangy herb-laden sauce is used as a table condiment; it perks up almost any savory dish. Its intense color and taste are appealing with baked, broiled, or grilled fish, egg dishes, and sandwiches.

Easy Artichoke Sauce

TOTAL TIME
15 minutes

SERVINGS
1½ to 2 cups

This is our most recent "emergency sauce" at Moosewood Restaurant. When we need something fast, we prepare this and serve it on cheese ravioli, spinach fettuccine, or linguine, topped with grated Parmesan cheese and chopped fresh tomatoes. It was concocted during a crisis, but now our customers ask for it. It's also good on baked or broiled fish.

¼ cup olive oil
¼ cup butter or margarine
4 – 6 garlic cloves, minced or pressed
5 artichoke hearts (14-ounce can), drained and quartered
   or chopped
2 tablespoons chopped fresh basil or other fresh herb
1 tablespoon fresh lemon juice
ground black pepper to taste

Heat the oil and butter in a nonreactive saucepan. When the butter has melted, add the garlic and sauté for 2 or 3 minutes, until golden but not brown. Add the artichoke hearts, basil, and lemon juice, and heat gently for about 10 minutes. Add black pepper to taste. Serve warm.

PER 2-OZ SERVING: 129 CALORIES, 1.6 G PROTEIN, 12 G FAT, 5.3 G CARBOHYDRATE, 101 MG SODIUM, 0 MG CHOLESTEROL.

FENNEL-MUSTARD SAUCE

¼ cup Dijon mustard
2 tablespoons fresh lemon juice
1 teaspoon ground fennel
1½ teaspoons chopped fresh tarragon (½ teaspoon dried)
1 tablespoon honey
¼ cup olive oil
salt and ground black pepper to taste

In a small bowl, whisk together the mustard, lemon juice, fennel, tarragon, and honey. Slowly drizzle in the oil, whisking constantly to form a thick sauce. Season to taste with salt and pepper.

PER 2-OZ SERVING: 201 CALORIES, 1.2 G PROTEIN, 19.9 G FAT, 6.5 G CARBOHYDRATE, 296 MG SODIUM, 0 MG CHOLESTEROL.

TOTAL TIME
5 minutes

SERVINGS
⅔ cup

*S*erve this tempting sauce with steamed vegetables or grilled or broiled fish. It also works very well on baked fish — simply pour the sauce over the fish, cover the pan, and bake.

HAZELNUT-RED PEPPERS SAUCE

TOTAL TIME

25 minutes

SERVINGS

about 6 cups

Use this fragrant sweet sauce with pasta or steamed vegetables (or a combination of both), or over a simple baked, broiled, or grilled fish. If you like, reserve a few of the roasted whole hazelnuts and coarsely chop them for a garnish just before serving.

1 cup whole hazelnuts

≈

2 red bell peppers (about 2 cups chopped)
3 cups undrained canned tomatoes (28-ounce can), or
    4 medium fresh tomatoes
4 garlic cloves
3 tablespoons olive oil
1 tablespoon red wine vinegar
pinch of cayenne

≈

2 small slices Italian or French bread, or
    ½ cake tofu (6 ounces)
salt to taste

Preheat the oven to 325°. A toaster oven will work fine.

Spread the hazelnuts on an unoiled baking sheet and bake for 10 minutes. While the nuts are baking, chop the bell peppers, tomatoes, and garlic. Heat the olive oil in a saucepan, then add the peppers, tomatoes, garlic, vinegar, and cayenne. Cook on high heat for 5 minutes and remove from the heat. The peppers should still be crunchy.

Cool the baked hazelnuts for several minutes, and then rub them briskly with a towel to remove most of the skins. Finely grind the hazelnuts in a food processor or nut grinder, or in several batches in a spice mill. If you are using bread rather than tofu, submerge it in water for a moment, then gently squeeze out the excess water. Place all of the ingredients in a food processor or blender and purée until smooth.

Reheat the sauce if necessary, and add salt to taste.

PER 2-OZ SERVING: 55 CALORIES, 1.1 G PROTEIN, 2.3 G FAT, 7.9 G CARBOHYDRATE, 71 MG SODIUM, 0 MG CHOLESTEROL.

MISO SAUCE

⅓ cup medium to light miso (see page 336)
⅓ – ½ cup water
2 tablespoons rice vinegar
1 teaspoon grated fresh ginger root

In a small bowl, blend together the miso and ⅓ cup of the water until smooth. Add the vinegar and ginger, and mix well. Add a little more water if necessary to reach a saucelike consistency.

PER 2-OZ SERVING: 70 CALORIES, 1.9 G PROTEIN, 0.2 G FAT, 15.6 G CARBOHYDRATE, 2 MG SODIUM, 0 MG CHOLESTEROL.

TOTAL TIME
5 minutes
SERVINGS
¾ cup
MENU
Excellent with Broiled Eggplant (see page 74), crudités, or rice and steamed vegetables. Garnish with sesame seeds and chopped scallions for added color and taste.

Richly flavored yet light, this is a classic Japanese dipping sauce.

MAIN DISH SALADS

MAIN DISH SALADS are a perennial favorite at Moosewood Restaurant, and the big, beautiful selections here are all substantial enough to stand on their own as a meal. Most can be prepared in 15 or 20 minutes, and almost all of them can also be made ahead for flexibility and convenience.

While we all value the low-fat, healthful aspects of a salad meal, we never want those to be the dominant features. (If you must say, "Well, at least it's good for me," a dish is not a success.) The salads in this chapter range from an earthy, peasant-type Mediterranean Lentil Salad to the sophisticated style of Caesar Salad or Mushroom Celery Parmesan Salad. The bright, assertive flavors in salads such as Green Bean Pesto Salad and White Bean and Tomato Salad capture the essence of summer, while others, such as Sweet Potato Salad, Beans and Greens, and Avocado Corn Salad, are hearty enough to be satisfying in winter.

Greek Diced Vegetable Salad and Soba Noodle Salad are fairly faithful renditions of traditional standards in their cuisines, whereas Greek Pasta Salad and Udon Noodles and Vegetables are faithful only to the Moosewood Restaurant tradition of mixing and matching different ethnic culinary elements.

Visual appeal is very important in a big salad. If you take an extra minute to choose the serving bowl best suited to display your creation and arrange the salad in it with artistry, you will appreciate this relaxed meal even more.

Antipasto Salad

TOTAL TIME

15 minutes

MENU

With a crusty peasant bread and a glass of red wine, this dish can be a satisfying meal in itself or can serve as an impressive first course followed by a simple pasta such as Spaghetti with Pecorino and Black Pepper (see page 194).

Choose as many or as few of our suggested ingredients as you like. If there's no jar of capers in your refrigerator, no matter. If the fresh tomatoes at the market are unappealing, forget them. No time to make croutons? It'll be fine without. Try adding cheese, toasted pine nuts, chopped fresh green herbs, or hot pepper flakes when they're handy.

CHOOSE ANY OF THE FOLLOWING:
artichoke hearts, drained and quartered
roasted red peppers, sliced
celery or fresh fennel, thinly sliced
cooked beans (garbanzos, lupini, canellini),
    rinsed and drained
pickled eggplant, drained and chopped
olives (black Gaeta, Calamata, Liguria, or green Sicilian)
fresh tomatoes, sliced or cut into wedges
red onion, thinly sliced or minced
cheese (sliced fresh mozzarella, crumbled feta, cubed
    Bel Paese, or shaved Parmesan)
croutons
capers, rinsed and drained

≈
extra-virgin olive oil
fresh lemon juice
freshly ground black pepper

≈
salad greens (romaine, arugula, watercress, shredded
    radicchio, or torn pale inner leaves of escarole)

Slice, dice, or otherwise prepare the ingredients you've chosen according to your taste. On a large platter — on a bed of greens if you like — arrange the ingredients in rows. Capers might be sprinkled on roasted red pepper strips, red onions on tomatoes, and celery mixed in with the beans. Drizzle everything with olive oil and lemon juice and top with black pepper. Or if you choose to serve the salad without greens, toss everything in a colorful jumble in a large serving bowl. Best served warm.

Prepared without lettuce and tomatoes, this salad will keep, refrigerated, for a week.

PER 8-OZ SERVING: 246 CALORIES, 6.6 G PROTEIN, 14.4 G FAT, 25.3 G CARBOHYDRATE, 664 MG SODIUM, 10 MG CHOLESTEROL.

Avocado Corn Salad

1 cup fresh or frozen cut corn
1 tablespoon vegetable oil
2 tablespoons water
1 teaspoon ground cumin
pinch of cayenne or red pepper flakes (optional)

≈

1 medium avocado (preferably Haas)
2 tablespoons fresh lime or lemon juice
½ medium red bell pepper
2 tablespoons minced red onion
salt to taste
dash of Tabasco or other hot pepper sauce (optional)
whole or chopped cilantro leaves (optional)

In a skillet or saucepan, combine the corn, oil, water, cumin, and optional cayenne or red pepper flakes. Cook, covered, on medium heat for 5 minutes, or until the corn is tender. Uncover and cook for an additional minute or two to evaporate the excess moisture. Set aside to cool.

Slice the avocado in half lengthwise, and gently twist to remove the pit. Make lengthwise and crosswise cuts in the flesh every ½ inch. Scoop the avocado cubes out of the shells and into a large bowl. Gently stir in the lemon or lime juice. Cut the bell pepper into ½-inch or smaller pieces and add to the bowl. Stir in the red onion and cooked corn. Add salt and the optional Tabasco to taste, and top with cilantro if you like.

Serve immediately, or chill for 30 minutes and then serve.

PER 8-OZ SERVING: 317 CALORIES, 5 G PROTEIN, 23.5 G FAT, 29.3 G CARBOHYDRATE, 315 MG SODIUM, 0 MG CHOLESTEROL.

TOTAL TIME
15 minutes (45 minutes served cold)

SERVINGS
2

MENU
This versatile salad can be a whole meal when served on a bed of lettuce with tomatoes, hard-boiled eggs, olives, and Seasoned Tempeh (see page 85). It's also delicious as a side dish for burritos, enchiladas, or quesadillas.

TIME-SAVING TIP
To hasten the ripening of an avocado, wrap it with newspaper or put it in a brown paper bag and leave it at room temperature.

Beans and Greens

TOTAL TIME

20 minutes

SERVINGS

4 to 6

MENU

For a satisfying, earthy
main dish, serve Beans
and Greens with bread,
olives, and Fresh
Mozzarella and Tomato
Salad (see page 68). Beans
and Greens can also be an
antipasto before Penne
with Sun-Dried Tomatoes
and Capers (see page 190)
or Broiled Eggplant
(see page 74). For crostini,
spread the beans on
toasted slices of French or
Italian bread and top with
the greens.

*The soothing
creaminess of
beans is
complemented by the
bracing sharpness of the
greens in this time-
honored classic from
southern Italy.*

BEANS

4 cups drained cooked Roman beans or cannellini
    (two 16-ounce cans)
juice of ½ lemon, or to taste
salt and ground black pepper to taste
¼ teaspoon crushed red pepper flakes (optional)

GREENS

1 large head curly endive or escarole (about 1 pound)
2 tablespoons olive oil
4 garlic cloves, minced
salt and ground black pepper to taste

≈

extra-virgin olive oil (optional)

Using a potato masher or a large slotted spoon, slightly mash the beans until they hold together. Stir in the lemon juice, salt, and pepper to taste. If you plan to serve the dish at room temperature, set it aside. If you plan to serve it hot, gently heat the beans in a covered saucepan on low heat, using a heat diffuser or a double boiler if necessary to prevent sticking.

Wash the greens and chop them into small pieces. In a large skillet or wok, heat the olive oil and garlic on medium heat until the garlic is just turning golden. Add the greens. You may have to wait for the first greens in the pan to wilt before you can add the rest. Raise the heat and cook, stirring frequently, until all of the greens are wilted and bright green. Add salt and pepper to taste.

Serve the beans and greens side by side in a serving bowl, or make a nest of the greens and mound the beans in the center. Drizzle the top with extra-virgin olive oil, if desired.

PER 8-OZ SERVING: 109 CALORIES, 5.5 G PROTEIN, 3.6 G FAT, 15.4 G CARBOHYDRATE, 155 MG SODIUM, 0 MG CHOLESTEROL.

Good — really different

BLACK BEANS AND RICE SALAD

2 cups drained cooked black beans (16-ounce can)
3 cups cooked brown rice
2 celery stalks, finely chopped
¼ cup sliced Spanish olives

DRESSING
1 teaspoon ground coriander
2 teaspoons ground cumin
½ cup chopped scallions
1–2 tablespoons chopped fresh cilantro
½ cup orange juice
1½ tablespoons cider vinegar
3 tablespoons olive oil
2 teaspoons freshly grated orange peel
2 tablespoons chopped fresh parsley
½ teaspoon cinnamon
salt and ground black pepper to taste

≈

½ cup chopped toasted walnuts (see page 354)
a few fresh cilantro or parsley leaves

In a mixing bowl, combine the drained beans with the rice, celery, and Spanish olives. In a small bowl, whisk together all of the dressing ingredients. Pour the dressing over the beans and rice mixture, and stir thoroughly.

Top with the toasted walnuts and the cilantro or parsley.

PER 8-OZ SERVING: 340 CALORIES, 10.9 G PROTEIN, 14.2 G FAT, 45.2 G CARBOHYDRATE, 238 MG SODIUM, 0 MG CHOLESTEROL.

TOTAL TIME
25 minutes

SERVINGS
4

MENU
Great for a summer barbecue served with grilled corn, Tomato-Orange Salsa (see page 106), and green salad.

T his beautiful dish, flavorful and substantial enough to stand on its own, is a good potluck or picnic salad.

CAESAR SALAD

TOTAL TIME

20 minutes

SERVINGS

4

MENU

For a flavorful meal, serve Caesar Salad with Herbed Green Pea Soup (see page 29) or Spanish Potato Onion Soup (see page 40).

*W*hy does *Caesar Salad have such a mystique? It is a brilliant combination of tastes and textures, and it can be assembled tableside in a showy manner. However, it can also be thrown together in the kitchen and enjoyed just as much. The component parts can all be prepared well ahead, so this classic salad can be served up in just minutes.*

1 head romaine lettuce or the inner leaves of
    2 heads (about 1 pound)
3 cups croutons (see below)
2 ounces Parmesan cheese (½ cup shaved or coarsely grated)
½– 1 cup Caesar Salad Dressing (see page 94)
freshly ground black pepper

Wash the romaine leaves well in cold water, shake them dry, wrap them in a clean, dry kitchen towel, and refrigerate until serving time. This can be done a day or two ahead.

If you're making your own croutons, prepare them as directed below. Coarsely grate the cheese, or shave it using a vegetable peeler. Prepare the dressing. Tear the lettuce into bite-sized pieces.

Place the lettuce in a large salad bowl or on individual salad plates. Top with the croutons and cheese, drizzle with the dressing, and toss until the lettuce is lightly coated. Add pepper to taste.

PER 8-OZ SERVING, WITH DRESSING AND CROUTONS: 553 CALORIES, 17.5 G PROTEIN, 38.8 G FAT, 34.6 G CARBOHYDRATE, 936 MG SODIUM, 135 MG CHOLESTEROL.

CROUTONS

3 cups ½-inch bread cubes
2 tablespoons olive oil
2 garlic cloves, pressed or minced

Preheat the oven to 350°.

Spread the bread cubes on an unoiled baking sheet and bake for 5 to 8 minutes, until completely dry and lightly toasted. Heat the oil in a large, heavy skillet. Add the toasted bread cubes and the garlic, and stir constantly until the bread is lightly coated and the garlic is just beginning to color. Remove from the heat.

The croutons can be served immediately, still warm. Or set them aside to cool and then store them tightly covered until serving time.

PER 2-OZ SERVING: 226 CALORIES, 4.9 G PROTEIN, 10.7 G FAT, 27.4 G CARBOHYDRATE, 265 MG SODIUM, 2 MG CHOLESTEROL.

CALIFORNIA DREAM SALAD

romaine, ruby, and/or Boston lettuce

red cabbage or radicchio

watercress or spinach

mung, alfalfa, and/or radish sprouts

avocado

tomato

carrots and/or beets

bell peppers and/or celery

fresh green peas, snow peas, and/or green beans

scallions or red onion

toasted sesame and/or sunflower seeds (see page 354)

whole-grain croutons (see page 122)

cooked chick peas and/or Tofu-Kan (see page 343)

Select enough of the listed ingredients to create a nice variety in texture, color, and taste. Clean and dry your choices of lettuce, cabbage, and other greens. Tear the lettuces into bite-sized pieces and put them in a big, good-looking salad bowl. Slice the cabbage or radicchio very thin and sprinkle it over the lettuce. Roughly chop the watercress or spinach, and add it to the bowl. Fluff some sprouts into the greens.

Cut the avocado flesh and the tomato into bite-sized chunks, and add them. Peel and shred the carrots and/or beets. Slice the bell pepper and/or celery into paper-thin strips or crescents. Slice the beans or scallions or whatever else you found fresh and appealing in the market. Scatter everything artfully onto the salad. Top the salad with toasted seeds or croutons, and chick peas or sliced or shredded tofu-kan.

Serve immediately, with your choice of dressing on the side.

PER 8-OZ SERVING: 124 CALORIES, 3.7 G PROTEIN, 8.1 G FAT, 12.7 G CARBOHYDRATE, 41 MG SODIUM, 0 MG CHOLESTEROL.

TOTAL TIME

15 minutes

MENU

To round out the meal, serve this salad with Multigrain Muffins (see page 56) and a Fruit Shake (see page 311).

Light, fresh, fibrous, low-fat—this salad is so big, generous, varied, colorful, and satisfying that you won't mind that it's healthful too. It's an appealing endless-summer supper, good any time of the year, that will help you get back on track if you've been overdoing it and is better than just California dreaming.

Dress your salad with one of these low-fat, low-cal dressings, which can be quickly prepared in a blender.

A tangy nonfat tomato dressing.

TOMATO HERB DRESSING

¾ cup canned plum tomatoes and their juice (about
　　2 tomatoes), or ¾ cup tomato juice or V8 juice
¼ cup fresh lemon juice or cider vinegar
2 garlic cloves, minced or pressed
2 tablespoons chopped scallions, chives, or fresh parsley
　　(singly or in combination)
½ teaspoon salt
¼ teaspoon dried thyme or oregano
ground black pepper
2 leaves fresh basil (optional)
dash of Tabasco or other hot pepper sauce, or pinch of
　　cayenne (optional)

Put all of the ingredients in a blender and whirl them until
smooth. Stored chilled in a covered jar, this dressing will keep for
about 2 weeks.

PER 2-OZ SERVING: 15 CALORIES, 0.7 G PROTEIN, 0.1 G FAT, 3.6 G CARBOHYDRATE, 282 MG SODIUM,
0 MG CHOLESTEROL.

Fresh tasting. Nonfat yogurt or cottage cheese may be used, but the low-fat versions have a nicer texture. When this dressing is made with cottage cheese, it is very thick and slightly sweeter than when it is made with yogurt.

GARLIC DRESSING

½ cup low-fat or nonfat cottage cheese or plain yogurt
1 teaspoon Dijon mustard
1 teaspoon vinegar if using yogurt, 2 teaspoons vinegar if
　　using cottage cheese
1 – 2 garlic cloves, minced or pressed
¼ cup chopped scallions and/or 2 tablespoons chopped
　　fresh parsley (optional)
¼ teaspoon salt (optional)
ground black pepper

Put all of the ingredients in a blender and whirl them until
smooth. If you are using cottage cheese and it's not blending easily,
add 1 to 2 teaspoons water (some cottage cheeses are drier than oth-

ers). Stored chilled in a covered jar, this dressing will keep for about a week.

PER 2-OZ SERVING: 55 CALORIES, 8 G PROTEIN, 1.2 G FAT, 2.9 G CARBOHYDRATE, 260 MG SODIUM, 5 MG CHOLESTEROL.

ORANGE MUSTARD DRESSING

⅓ cup frozen orange juice concentrate
¼ cup red wine vinegar
2 teaspoons Dijon mustard
2 tablespoons chopped scallions (optional)
¼ teaspoon ground fennel (optional)
¼ teaspoon anise seed (optional)

Put all of the ingredients in a blender and whirl them until smooth. Stored chilled in a covered jar, this dressing will keep for about 2 weeks.

PER 2-OZ SERVING: 45 CALORIES, 0.8 G PROTEIN, 0.2 G FAT, 10.8 G CARBOHYDRATE, 40 MG SODIUM, 0 MG CHOLESTEROL.

SERVINGS
⅔ cup

Flavorful and aromatic, this dressing is more sweet than sour. Good on artichokes or sliced fresh fennel.

JAPANESE CARROT DRESSING

1 small carrot, shredded (about ½ cup)
2 tablespoons mirin (see page 336)
2 tablespoons rice vinegar and/or cider vinegar
1 tablespoon soy sauce
½ teaspoon dark sesame oil (optional)
1 tablespoon grated fresh ginger root (optional)
¼ cake silken tofu (about 3 ounces) (optional)

Put all of the ingredients in a blender and whirl them until smooth. Stored chilled in a covered jar, this dressing will keep for a week (less, if you use the tofu).

PER 2-OZ SERVING: 28 CALORIES, 0.6 G PROTEIN, 0.1 G FAT, 4.2 G CARBOHYDRATE, 332 MG SODIUM, 0 MG CHOLESTEROL.

SERVINGS
½ (¾ cup with tofu)

Mirin is expensive, but it's worth it: using just a little will add a special flavor. The addition of tofu makes the dressing very thick and creamy and provides extra protein.

COUSCOUS WITH ARTICHOKE HEARTS AND WALNUTS

TOTAL TIME

15 minutes

SERVINGS

4 to 6

MENU

Serve with Yogurt Cheese (see page 52), Borani (see page 47), or Broiled Eggplant (see page 74).

Quick-cooking couscous is a great time saver, requiring just 5 minutes to prepare. Good with saucy dishes or with just butter or olive oil, here it's dressed up with savory ingredients. Also delicious topped with chèvre.

1 cup water
1½ cups quick-cooking couscous *
1 tablespoon olive oil
1 teaspoon salt

≈

5 artichoke hearts, cut into eighths (14-ounce can)
½ cup minced scallions
1 large garlic clove, minced or pressed
1 cup chopped fresh parsley
1 – 2 tablespoons chopped fresh dill (1 teaspoon dried)
1 tablespoon chopped fresh mint and/or tarragon
3 tablespoons olive oil
juice of ½ lemon (or more to taste)
½ cup chopped toasted walnuts (see page 354)
salt and ground black pepper to taste

≈

fresh greens (optional)

* Or use 1 cup bulghur; see page 356 for cooking directions.

Bring the water to a boil. Place the couscous in a large heatproof bowl, and cover with the boiling water. Using a fork, stir in the olive oil and salt. Cover, and set aside for about 5 minutes.

Mix the artichoke hearts, scallions, garlic, parsley, dill, and optional mint and/or tarragon into the cooked couscous. Stir in the oil, lemon juice, and walnuts. Add salt and pepper to taste.

Serve plain or on a bed of fresh greens, either at room temperature or chilled.

PER 8-OZ SERVING: 249 CALORIES, 7.1 G PROTEIN, 8.6 G FAT, 36.7 G CARBOHYDRATE, 319 MG SODIUM, 0 MG CHOLESTEROL.

GREEK DICED VEGETABLE SALAD

1 cucumber, peeled, seeded, and diced
1 large ripe tomato, diced
1 red bell pepper, diced
1 scallion, finely sliced or minced
2 tablespoons minced fresh parsley
2 tablespoons extra-virgin olive oil
juice of ½ lemon (or more to taste)
1 garlic clove, pressed
¼ teaspoon dried oregano, crumbled
8 black Calamata olives, whole or pitted and sliced
salt and ground black pepper to taste

≈

romaine lettuce leaves
crumbed or grated feta cheese (optional)

Combine the cucumbers, tomatoes, bell peppers, scallions, parsley, oil, lemon juice, garlic, oregano, and olives in a large bowl. Add salt and pepper, and toss well. Although you can serve the salad immediately, it is even better if it sits for about 30 minutes before serving.

Mound the salad on lettuce leaves, and top with feta if you like.

PER 8-OZ SERVING: 192 CALORIES, 2 G PROTEIN, 17 G FAT, 11.2 G CARBOHYDRATE, 860 MG SODIUM, 0 MG CHOLESTEROL.

NOTE: This salad is good with or without the feta. If you mix the feta into the salad, the cheese will absorb the marinade, which is delicious. For a more decorative presentation, sprinkle the feta on top. This salad will keep better if the cheese is not mixed into it.

TOTAL TIME
15 minutes

SERVINGS
2

MENU
Serve this with a crusty bread, or stuff a pita with it. North African Cauliflower Soup (see page 33) or Portuguese White Bean Soup (see page 34) is excellent with Greek Diced Vegetable Salad.

A light, refreshing, and flavorful salad. The intensity of the Calamata olives will be more evenly distributed if you take the time to pit and slice them. A heartier salad can be created by the addition of chick peas and slices of hard-boiled egg.

GREEK PASTA SALAD

TOTAL TIME
35 minutes

SERVINGS
4

MENU
For a Mediterranean meal, serve this salad with a soup such as Simple Garlic Broth (see page 38) with croutons and cheese.

A pasta salad generous with vegetables and bright flavors.

½ pound pasta shells

≈

¼ cup olive oil
1 medium eggplant, cut into 1-inch cubes
½ teaspoon salt
2 garlic cloves, minced or pressed
juice of 1 lemon
2 tablespoons water
1 green or red bell pepper, diced

≈

5 artichoke hearts, drained and quartered (14-ounce can)
1 cucumber, peeled, seeded, and diced
2 tomatoes, diced
1 celery stalk, sliced
2 scallions, chopped
2 tablespoons chopped fresh dill (2 teaspoons dried)
1 tablespoon chopped fresh oregano (1 teaspoon dried)
salt and ground black pepper to taste

≈

1 cup grated or crumbled feta cheese
Greek olives

Bring a large covered pot of water to a rapid boil. Cook the pasta shells, uncovered, until al dente, and then drain. Rinse them under cold water until cool, and drain again.

Heat the oil in a large saucepan and add the eggplant. Cover and cook for 3 minutes on medium heat. Stir in the salt, garlic, lemon juice, and water. Cover and simmer for 6 to 8 minutes, until the eggplant is almost tender. Add the diced red bell peppers, and if you are using dried herbs, add the dill and oregano. Simmer a few minutes more, until the peppers are cooked but still have some crunch.

While the eggplant and peppers are cooking, place the artichoke hearts, cucumbers, tomatoes, celery, scallions, fresh dill, and fresh oregano in a large salad bowl. Add the cooked eggplant and peppers. Stir in the pasta and toss well. Add salt and pepper and more lemon juice or olive oil to taste.

Serve at room temperature topped with the feta and some olives.

PER 8-OZ SERVING: 200 CALORIES, 5.7 G PROTEIN, 9.3 G FAT, 25.6 G CARBOHYDRATE, 491 MG SODIUM, 8 MG CHOLESTEROL.

N O T E : This salad can be refrigerated to serve later, but the pasta may absorb the flavors and need an additional dash of lemon juice and olive oil just before serving.

GREEN BEAN PESTO SALAD

TOTAL TIME

30 minutes

SERVINGS

4

MENU

Serve this salad with
bread or crackers for
lunch or a summer picnic,
or with soup and bread
for a complete meal.

A *felicitous
combination
of ingredients
that transforms simple
elements into a
beautiful, delicious
salad. To prepare it
even more quickly, use
commercial pesto or
pull your own out of the
freezer. (To freeze
homemade pesto,
prepare it without the
cheese; then add the
cheese to the thawed
sauce when you're ready
to serve it.)*

4 large eggs

PESTO
2 cups loosely packed fresh basil leaves
⅓ cup loosely packed fresh parsley leaves
3 garlic cloves, minced or pressed
½ cup olive oil
½ cup grated Pecorino, Parmesan, or Romano cheese
⅓ cup pine nuts

≈
2 cups stemmed fresh green beans (about ¾ pound)
8 small potatoes, quartered
2 tomatoes, cut into wedges
½ cup thinly sliced red onion
sliced Fontina, fresh mozzarella, or Jarlsberg cheese

In a small saucepan, cover the eggs with cool water, bring to a boil, and simmer for 5 minutes. Place the pesto ingredients in a food processor or blender, and purée (if you're using a blender, first chop the basil and parsley and add a tablespoon of water). Set the pesto aside. Drain the hard-boiled eggs and cover them with cold water.

In a saucepan, bring about 2 quarts of water to a boil. Add the green beans to the boiling water and cook until tender, about 3 to 5 minutes. Remove the beans with a slotted spoon, and ease the potatoes into the boiling water. Cook the potatoes until they are easily pierced with a knife. Peel and halve the eggs. Drain the potatoes and arrange them on a platter surrounded by the green beans, tomatoes, onions, cheese, and hard-boiled eggs. Mound the pesto in the center.

Serve while still warm, or cover tightly and refrigerate to serve later.

PER 8-OZ SERVING, INCLUDING PESTO: 399 CALORIES, 9.6 G PROTEIN, 27.5 G FAT, 33 G CARBOHYDRATE, 230 MG SODIUM, 10 MG CHOLESTEROL.

MEDITERRANEAN LENTIL SALAD

1 cup brown or green lentils
4 cups water
2 bay leaves
1 teaspoon fresh thyme (½ teaspoon dried)
2 garlic cloves, peeled

≈

⅓ cup sun-dried tomatoes (not packed in oil)
boiling water
½ cup diced celery
½ cup diced red or yellow bell pepper
¼ cup minced red onion
½ cup chopped fresh parsley

DRESSING
⅓ cup olive oil
3 tablespoons red wine vinegar
1 teaspoon ground fennel
1 rounded teaspoon Dijon mustard
salt and ground black pepper to taste

Rinse the lentils. In a medium saucepan, bring the lentils, water, bay leaves, thyme, and garlic to a boil. Reduce the heat and simmer for about 20 minutes, until tender, stirring occasionally.

While the lentils simmer, cover the sun-dried tomatoes with boiling water in a heatproof bowl and set aside. Combine the celery, peppers, onions, and parsley in a large bowl. In a separate bowl, whisk the dressing ingredients until smooth. When the sun-dried tomatoes have softened, drain and mince them, and add to the vegetables.

Drain the lentils and discard the bay leaves. Remove the garlic, mash it, and mix it back into the lentils. Toss the lentils with the vegetables and dressing, and adjust the seasonings if necessary.

Serve immediately, or cover and chill to serve later.

PER 8-OZ SERVING: 277 CALORIES, 15.3 G PROTEIN, 6.3 G FAT, 44.8 G CARBOHYDRATE, 120 MG SODIUM, 0 MG CHOLESTEROL.

DRESSING PER 2-OZ SERVING: 343 CALORIES, 0.3 G PROTEIN, 38.1 G FAT, 1.9 G CARBOHYDRATE, 602 MG SODIUM, 0 MG CHOLESTEROL.

TOTAL TIME
30 minutes

SERVINGS
4

MENU
Serve this nutritious salad on a bed of lettuce, topped with feta cheese and olives and surrounded by tomato wedges and cucumber slices. Broccoli Egg-Lemon Soup (see page 24), Curried Cauliflower (see page 75), or Curried Corn and Peppers (see page 76) are agreeable companions for this salad.

Perhaps not gorgeous, but definitely tasty. With a little stock and some extra seasonings, leftovers can easily become lentil soup.

Mediterranean Potato Salad

TOTAL TIME
30 minutes

SERVINGS
4

MENU
Serve as a main dish with sliced cheese or hard-boiled eggs and tomatoes. Or use as a side salad with a simple grilled fish, or with Greek or French Fish in a Packet (see pages 247, 246).

Tart-sweet sun-dried tomatoes, fragrant cumin, and olive oil give this potato salad its special flavor. Red potatoes are nice for color, taste, and texture. This salad is good warm, but even better after a couple of hours, when the flavors have "married."

⅓ cup firmly packed sun-dried tomatoes (not packed in oil)
boiling water

≈

1 – 1½ pounds cubed potatoes (5 cups cubed)

≈

1½ cups finely chopped scallions
½ teaspoon ground cumin
¼ cup olive oil
2 tablespoons fresh lemon juice
salt and ground black pepper to taste

In a small heatproof bowl, cover the sun-dried tomatoes with boiling water and set aside.

Cut the potatoes into ½-inch cubes. As you do so, place them in a saucepan of salted water to prevent discoloration. Then cover the pan and bring the water to a boil. Lo er the heat, and simmer until the potatoes are tender.

Place the scallions in a large serving bowl with the cumin, olive oil, and lemon juice. Drain the sun-dried tomatoes and gently squeeze them to remove excess moisture. Finely chop the tomatoes and add them to the bowl. When the potatoes are tender, drain them thoroughly and add them to the bowl. Toss the salad, and add salt and pepper to taste.

PER 8-OZ SERVING: 384 CALORIES, 6.9 G PROTEIN, 17.6 G FAT, 55 G CARBOHYDRATE, 211 MG SODIUM, 0 MG CHOLESTEROL.

Mushroom Celery Parmesan Salad

12 – 16 ounces mushrooms *
pale center stalks of 1 head celery (without leaves)†
2 ounces Parmesan cheese (½ cup shaved)
juice of 2 lemons
⅓ cup olive oil (preferably extra-virgin)
salt and freshly ground black pepper to taste

When they're available, wild or imported fresh mushrooms (chanterelles, porcini, ovali) are good.

† *For a sweeter flavor, use fennel in place of the celery.*

Wash or wipe the mushrooms, if necessary. Cut off the stems and discard them. Thinly slice the mushroom caps. Cut the celery into thin diagonal slices. Use a vegetable peeler or small knife to shave the Parmesan into thin slivers.

Combine the mushrooms, celery, and Parmesan in a serving bowl. Drizzle with the lemon juice and olive oil, and season with salt and pepper. Toss gently. Taste, and adjust the seasonings. This is best served immediately, but it can be kept, refrigerated, for up to an hour before serving.

PER 8-OZ SERVING: 234 CALORIES, 8.1 G PROTEIN, 19.5 G FAT, 9.5 G CARBOHYDRATE, 428 MG SODIUM, 10 MG CHOLESTEROL.

TOTAL TIME
15 minutes

SERVINGS
2

MENU
Serve with Chilled Moroccan Tomato Soup (see page 26) or North African Cauliflower Soup (see page 33).

Crunchy, chewy, refreshing, and satisfying—this is a good appetizer, light lunch, summer supper, or salad to end a meal. This simple recipe could be enhanced with green olives, parsley, mustard, pears, walnuts, or—if you are fortunate enough to be able to find and afford the real thing—truffles.

SOBA NOODLE SALAD

OK

TOTAL TIME

20 minutes

SERVINGS

4

MENU

Serve with Broiled Tofu (see page 261) or Broiled Eggplant (see page 74).

The hearty flavor of buckwheat noodles and miso stand out in this version of a traditional Asian salad.

2 cups snow peas
1 pound soba noodles

SAUCE
2 tablespoons white or rice miso (see page 336)
⅓ cup water
2 tablespoons unsweetened apple juice
2 tablespoons dark sesame oil
¼ cup soy sauce
1 tablespoon grated peeled fresh ginger root
2 tablespoons rice vinegar

≈

⅔ cup chopped scallions

Bring a large covered pot of water to a rapid boil. Blanch the snow peas, uncovered, for a minute, until tender but still bright green. Remove the snow peas with a slotted spoon or a strainer, place them in a large serving bowl, and set aside. Cook the noodles in the same water until just tender, about 3 minutes. Drain, rinse under cold water, and drain again.

While the pasta cooks, prepare the sauce: In a small bowl, dissolve the miso in the water. Whisk in the apple juice, sesame oil, soy sauce, ginger, and vinegar. Chop the scallions.

In the serving bowl, toss the snow peas, sauce, and scallions with the noodles.

PER 8-OZ SERVING: 203 CALORIES, 9.4 G PROTEIN, 3.5 G FAT, 36.6 G CARBOHYDRATE, 562 MG SODIUM, 0 MG CHOLESTEROL.

SWEET POTATO SALAD

2 large sweet potatoes, peeled and cut into ¼-inch cubes
(about 3 cups)

≈

1½ tablespoons wine vinegar or cider vinegar
1½ tablespoons Dijon mustard
1 tablespoon honey
¼ cup vegetable oil

≈

1 cup diced celery
¾–1 cup diced red bell peppers
salt and ground black pepper to taste
2 tablespoons chopped fresh parsley
1 scallion, thinly sliced

≈

salad greens
½ cup ricotta cheese (optional)

TOTAL TIME
20 minutes

SERVINGS
2

MENU
Serve with Mexican Tomato Lime Soup (see page 30) or Black Bean Soup (see page 23).

A beautifully colored salad of contrasting textures and tastes — smooth and crunchy, sweet and savory.

Steam the sweet potato cubes for 6 to 8 minutes, until just tender (see page 353). Take care not to overcook them. While the potatoes steam, whisk the vinegar, mustard, and honey in a small bowl. Slowly add the oil in a thin stream, whisking until the dressing emulsifies. Place the diced celery and red peppers in a serving bowl. Add the steamed potatoes and the dressing. Stir gently, add salt and pepper to taste, and set aside for a few minutes. When the salad has cooled a little, toss in the parsley and scallions.

Serve on crisp salad greens, topped with a dollop of ricotta if you like. (If you use the ricotta, you may wish to add another scallion and additional salt and pepper.)

PER 8-OZ SERVING: 294 CALORIES, 3.2 G PROTEIN, 14.7 G FAT, 39.6 G CARBOHYDRATE, 247 MG SODIUM, 0 MG CHOLESTEROL.

Udon Noodles and Vegetables

Accompany with Broccoli and Carrots with Lime Dressing (see page 73) and Tropical Fruit Salad (see page 324).

A *Moosewood variation of an Asian pasta salad, combining elements of Chinese, Southeast Asian, and Japanese cuisines.*

8 ounces udon noodles or linguini

SAUCE
¼ cup peanut butter
⅓ cup rice vinegar or cider vinegar
¼ cup soy sauce
⅓ cup warm water
⅓ cup dark sesame oil
2 garlic cloves, minced or pressed
1 small fresh chile, seeded and minced, or a few splashes of chili oil, Tabasco, or other hot pepper sauce
½ teaspoon five-spice powder or ground fennel
¼ cup chopped fresh basil

≈

⅔ cup chopped scallions
1 cucumber, peeled, seeded, and diced
1 cake Tofu-Kan (see page 343) or five-spice tofu, cubed (about 6 ounces)

≈

fresh spinach or lettuce leaves
1 small carrot, grated

Bring a large covered pot of water to a boil. While the water heats, mix the sauce ingredients together until smooth, using a whisk or food processor. Set aside. Cook the noodles or linguini in the boiling water, uncovered, until tender but still firm to the bite (al dente). Drain, rinse under cold water, and drain again. In a large bowl, toss the noodles with the sauce, scallions, cucumbers, and tofu. Serve at once or refrigerate.

Serve on fresh greens and top with the grated carrots.

PER 8-OZ SERVING: 281 CALORIES, 9.2 G PROTEIN, 15.9 G FAT, 28.5 G CARBOHYDRATE, 528 MG SODIUM, 25 MG CHOLESTEROL.

WHITE BEAN AND TOMATO SALAD

4 cups cooked cannellini (two 16-ounce cans)

≈

2 garlic cloves, minced or pressed
½ red onion, minced (about ¼ cup)
6 pale center celery stalks, with leaves, thinly sliced
    crosswise
juice of 1 lemon
2 tablespoons extra-virgin olive oil
1 tablespoon chopped fresh mint or basil
    (1 teaspoon dried)
4 or 5 tomatoes, cut into ½-inch cubes
salt and freshly ground black pepper to taste

Drain the beans. If you are using canned beans, rinse them very gently in a colander and then set them aside to drain.

Combine the garlic, red onion, celery, lemon juice, olive oil, mint or basil, tomatoes, and salt and pepper in a large salad bowl. Add the beans and carefully stir with a wooden spoon, or with your hands, so that the beans don't break apart.

Serve at room temperature.

PER 8-OZ SERVING: 191 CALORIES, 9.2 G PROTEIN, 5 G FAT, 29.5 G CARBOHYDRATE, 119 MG SODIUM, 0 MG CHOLESTEROL.

TOTAL TIME
15 minutes

SERVINGS
4

MENU
Serve with Crostini (see page 263), Yogurt Cheese (see page 52), or Easiest Artichokes (see page 77).

A basic Mediterranean-style bean salad that can be the centerpiece of a summer supper or lunch.

Leftovers make a satisfying soup with the simple addition of vegetable stock: cook briefly, purée, and serve with croutons.

GRAINS

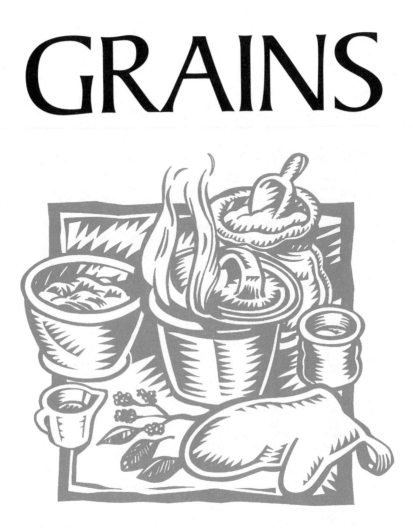

ONLY RECENTLY, the USDA finally put its official stamp of health on grains, making them the nutritional foundation of the recommended diet — the wide base of the Food Guide Pyramid, in fact, calling for six to eleven servings of grain, cereals, and breads a day. Although this new Food Guide Pyramid was announced with great fanfare and precipitated a flurry of news stories, there is really nothing new about this diet.

Throughout history, most cultures around the world have relied on grains for the basis of their diet. Whether wheat, corn, rice, rye, oats, millet, buckwheat, or quinoa, grains have fed people and kept them healthy for thousands of years.

For twenty years at Moosewood Restaurant, we have looked to the world's ethnic cuisines for inspiration for our own diet. The grain we have most often relied upon is brown rice. But the 45-to-50-minute cooking time for brown rice is a definite drawback when a meal must be on the table quickly.

One obvious solution is to create deliberate leftovers. In the same amount of time, a well-organized cook can steam double or triple the amount of rice needed for one meal and set it aside to be used later. Cooked brown rice can be refrigerated for about a week and frozen for a couple of months. It can be easily and quickly resteamed or microwaved to accompany a stir-fry, stew, fish, or bean entrée. Or it can be incorporated into pilafs, soups, and casseroles, giving the family cook a head start on the week's meals.

When you are strapped for time and no leftovers await you, or if you simply want some variety, thumb through this chapter for an interesting selection of grains. Bulghur, or cooked cracked wheat, is tasty and tempting in pilafs and burgers. Aromatic basmati rice, either brown or white, is another option. Couscous and orzo, actually grain-like pastas made from durum semolina wheat, are now reaching gourmet status. Quinoa, the extra-nutritious grain from the mountains of Peru, has a nutty whole-grain flavor and fluffy texture. Kasha, made from buckwheat groats, has a distinctive earthy taste that mixes especially well with savory vegetables. Arborio rice, with its creamy yet firm texture, combines with vegetables and cheese in risottos for a quick and uniquely toothsome entrée. Grits, made from hominy, are the most appropriate sidekick for certain Southern dishes and couldn't be easier to make. Polenta, a thick golden cornmeal porridge, is extremely adaptable and one of our favorites.

Taking from 5 to 20 minutes to cook, each of these grains is an economical, nutritious, versatile, and readily available staple. With these tasty and satisfying resources in your pantry, you can easily enrich your diet, even at a moment's notice, whenever inspiration strikes or hunger beckons, and you'll enjoy an amazing range of textures and tantalizing flavors.

Whole grains, such as arborio or brown rice and quinoa, should be stored in a dry, cool, insect-free space. Cracked and ground grains, such as bulghur and cornmeal, may show their age sooner and are best stored in a jar in the refrigerator or freezer. Couscous and orzo have an almost indefinite shelf life.

APRICOT BULGHUR PILAF

2 tablespoons olive oil
1½ cups chopped onions
1½ cups bulghur
2¼ cups boiling water
½ cup chopped dried apricots (preferably unsulfured)
1½ tablespoons fresh spearmint leaves, minced
     (2 teaspoons dried)
2 tablespoons chopped fresh dill (1½ teaspoons dried)
½ cup chopped fresh parsley
juice of 1 lemon
salt and ground black pepper to taste

≈

1 tomato, cut into wedges
lemon wedges
½ cup grated feta cheese (optional)

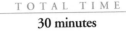

TOTAL TIME
30 minutes

SERVINGS
4 to 6

MENU
Serve with Black Bean
Dip (see page 46) and
crudités, or with North
African Cauliflower Soup
(see page 33).

*S*weet, aromatic
apricots and
mint enliven a
hearty bulghur pilaf.
This pilaf can be
transformed into a
perfect protein dish
with the addition of
cooked lentils.

   In a saucepan with a tight-fitting lid, heat the oil and sauté the onions for 3 minutes. Stir in the bulghur and sauté for 2 more minutes. Add the boiling water, cover, and bring to a boil. Reduce the heat and gently simmer for 10 minutes. Add the apricots without stirring them in, cover, and cook for another 5 to 10 minutes, until the water is absorbed and the bulghur is fluffy. Stir in the mint, dill, parsley, and lemon juice. Add salt and pepper to taste.

   Serve garnished with wedges of fresh tomato and lemon, and top with grated feta if you like.

PER 8-OZ SERVING: 294 CALORIES, 7.7 G PROTEIN, 6.6 G FAT, 56.3 G CARBOHYDRATE, 48 MG SODIUM, 0 MG CHOLESTEROL.

NOTE: If you plan to top the pilaf with feta, use less salt in the pilaf.

BULGHUR BURGERS

TOTAL TIME
40 minutes

SERVINGS
6 to 8 burgers

MENU
Serve with lettuce,
tomato, red onion rings,
and catsup, or with just a
splash of soy sauce, and
with Roasted Vegetable
Salad with Garlic and
Rosemary (see page 84).

Inspired by a recipe from former Moosewood Collective member Allan Warshawsky's first years in Ithaca, these hearty, nutty burgers are crunchy on the outside but moist and creamy inside.

3 cups water
2 garlic cloves, minced or pressed
1½ cups bulghur
2 tablespoons vegetable oil

½ cup chopped scallions
½ cup grated carrots
¼ cup chopped fresh parsley
¼ cup tahini
2 tablespoons tomato paste
2 tablespoons soy sauce
1 teaspoon Dijon mustard
dash of ground black pepper

Bring the water to a boil. While it is heating, use a heavy pan or skillet to sauté the garlic and bulghur in the oil on medium-high heat for 2 minutes, stirring frequently. Add the boiling water. Return to a boil, cover, and reduce the heat to low. Simmer for 15 to 20 minutes, until all of the water is absorbed and the bulghur is soft but still chewy.

Preheat the oven to 375° if you plan to bake the burgers.

When the bulghur is ready, stir in the scallions, carrots, parsley, tahini, tomato paste, soy sauce, mustard, and pepper. With moistened hands, form the bulghur mixture into 6 to 8 burgers. Cook them in a lightly oiled heavy skillet on medium-low heat for about 10 minutes, flipping the burgers once when the outside is crunchy, or bake on an oiled baking sheet for 20 minutes.

PER 8-OZ SERVING: 367 CALORIES, 9.3 G PROTEIN, 24.1 G FAT, 33.8 G CARBOHYDRATE, 927 MG SODIUM, 0 MG CHOLESTEROL.

VARIATION

For a different flavor and more protein, add 1 cup of mashed cooked chick peas to the cooked bulghur along with the other ingredients, before forming the burgers.

COUSCOUS WITH SUN-DRIED TOMATOES *Very good*

1 medium onion, finely chopped (about 1 cup)
2 tablespoons olive oil
8 sun-dried tomatoes
rounded ¼ teaspoon dried thyme
1¼ cups water
¼ teaspoon salt
1 cup whole wheat couscous

In a medium saucepan with a tightly fitting lid, sauté the onions in the oil on medium heat. When the onions are beginning to soften, add the sun-dried tomatoes and thyme, and continue to sauté for about 5 minutes more. Bring the water to a boil. When the onions are translucent, add the boiling water and the salt and return to a boil. Stir in the couscous, cover, and simmer on low heat for 5 minutes. Stir with a fork to fluff the couscous, and serve.

PER 4-OZ SERVING: 175 CALORIES, 5.1 G PROTEIN, 4.1 G FAT, 30.1 G CARBOHYDRATE, 89 MG SODIUM, 0 MG CHOLESTEROL.

TOTAL TIME
20 minutes

SERVINGS
4

MENU
Serve with Fish with Saffron and Garlic (see page 252) or a moist vegetable stew.

This is a simple yet sophisticated side dish. We prefer the nuttier taste, texture, and nutritional value of quick-cooking whole wheat couscous, although other types could be used.

If you use oil-packed sun-dried tomatoes, be sure to first drain them well.

NORTH AFRICAN COUSCOUS PAELLA

Excellent Wonderful

TOTAL TIME

20 minutes

SERVINGS

2

MENU

Fresh Orange Compote
(see page 309) is a perfect
dessert for this sunny
dish.

This recipe reminds us of one of those "magic" paper flowers that swell up and blossom when dropped in water. Five minutes after you add the couscous to the pot, you take off the lid and— voilà!—a colorful, delicious meal-in-a-pot is ready to serve!

2 tablespoons vegetable oil
½ cup chopped red bell pepper
4 scallions, chopped (about ½ cup)
2 garlic cloves, minced or pressed
1 teaspoon ground coriander
½ teaspoon turmeric
pinch of cayenne

2 cups hot vegetable stock or hot water
¾ pound tofu-kan (see page 343) or five-spice tofu, cut
        into ½-inch cubes, or ½ pound shelled shrimp
1 cup fresh or frozen green peas
1 cup quick-cooking couscous
1 tablespoon margarine or butter
salt and ground black pepper to taste

coarsely chopped toasted almonds (see page 354)
chopped fresh parsley
lemon wedges

Heat the oil in a 2-quart saucepan. Add the peppers, scallions, garlic, coriander, turmeric, and cayenne, and sauté on medium heat for 3 to 4 minutes, stirring occasionally. Stir in the stock or water. Add the tofu or shrimp and cook for another 3 to 4 minutes, until the tofu is hot or the shrimp are pink. Stir in the peas and cook for another minute. Mix in the couscous and the margarine or butter. Cover, remove from the heat, and let stand for 5 minutes.

Uncover the pan and using a fork, stir thoroughly to fluff up the couscous and break up any lumps. Add salt and pepper to taste. Serve on a platter, topped with toasted almonds, parsley, and lemon wedges.

PER 8-OZ SERVING: 264 CALORIES, 13 G PROTEIN, 7.2 G FAT, 36.8 G CARBOHYDRATE, 128 MG SODIUM, 50 MG CHOLESTEROL.

CHEESE GRITS

3 cups water
¼ teaspoon salt (optional)
¾ cup quick grits *
1 cup shredded cheddar cheese (or 3 ounces cubed)
ground black pepper (optional)

This recipe calls for "quick" grits, because they are quick and because they seem to be the most readily available around the country. Do not confuse "quick" grits with "instant" grits, however, which often contain a host of chemical additives. If you live in a part of the country where grits come in different speeds, you'll know what to do with them already or can easily find somebody to tell you all about it.

Bring the water, and salt if you are using it, to a boil in a medium saucepan. When the water boils, slowly stir in the grits. Lower the heat to medium, cover, and cook for about 5 minutes, stirring occasionally, until the grits are soft and thickened. Add the cheese and continue to stir until it melts. Add the pepper. Serve immediately, or keep warm on low heat using a heat diffuser or a double boiler.

PER 8-OZ SERVING: 266 CALORIES, 12.2 G PROTEIN, 12.7 G FAT, 24.9 G CARBOHYDRATE, 707 MG SODIUM, 40 MG CHOLESTEROL.

TOTAL TIME
10 minutes

SERVINGS
4

MENU
Try Cheese Grits with Black-Eyed Peas with Spinach (see page 166) and fried green tomatoes.

Those of us who were raised in the South still experience periodic, but strong, cravings for grits. It's not the bland corn taste we get a yen for, but the texture — not quite creamy smooth, just a bit nubbly . . . gritty.

KASHA WITH MUSHROOMS

TOTAL TIME
25 minutes

SERVINGS
4

MENU
Serve with pickled beets
and Sweet Peppers Soup
(see page 41) or
Cauliflower Paprikash
(see page 202).

Kasha is a
traditional high-
protein, high-
fiber, lysine-rich grain
that is a staple in
Eastern Europe. In this
dish the egg or egg
white could be optional,
but using it creates a
fluffier, lighter grain.

3 tablespoons vegetable oil
1 onion, chopped (1 heaping cup)
2 cups water or vegetable stock
1 large egg or 1 egg white (for less fat), lightly beaten
1 cup kasha
¾ pound mushrooms, sliced (about 4 cups)
2 tablespoons soy sauce
1 tablespoon chopped fresh dill (1 teaspoon dried)
⅛ teaspoon ground black pepper

≈

diced red bell pepper
sprig of fresh dill (optional)

Heat 1 tablespoon of the oil in a medium skillet. Add the chopped onions and sauté on medium heat stirring occasionally. While the onions sauté, heat the water or stock to boiling. In a small bowl, combine the egg and kasha. When the onions have softened, add the kasha mixture to the skillet and stir well. Continue to stir for a minute or two, until the kasha kernels are separate and dry. When the water or stock boils, pour it into the skillet, cover, and simmer gently on low heat for about 10 minutes, until the liquid is absorbed and the kasha is cooked.

While the kasha cooks, heat the remaining 2 tablespoons of oil in a medium skillet and sauté the mushrooms on high heat, stirring often, until they release their juices. Remove the mushrooms from the heat and drain, reserving their liquid. When the kasha is tender, add the mushrooms and 2 or 3 tablespoons of their reserved liquid. Stir in the soy sauce, dill, and pepper.

Top with some diced bell pepper, and a sprig of fresh dill if you like, and serve hot.

PER 8-OZ SERVING: 387 CALORIES, 11.8 G PROTEIN, 21.2 G FAT, 42.7 G CARBOHYDRATE, 466 MG SODIUM, 85 MG CHOLESTEROL.

SAFFRON ORZO

generous pinch of saffron, crumbled (about ½ teaspoon)
½ pound orzo *
½ cup finely grated Pecorino or Parmesan cheese
salt and ground black pepper to taste

* Orzo is known as Rosamarina in Italian, because the little grains of
pasta resemble rosemary leaves.

Bring about 3 quarts of water to a rapid boil in a large covered pot.
Crumble the saffron into a small heatproof bowl and stir in about
3 tablespoons of the boiling water. Set aside. Stir the orzo into the pot
of boiling water, cover, and return it to a boil. Cook for about 8 minutes, until al dente. Taste it frequently, and when the grains of pasta
are cooked, but still firm and separate, drain the orzo and quickly toss
it in a serving bowl with the saffron water and Pecorino. Add salt and
pepper to taste, and serve hot.

PER 8-OZ SERVING: 315 CALORIES, 9.9 G PROTEIN, 3.9 G FAT, 58.2 G CARBOHYDRATE, 238 MG SODIUM,
9 MG CHOLESTEROL.

TOTAL TIME
20 minutes

SERVINGS
4

MENU
Serve Saffron Orzo with
Cajun Skillet Beans
(see page 167) and Spicy
Kale (see page 88), or
with Caribbean Black
Beans (see page 168) and
Mango Salsa
(see page 103).

This golden,
fragrant side
dish is a good
alternative to rice when
you are either in a
hurry or just in the
mood for a change. It is
especially suited to
Spanish, Caribbean,
and North African
cuisines.

POLENTA

TOTAL TIME

15 minutes

SERVINGS

about 3 cups

MENU

Polenta is wonderful plain or topped with Peperonata (see page 83), Porcini Mushroom Sauce (see page 192), or Salsa Verde (see page 105). Cooked polenta can be sliced and then baked, broiled, grilled, or pan-fried. It can be cut into small cubes and used like dumplings in a stew.

Long a staple of northern Italian cuisine, this simple golden cornmeal mush is nourishing and heartwarming. We love the pure corn taste. In the winter especially, we can't get enough of it.

CLEANUP TIP: Almost inevitably some polenta sticks to the bottom of the cooking pot. To make it easier on the pot washer, fill the empty pot immediately with cold water and a few drops of detergent and let it soak for about an hour.

3 cups water
½ teaspoon salt
1 cup cornmeal
2 tablespoons butter or margarine
⅛ teaspoon crushed red pepper flakes (optional)
½ cup grated Parmesan cheese

In a saucepan, bring the water and salt to a boil. Add the cornmeal in a thin, steady stream while whisking briskly. Stir in the butter and optional crushed red pepper. Simmer for about 10 minutes, stirring often, until thickened. Polenta sputters as it cooks, so cover the pan when you're not stirring it. Remove from the heat, stir in the Parmesan, and serve.

PER 8-OZ SERVING: 263 CALORIES, 10 G PROTEIN, 11.2 G FAT, 30 G CARBOHYDRATE, 647 MG SODIUM, 28 MG CHOLESTEROL.

NOTE: Finely ground cornmeal cooks very rapidly—5 minutes should do it. Coarse-textured cornmeal will take a longer time to cook, but many people prefer its texture.

POLENTA WITH ENDIVE

3 cups water
½ teaspoon salt
1 cup fine cornmeal

≈

1 head curly endive (about 1 pound; 8 cups, chopped)
3 garlic cloves, minced or pressed
1½ tablespoons olive oil
dash of salt
pinch of crushed red pepper flakes (optional)
½ cup grated Pecorino, Parmesan, or Romano cheese
dash of ground black pepper

Preheat the broiler.

Bring the water to a boil and add the salt. When the water is boiling rapidly, pour in the cornmeal in a thin, steady stream, whisking constantly to prevent lumps. Lower the heat and simmer for about 10 minutes, stirring often to prevent sticking, until the polenta thickens.

While the polenta cooks, rinse the endive well, shake it dry, and finely chop it. In a skillet, lightly sauté the minced garlic in 1 tablespoon of the oil. Add the chopped endive and continue to sauté for 3 to 5 minutes, until the endive turns bright green and is somewhat reduced in volume. Stir the salt and optional red pepper flakes into the endive, and remove the skillet from the heat.

When the polenta is thickened, stir in the sautéed endive and the grated cheese. Spread the mixture in an unoiled flameproof 10-inch pie pan, brush the top with the remaining ½ tablespoon of oil, and sprinkle with black pepper. Broil for about 4 minutes, until the top is crisp and browned.

PER 8-OZ SERVING: 188 CALORIES, 7.7 G PROTEIN, 7.4 G FAT, 23 G CARBOHYDRATE, 438 MG SODIUM, 9 MG CHOLESTEROL.

TOTAL TIME
25 minutes

SERVINGS
4 to 6

MENU
Serve with Fresh Mozzarella and Tomato Salad (see page 68) or White Bean and Tomato Salad (see page 137). When giant portobello mushrooms appear in the market, grill them and serve them with Polenta with Endive and Easiest Artichokes (see page 77) for a very special meal.

In this recipe the smooth sweetness of the corn is offset by the slightly bitter crunch of the endive.

Leftover Polenta with Endive reheats quite nicely in the oven, or the cold polenta can be sliced and then grilled or pan-fried.

BROILED POLENTA WITH MUSHROOMS AND CHEESE

·TOTAL TIME·
30 minutes

SERVINGS
6

MENU
Accompany with Caesar Salad (see page 122) and fruit sorbet with Gingered Plum Sauce (see page 312).

The concentrated, woodsy flavor of porcini combines wonderfully with smoked cheese and cornmeal, but even if you use only the more economical and convenient domestic fresh mushrooms, the results are still pleasing.

This dish can be prepared early and broiled at serving time.

½ cup boiling water (optional)
½ cup dried porcini mushroom pieces (optional)

≈

3 cups water
½ teaspoon salt
1 cup cornmeal

≈

3 tablespoons olive oil
1½ cups diced domestic mushrooms (about 6 ounces), or 2 cups if omitting the porcini
1 large garlic clove, minced or pressed
1 tablespoon dry white wine, water, or reserved porcini soaking liquid
⅛ teaspoon salt

≈

½ cup shredded mozzarella cheese
½ cup shredded smoked cheddar or mild provolone cheese (or a combination)
ground black pepper to taste

≈

dash of basil, marjoram, or tarragon (optional)

If you are using the porcini mushrooms, place them in a heatproof bowl, cover with the boiling water, and set aside for about 10 minutes.

In a saucepan, bring the 3 cups of water and the salt to a boil. When the water is boiling rapidly, add the cornmeal in a thin, steady stream, whisking constantly to prevent lumps. Lower the heat and simmer for about 10 minutes, stirring often to prevent sticking, until the polenta thickens.

While the polenta cooks, strain the porcini mushrooms, reserving 1 tablespoon of the soaking liquid, and rinse them. Heat the oil in a skillet and sauté the domestic mushrooms, garlic, and porcini on medium heat until the oil is absorbed, stirring occasionally. Stir in the wine, water, or reserved porcini liquid, and add the salt. Simmer gently for another minute or two.

Preheat the broiler.

Spread the polenta evenly in an oiled or buttered flameproof pie plate or casserole dish. Sprinkle the shredded mozzarella on the polenta. Spoon the sautéed mushrooms over the mozzarella, and finish with a layer of the smoked cheddar and/or provolone cheese. Add pepper to taste. Broil for 3 to 5 minutes, until the cheese is golden brown. Top with a sprinkling of basil, marjoram, or tarragon if you like, and serve bubbling hot.

PER 8-OZ SERVING: 278 CALORIES, 9.1 G PROTEIN, 15.6 G FAT, 25.4 G CARBOHYDRATE, 604 MG SODIUM, 21.5 MG CHOLESTEROL.

very good

CARIBBEAN YELLOW RICE AND PIGEON PEAS

PREPARATION TIME
20 minutes

TOTAL TIME
40 minutes

SERVINGS
6 to 8

MENU
This dish is at its best when paired with a spicy, flavorful salsa, such as Mango Salsa (see page 103) or Tomato-Orange Salsa (see page 106).

3 tablespoons olive oil or vegetable oil
1 medium onion, chopped (about 1 cup)
2 garlic cloves, minced or pressed
1 teaspoon turmeric
2 cups white rice
3½ cups water
1½ teaspoons salt
1½ cups drained cooked pigeon peas* (16-ounce can)
1 cup fresh or frozen cut corn

≈

ground black pepper to taste

* Cooked dried peas, not green.

Heat the oil in a 3-quart saucepan. Sauté the onions and garlic for 2 to 3 minutes on medium heat until just beginning to soften. Mix in the turmeric and then the rice, stirring until the rice is uniformly yellow. Add the water, salt, drained pigeon peas, and corn. Cover and bring to a boil. Reduce the heat to low and cook for 15 to 20 minutes, until the liquid is absorbed. Season to taste with black pepper, and serve.

PER 8-OZ SERVING: 270 CALORIES, 6 G PROTEIN, 5.5 G FAT, 48.9 G CARBOHYDRATE, 418 MG SODIUM, 0 MG CHOLESTEROL.

COCONUT BASMATI RICE

1¼ cups water
1 cup white basmati rice
½ cup coconut milk (see page 333)
½ teaspoon turmeric
¼ teaspoon salt
1 piece cinnamon stick (1–1½ inches)
¼ cup currants or raisins
1 dried chile (optional)

In a heavy saucepan with a tightly fitting lid, bring the water to a boil. While the water heats, rinse the rice well. When the water boils, stir in the rice and all of the remaining ingredients. Return to a boil. Stir, cover, reduce the heat to low, and simmer for 15 minutes. Remove the cinnamon stick and the optional chile, stir to fluff the rice, and serve.

PER 8-OZ SERVING: 327 CALORIES, 5.4 G PROTEIN, 9.5 G FAT, 56 G CARBOHYDRATE, 204 MG SODIUM, 0 MG CHOLESTEROL.

PREPARATION TIME
5 minutes

TOTAL TIME
20 minutes

SERVINGS
3 or 4

MENU
Serve with Curried Chick Peas and Tofu (see page 169) or Curried Vegetables with Dahl (see page 206). Leftovers can be used for Curried Fried Rice (see page 226).

A sweetly aromatic golden rice perfect with curried dishes.

GOLDEN SPANISH RICE

TOTAL TIME
20 minutes

SERVINGS
4

MENU
Serve with
Simple Quesadillas
(see page 268), Mexican
Seitan (see page 80), or
Caribbean Black Beans
(see page 168), or as a
simple meal with avocado
wedges and Monterey
Jack cheese.

*A*nnatto seeds
add a golden
hue to this
easily prepared, tasty
treatment for leftover
rice.

1 tablespoon vegetable oil
1 teaspoon annatto seeds

≈

4 cups cooked rice (preferably brown)
½ cup fresh or frozen cut corn (optional)
1 tomato, diced
2 – 3 scallions, finely chopped (about ⅓ cup)
¼ cup chopped Spanish olives
2 tablespoons chopped fresh cilantro
salt and ground black pepper to taste

In a medium skillet, heat the oil and annatto seeds. Cook for a minute or two on medium heat, until the oil becomes a golden-orange color. Strain the oil through a sieve to remove the seeds. Discard the seeds and return the strained oil to the skillet.

Add the rice and corn to the pan and stir well. Cover and cook on low heat, stirring occasionally, for about 5 minutes. Stir the tomato, scallions, olives, and cilantro into the rice and cook for about 10 minutes, until hot. Stir occasionally, and add a dash or two of water if needed to prevent the rice from sticking. Add salt and pepper to taste, and serve hot.

PER 8-OZ SERVING: 274 CALORIES, 5.8 G PROTEIN, 7 G FAT, 48.3 G CARBOHYDRATE, 253 MG SODIUM, 0 MG CHOLESTEROL.

GREEK RICE PILAF

1 large onion, chopped (about 1½ cups)
2 tablespoons olive oil
1 – 2 garlic cloves, minced or pressed
1 tablespoon dried mint leaves
⅛ teaspoon ground black pepper (or to taste)
4 cups chopped washed spinach (about 5 ounces)
3 tablespoons fresh lemon juice
4 cups cooked rice
1 cup fresh or frozen green peas
2 tablespoons chopped fresh dill
1 cup grated or crumbled feta cheese

TOTAL TIME
25 minutes

SERVINGS
4

MENU
This pilaf can be the centerpiece of a meal or an accompaniment to grilled fish, Broiled Eggplant (see page 74), or Red Lentil Soup (see page 36).

In a heavy skillet, sauté the onions in the oil on medium heat for about 5 minutes, until the onions begin to soften. Add the garlic, mint, and pepper, and continue to sauté for 2 minutes. Stir in the spinach, lemon juice, rice, and green peas. Add the dill. Cover and cook for 3 or 4 minutes, stirring occasionally.

When the spinach is limp and the rice is hot, top with the feta and serve immediately.

Sweet, salty, and savory, this flavorful pilaf can be served hot or at room temperature.

PER 8-OZ SERVING: 305 CALORIES, 8.7 G PROTEIN, 9.4 G FAT, 46.5 G CARBOHYDRATE, 254 MG SODIUM, 17 MG CHOLESTEROL.

VARIATIONS

• Add 2 chopped tomatoes along with the spinach and peas.
• Add 1 cup of drained cooked chick peas along with the spinach and green peas.

HERBED LEMON PILAF WITH ALMONDS

TOTAL TIME
20 minutes

SERVINGS
4

MENU
Serve with steamed green beans tossed with Honey Mustard Vinaigrette (see page 97).

H*ere leftover brown rice transcends the* ordinary.

2 tablespoons olive oil
1 medium onion, chopped
2 garlic cloves, minced or pressed
1 teaspoon turmeric
juice of ½ lemon
2 tablespoons soy sauce
½ cup chopped fresh basil
1 – 2 teaspoons fresh thyme
½ cup chopped fresh parsley
3 cups cooked brown rice
¼ cup hot water

≈

⅔ cup chopped almonds
salt and ground black pepper to taste
1 tablespoon butter or margarine (optional)

Heat the olive oil in a saucepan. Add the onions and garlic, and sauté on medium heat for 5 or 6 minutes. Stir in the turmeric, lemon juice, and soy sauce. Lower the heat and add the chopped basil, thyme, and parsley. Add the rice and mix it well with the seasonings. Drizzle in the hot water. Cover the pot and steam the rice on low heat for 5 minutes.

While the pilaf steams, toast the chopped almonds (see page 354). (If you're using already toasted almonds, warm them before serving.) Season the pilaf to taste with salt and pepper. Toss it with the butter or margarine if you like, top with the warm toasted almonds, and serve.

PER 8-OZ SERVING: 292 CALORIES, 7.6 G PROTEIN, 8.6 G FAT, 50.8 G CARBOHYDRATE, 433 MG SODIUM, · 0 MG CHOLESTEROL.

Mediterranean Rice

1 cup chopped onions
2 garlic cloves, minced or pressed
2 tablespoons olive oil
3 celery stalks, thinly sliced (about 1 cup)
2 teaspoons fresh thyme (1 teaspoon dried)
1 teaspoon fresh marjoram (½ teaspoon dried)
1 bell pepper, diced (about 1 cup)
2 cups canned tomatoes (15-ounce can)
1 tablespoon tomato paste (optional)
salt and ground black pepper to taste
3 cups cooked rice

*T*his dish makes
good use of
leftover rice with
its classic combination
of aromatic ingredients.

In a large skillet, sauté the onions and garlic in the oil on medium heat for about 5 minutes, until softened. Stir in the celery, thyme, and marjoram and sauté for 2 more minutes. Add the bell pepper and continue to cook for another 2 or 3 minutes. Drain the tomatoes, reserving the juice. Stir in the drained tomatoes and the optional tomato paste. Add salt and pepper to taste. Stir in the rice and mix thoroughly. If the rice is too dry or firm, add some of the reserved tomato juice to reach an agreeable texture. When the rice is hot and the juice has been absorbed, the dish is ready to serve.

PER 8-OZ SERVING: 204 CALORIES, 3.9 G PROTEIN, 5.3 G FAT, 35.4 G CARBOHYDRATE, 122 MG SODIUM, 0 MG CHOLESTEROL.

VARIATIONS

• If you like a slightly sweeter flavor, substitute canned stewed tomatoes for the plain tomatoes.
• For an even quicker Mediterranean Rice, substitute scallions for the onions (sautéing about 3 minutes), eliminate the celery, and use canned sweet pimientos instead of the bell pepper.

RICE PILAF WITH DATES AND ALMONDS

TOTAL TIME

25 minutes

SERVINGS

4

MENU

Serve with Curried
Cauliflower
(see page 75) or simple
steamed vegetables.

*T*urn leftover rice
into an elegant
golden pilaf
seasoned with spices,
crisp almonds, and the
subtle sweetness of dates.
Inspired by the more
labor-intensive and
elaborate pilafs of Iraqi
cooking, this is
nontraditional but
delightful.

1 tablespoon butter
1 tablespoon vegetable oil
1 medium onion, chopped (about 1 cup)
1 large garlic clove, minced or pressed
1 red, green, or yellow bell pepper

≈

1 teaspoon turmeric
½ teaspoon cinnamon
½ teaspoon ground allspice or nutmeg

≈

½ cup dates
3 cups cooked brown, white, or basmati rice
2 tablespoons chopped fresh parsley
¼ cup hot water
½ cup chopped toasted almonds (see page 354)
salt and ground black pepper to taste

In a large heavy skillet, heat the butter and oil. Sauté the onions and garlic on medium heat until just tender. Finely chop the bell pepper, and add it to the sautéing onions. Stir in the turmeric, cinnamon, and allspice or nutmeg. Finely chop the dates, and add them to the onions. Stir in the rice and parsley, sprinkle on the water, and heat, uncovered, for a few minutes. When the rice is hot, stir in the almonds, add salt and pepper to taste, and serve.

PER 8-OZ SERVING: 290 CALORIES, 5.3 G PROTEIN, 8.5 G FAT, 50 G CARBOHYDRATE, 75 MG SODIUM, 7 MG CHOLESTEROL.

RISOTTO WITH CARROTS AND FETA

5 cups vegetable stock, or 1 – 2 vegetable bouillon cubes
    and 5 cups water

4 carrots, cut into matchsticks (about 4 cups)

≈

1 small onion, diced (about ⅔ cup)

1 tablespoon olive oil

1½ cups arborio rice (see page 339)

1 tablespoon chopped fresh dill (1 teaspoon dried)

≈

juice of 1 lemon

1 cup crumbled or grated feta cheese

2 tablespoons chopped fresh parsley (optional)

Bring the stock to a boil in a covered pot. Ease the carrots into the boiling stock, lower the heat, and very gently simmer.

In a large saucepan, sauté the onions in the oil for about 5 minutes on medium heat, until softened but not browned. Using a wooden spoon to avoid breaking the individual kernels, carefully add the rice, stirring gently until it is thoroughly coated with oil. Add the dill. Ladle 1 cup of the simmering stock and carrots into the saucepan and stir it into the rice. When the rice has absorbed the liquid, stir in another cup of the stock. Stir in the stock and carrots, a cup at a time every few minutes, until all of the stock has been absorbed and the rice is tender but al dente. This will take 15 to 20 minutes.

When the risotto is ready, remove it from the heat and stir in the lemon juice, feta, and optional parsley. Serve immediately.

PER 8-OZ SERVING: 155 CALORIES, 4.6 G PROTEIN, 5.8 G FAT, 21.8 G CARBOHYDRATE, 188 MG SODIUM, 12 MG CHOLESTEROL.

TOTAL TIME
30 minutes

SERVINGS
2

MENU
Serve this risotto with Easiest Artichokes (see page 77) or a salad of tomatoes and cucumbers.

Risotto has a mystique. In this country it seems to be found only in trendy Northern Italian restaurants, where it is prepared by skilled chefs. However, in Italy it is a familiar home-style dish. Once you understand the technique, making risotto becomes as easy as cooking pasta, and almost as various.

Add a beaten egg to cold leftover risotto and either pan-fry it for a risotto frittata or bake it for a rice "cake."

RISOTTO WITH GREEN BEANS AND PESTO

TOTAL TIME
30 minutes

SERVINGS
2

MENU
Serve with Carrot
and Parsley Salad
(see page 65) or Fennel
and Orange Salad
(see page 67).

A risotto that uses ordinary ingredients with extraordinary results. Jars of pesto are usually available anywhere that Italian specialty foods are sold, or you can choose from our selection of herb pestos (see pages 362–63) to make your own.

5 cups vegetable stock, or 1 – 2 vegetable bouillon cubes
 and 5 cups water

≈

1 small onion, diced (about ⅔ cup)
1 tablespoon olive oil
1½ cups arborio rice (see page 339)
9 ounces frozen french-cut green beans

≈

¼ cup prepared pesto
1 cup chopped tomatoes, or 1 cup halved cherry tomatoes
½ cup grated Pecorino or Parmesan cheese

Bring the stock to a boil in a covered pot, then lower the heat to maintain a simmer.

While the stock heats, sauté the diced onions in the oil in a large saucepan for about 5 minutes, until softened but not browned. Using a wooden spoon to avoid breaking the kernels, add the rice and stir gently to thoroughly coat it with oil. Ladle a cup of the simmering stock into the pan, and stir it into the rice. When the rice has absorbed the liquid, stir in another cup of the stock. Continue to add the stock, a cup at a time, every few minutes for about 10 minutes. When there are about 2 cups of stock remaining, add the frozen green beans to the stock and cook them for a minute or two. Then continue to add the stock, with the beans, to the rice as before, until all of the stock has been absorbed and the rice is tender but al dente. This will take about 10 more minutes.

When the rice is ready, stir in the pesto, tomatoes, and grated cheese. Serve immediately.

PER 8-OZ SERVING: 188 CALORIES, 6.6 G PROTEIN, 9.4 G FAT, 20.3 G CARBOHYDRATE, 194 MG SODIUM, 7 MG CHOLESTEROL.

BEANS

BEANS AND BEAN PRODUCTS (tofu, tempeh, sprouts, miso, tamari, soy sauce, soy milk, and so on) are indispensable to the vegetarian cook. An excellent source of protein, minerals, B vitamins, fiber, and complex carbohydrates, they also are low in fats, don't contain many calories, and have relatively lower cholesterol levels.

For the cook, beans have the additional benefits of being both versatile and inexpensive. The bean recipes we have included here are very quick and mostly call for previously cooked beans. Most recipes in this book will be adequately served by canned beans. We have been pleased with Goya and Progresso brand products. Always rinse canned beans — they are often salty. When shopping, be sure to check the label for preservatives and other additives: the less, the better!

BLACK-EYED PEAS WITH SPINACH

TOTAL TIME
25 minutes

SERVINGS
4

MENU
For a speedy supper, serve
with sliced tomatoes and
Cheese Grits
(see page 147) or Saffron
Orzo (see page 149).

This skillet bean dish was inspired by Southern-style black-eyed peas. This recipe calls for canned beans, but fresh are best if you can get them. Some of us prefer frozen, and some of us use dried, but once they're cooked, the recipe is the same. A brand of canned beans that we recommend is The Allen's Fresh Shelled Black-eyed Peas, which are small and firm. Almost any greens could be used in place of spinach.

1 medium onion, chopped
1 tablespoon vegetable oil
10 ounces fresh spinach, rinsed, stemmed, and
    coarsely chopped
3 cups drained cooked black-eyed peas
    (two 16-ounce cans)
ground black pepper to taste
pinch of cayenne or crushed red pepper flakes (optional)

In a large skillet, sauté the onions in the oil for a few minutes, until soft. Add the spinach to the skillet. Stir for a minute or two until it wilts. Add the black-eyed peas, black pepper, and cayenne if desired. Bring to a simmer on medium heat.

Serve right away, or cover and keep warm on low heat.

PER 8-OZ SERVING: 256 CALORIES, 15.3 G PROTEIN, 4.7 G FAT, 40.7 G CARBOHYDRATE, 46 MG SODIUM, 0 MG CHOLESTEROL.

CAJUN SKILLET BEANS

1 medium onion, chopped
3 garlic cloves, minced or pressed
2 tablespoons vegetable oil
3 celery stalks (about 1 cup chopped)
2 green or red bell peppers (about 1½ cups chopped)
1 teaspoon chopped fresh thyme (½ teaspoon dried)
1 tablespoon chopped fresh basil (1 teaspoon dried)
1 teaspoon chopped fresh oregano (½ teaspoon dried)
¼ teaspoon ground black pepper (or more to taste)
pinch each of cayenne and salt
2 cups chopped fresh or canned tomatoes (14½-ounce can)
1 tablespoon honey or molasses
1 tablespoon Dijon mustard
4 cups cooked black-eyed peas or butter beans (two 10-
    ounce frozen packages or two 16-ounce cans, drained)

≈

chopped scallions (optional)
grated cheddar cheese (optional)

In a heavy saucepan or skillet, sauté the onions and garlic in the oil on medium heat. Chop the celery and bell peppers, and add them to the pan. Continue to sauté for about 5 minutes, stirring occasionally. Add the thyme, basil, oregano, black pepper, cayenne, and salt. Cover and cook for 5 minutes or until the onions are golden, stirring once or twice. Add the tomatoes, honey or molasses, and mustard, and simmer for 5 more minutes. Add the beans, cover, and stir occasionally until thoroughly heated. Canned beans will be hot in less than 10 minutes, but frozen beans need to simmer for 15 to 20 minutes.

Top with scallions or grated cheese if you like, and serve.

PER 8-OZ SERVING: 200 CALORIES, 10.2 G PROTEIN, 4.5 G FAT, 31.7 G CARBOHYDRATE, 143 MG SODIUM, 0 MG CHOLESTEROL.

TOTAL TIME
20 minutes (35 minutes
for frozen beans)

SERVINGS
6

MENU
Serve Cajun Skillet Beans
with Corn Scones
(see page 53) or Cheese
Grits (see page 147), or
over rice or Saffron Orzo
(see page 149). Spicy Kale
(see page 88) is an
appropriate side dish.
How about Coffee
Ricotta Mousse
(see page 307) for dessert?

Similar in taste to the pungent, cooked-forever beans found in Southern barbecue joints, this attractive, colorful dish can probably be made even faster if you put some zydeco on the hi-fi while you cook.

CARIBBEAN BLACK BEANS

TOTAL TIME
30 minutes

SERVINGS
4

MENU
**Serve Caribbean Black
Beans on rice or Golden
Spanish Rice
(see page 156), topped
with Mango Salsa
(see page 103).**

*A Moosewood
Restaurant
favorite that
requires minimal
preparation but results
in a sophisticated dish.*

**1½ cups chopped onions
3 garlic cloves, minced or pressed
2 tablespoons olive oil
1 tablespoon grated fresh ginger root
1 teaspoon fresh thyme (½ teaspoon dried)
½ teaspoon ground allspice
4½ cups drained cooked black beans (three 16-ounce cans)
¾ cup orange juice
salt and ground black pepper to taste**

Sauté the onions and garlic in the oil for about 5 minutes, until the onions begin to soften. Add the ginger, thyme, and allspice and sauté, stirring often to prevent sticking, until the onions are very soft, for about 5 more minutes. Stir in the beans and orange juice and cook on low heat for about 15 minutes, stirring occasionally, until the mixture thickens slightly. Use a heat diffuser or a double boiler if necessary to prevent scorching. Mash a few of the beans with the back of a spoon for a thicker consistency. Add salt and pepper to taste, and serve.

PER 8-OZ SERVING: 252 CALORIES, 5.3 G PROTEIN, 13.1 G FAT, 26.1 G CARBOHYDRATE, 1,606 MG SODIUM, 0 MG CHOLESTEROL.

CURRIED CHICK PEAS AND TOFU

1 medium onion, chopped
1 garlic clove, minced or pressed
2 tablespoons vegetable oil
2 teaspoons ground cumin
1 teaspoon ground coriander
½ teaspoon turmeric
¼ teaspoon ground black pepper
pinch of cayenne (optional)
1 cake tofu (¾ pound), cut into ½-inch cubes
2 cups undrained cooked chick peas (16-ounce can)
2 tomatoes, chopped (about 1½ cups)
pinch of salt (or more to taste)

≈

chopped fresh cilantro (optional)
plain yogurt (optional)

Sauté the onion and garlic in the oil until the onions are translucent, stirring occasionally. Stir in the cumin, coriander, turmeric, black pepper, and optional cayenne. Add the cubed tofu and cook for a minute or so, stirring constantly. Add the chick peas and about ½ cup of their liquid, and simmer for 5 minutes. Add the tomatoes and continue to cook until thoroughly heated. Add salt to taste.

Serve topped with cilantro and/or yogurt if you like.

PER 8-OZ SERVING: 253 CALORIES, 11.7 G PROTEIN, 10.5 G FAT, 30.5 G CARBOHYDRATE, 360 MG SODIUM, 0 MG CHOLESTEROL.

TOTAL TIME
20 minutes
SERVINGS
4
MENU
Curried Chick Peas and Tofu is at its best served over rice. Try Coconut Basmati Rice (see page 155). Think green for a side dish — steamed broccoli or a spinach salad, perhaps. Try Inside-Out Mango (see page 314) or Sautéed Bananas (see page 320) for dessert.

In this pretty yellow and red curry, we've adapted the traditional Indian dish by replacing the usual chenna (cheese) with tofu. Curried Chick Peas and Tofu is so easy to prepare that several uncomplicated side dishes can be made at the same time.

FIELD PEAS WITH KALE AND SWEET POTATOES

TOTAL TIME

25 minutes

SERVINGS

4 to 6

MENU

Serve with sliced tomatoes and a grain or Saffron Orzo (see page 149). Put the pot of water for the grain or orzo on the heat when you begin the recipe, and everything will be ready in just 25 minutes. Either Fresh Orange Compote (see page 309) or Creamy Banana Ice (see page 308) would be a perfect dessert.

*S*ort of Southern, could be Caribbean, absolutely African-influenced, this is a colorful, tasty meal in a skillet.

2 cups water
1 large sweet potato (about 2 cups cubed)
1 large onion (1½–2 cups chopped)
1 tablespoon vegetable oil

≈

1 pound kale (4–5 cups)
3½ cups cooked field peas or green pigeon peas (two 15½-ounce cans)
freshly ground black pepper to taste

≈

cider vinegar
Tabasco or other hot pepper sauce

In a saucepan, bring the water to a boil. While the water heats, peel the sweet potato and cut it into ½-inch cubes. When the water boils, cook the sweet potato cubes for about 10 minutes, until barely tender. While the potatoes cook, chop the onion and sauté it in the oil in a large skillet until translucent. Drain the potatoes, reserving a few tablespoons of the cooking liquid, and set aside.

Wash the kale leaves, shake them dry, and remove and discard the tough bottom parts of the stems. Cut through the stems lengthwise and finely chop the leaves. Add the kale to the onions and sauté for 1 or 2 minutes, until the leaves are still bright green but much reduced. Add the reserved potato water to the skillet to steam the kale. Drain and rinse the field peas or pigeon peas (canned pigeon peas are especially salty and must be well rinsed). Add them to the skillet along with the drained cooked sweet potatoes and heat for a minute or two. Add pepper to taste.

Serve immediately, offering vinegar and Tabasco at the table for a little extra zing.

PER 8-OZ SERVING: 142 CALORIES, 6.9 G PROTEIN, 2.3 G FAT, 24.5 G CARBOHYDRATE, 19 MG SODIUM, 0 MG CHOLESTEROL.

Greek-Style Cannellini and Vegetables

TOTAL TIME

40 minutes

SERVINGS

4

MENU

This dish can stand on its own, but to make a no-fuss feast, serve it with olives, bread, red wine, Fennel and Orange Salad (see page 67), and Goat Cheese with Honey and Walnuts (see page 313) for dessert.

*S*erve this hearty, colorful one-dish meal in the Greek style — with a splash of red wine vinegar. Look in the pasta section of your supermarket for orzo; an imported brand will be best. Look in the "Two for $1" bin at the record store for good bazouki music.

2 quarts water
2 garlic cloves, minced or pressed
1 large onion, chopped (about 1½ cups)
3 tablespoons olive oil
2–3 carrots (about 2 cups diced)
1 red or green bell pepper
1 cup orzo (see page 358)
1 zucchini (6 inches long)
1 tablespoon minced fresh mint (1 teaspoon dried)
1 tablespoon minced fresh dill (1 teaspoon dried)
½ teaspoon fresh marjoram (sprinkling of dried)
5 artichoke hearts, drained and chopped (14-ounce can) (optional)
1½–2 cups drained cooked cannellini or white kidney beans (15-ounce can)
1½–2 cups Italian-style stewed tomatoes (14½-ounce can)
salt and ground black pepper to taste

≈

red wine vinegar

Bring the water to a boil in a large covered pot.

While the water heats, sauté the garlic and onions in 2 tablespoons of the oil in a large skillet on medium-high heat. While the garlic and onions sauté, dice the carrots and chop the pepper. Add them to the onions and stir. When the water boils, add the orzo, return to a boil, and simmer for about 10 minutes, until al dente. Dice the zucchini and stir it into the skillet of vegetables. Add the mint, dill, and marjo-ram. Add the artichoke hearts, if you are using them. Gently stir in the beans and the stewed tomatoes. Simmer for several minutes, stir-ring occasionally.

When the pasta is al dente, drain it and stir in the remaining table-spoon of oil. When the beans and vegetables are hot, add the orzo. Season with salt and pepper to taste. Serve with a cruet of red wine vinegar at the table for a splash of flavor.

PER 8-OZ SERVING: 181 CALORIES, 6.9 G PROTEIN, 5.7 G FAT, 26.7 G CARBOHYDRATE, 93 MG SODIUM, 0 MG CHOLESTEROL.

HONOLULU SKILLET BEANS

TOTAL TIME

25 minutes

SERVINGS

4

MENU

These beans can easily be the centerpiece for many different menus. We like them served with sweet potatoes and Asian Cabbage Slaw (see page 64). Or pair them with Polenta with Endive (see page 151). For an all-American Saturday night supper, slice some vegetarian hot dogs into the beans and serve them with purchased steamed brown bread, applesauce, and cheddar cheese.

*S*picy, sweet, and aromatic, these richly flavored beans are a tropical variation of a New England classic. Catsup will give the beans a tangy flavor; use tomato paste for a mellower taste. Choosing two or three kinds of beans can add color and variety.

1 large onion, finely chopped (about 1½ cups)
2 teaspoons vegetable oil
4 cups cooked small firm beans, such as Roman or small
    pink, red, or white beans (two 16-ounce cans)
2 tablespoons hoisin sauce *
2 teaspoons prepared yellow mustard
2 tablespoons catsup or tomato paste
1 tablespoon soy sauce
1 teaspoon dark sesame oil
1 teaspoon ground cumin
grated peel of 1 orange (about 1 tablespoon)
¾ cup fresh or canned crushed pineapple (optional)

* Good commercial hoisin sauces are available in Asian markets and most supermarkets. We prefer the distinctive flavor that hoisin gives these beans, but if it's unavailable to you, substitute 1 tablespoon of molasses or brown sugar, 1 tablespoon of white vinegar, and 1 teaspoon of chili oil or hot pepper sauce.

In a skillet or saucepan, sauté the onions in the oil until soft and beginning to brown, about 10 minutes. While the onions cook, drain the beans in a colander and rinse them under running water. In a small bowl, stir together the hoisin sauce, mustard, catsup, soy sauce, sesame oil, cumin, orange peel, and optional pineapple. When the onions are soft, add the beans and the sauce. Stir gently to distribute the sauce. Bring to a gentle simmer on low heat.

Remove the beans from the heat and serve right away, or set them aside to reheat later.

PER 8-OZ SERVING: 317 CALORIES, 18.7 G PROTEIN, 4.5 G FAT, 52.9 G CARBOHYDRATE, 336 MG SODIUM, 0 MG CHOLESTEROL.

Red, Gold, Black, and Green Chili

½ cup bulghur
½ cup hot water
3 cups undrained canned tomatoes (28-ounce can)

3 tablespoons olive oil or vegetable oil
3 cups chopped onions
3 garlic cloves, minced or pressed
1 generous teaspoon ground cumin
1 generous teaspoon chili powder
1 tablespoons Tabasco or other hot pepper sauce, or
    ¼ teaspoon cayenne

2 green bell peppers, chopped
2 cups fresh or frozen cut corn
1½ cups drained cooked black beans (14-ounce can)
1½ cups drained cooked red kidney beans (14-ounce can)
salt to taste

grated cheddar or Monterey Jack cheese (optional)
chopped fresh cilantro (optional)

TOTAL TIME
35 minutes

SERVINGS
4 to 6

MENU
Serve with warmed tortillas or tortilla chips and crudités. Try a Mango Shake (see page 311) to finish the meal. Leftovers can be either used for a burrito or pita bread filling or thinned with stock or water for a soup.

With its variety of flavors and colors, we think this is one good-tasting, good-looking chili.

Place the bulghur, hot water, and about a cup of the juice from the canned tomatoes in a small saucepan. Cover and bring to a boil on high heat, then lower the heat and simmer gently.

While the bulghur cooks, heat the olive oil in a large saucepan. Sauté the onions, garlic, cumin, chili powder, and Tabasco or cayenne. When the onions are soft, stir in the bell peppers and sauté for 2 to 3 minutes more. Chop the tomatoes right in the can and add them to the pan. Stir in the corn and beans, and heat thoroughly on low heat. Taste the bulghur. When it is cooked but still chewy, add it to the pan with its liquid. Cover and simmer for a few minutes for the flavors to meld. Add salt to taste.

Serve plain or topped with grated cheese and fresh cilantro.

PER 8-OZ SERVING: 190 CALORIES, 6.8 G PROTEIN, 5.8 G FAT, 30.4 G CARBOHYDRATE, 291 MG SODIUM, 0 MG CHOLESTEROL.

TANGY LIMAS WITH SQUASH AND TOMATOES

TOTAL TIME

25 minutes

SERVINGS

4

MENU

Serve with Easiest
Artichokes (see page 77)
or Carrot and Parsley
Salad (see page 65), olives,
a crusty bread or wedges
of pita bread, and Lemon
Date Bars (see page 315)
for dessert.

H*ere's a savory,
colorful dinner
in a skillet.*

*This dish may be made
ahead for reheating
later, but it should be
removed from the skillet
and stored in an
ovenproof ceramic
casserole dish, since the
skillet may react with
the tomato and lemon
over time.*

SHOPPING TIP: Buy 1- or 2-pound plastic bags of frozen lima beans rather than the smaller cardboard packages. It's more economical, and the bags are easy to reseal for handy storage in the freezer.

2 cups water
2 cups frozen lima beans (10-ounce package)
2 onions, chopped (about 2 cups)
2 teaspoons olive oil
4 small yellow summer squash, thinly sliced into half-circles (about 3½ cups), or 2 zucchini, thinly sliced into half-circles (about 3½ cups), or a combination of the two
3 sprigs fresh thyme (1 teaspoon dried)
2 teaspoons chopped fresh dill (½ teaspoon dried)
2 cups chopped fresh or canned tomatoes
juice of 1 lemon
½ cup crumbled feta cheese (about 3 ounces)
ground black pepper to taste

Bring the water to a boil in a saucepan and add the limas. Following the package instructions, cook about 10 minutes, until tender. While the limas cook, sauté the onions in the oil in a large skillet until translucent. Add the squash, thyme, and dill and continue to sauté for 2 to 3 minutes. Add the tomatoes. When the limas are tender, drain them and stir them into the sautéing vegetables along with the lemon juice and crumbled feta cheese. Add plenty of black pepper. Cook until the feta begins to soften, remove the thyme sprigs, if used, and serve immediately.

PER 8-OZ SERVING: 117 CALORIES, 5.6 G PROTEIN, 2.8 G FAT, 19.5 G CARBOHYDRATE, 80 MG SODIUM, 6 MG CHOLESTEROL.

PASTAS

P ASTA IS PROBABLY THE FIRST DISH we think of as "quick and easy." It's a snap to prepare, and you need little more than a salad to round out a meal. But even if pasta required a longer, more arduous preparation, most of us in the Moosewood Collective would still make it our first choice at least once or twice a week. We can't get enough of it.

With scores of shapes and sizes from which to choose, and because it can be topped with almost anything, pasta is a perfect medium for improvisation. You could eat pasta every day of the year without repeating a dish. Some of the best toppings can be prepared in no more time than it takes to cook the pasta, so you can have a fresh, endlessly variable dinner in a flash.

Pasta is both economical and packed with nutritional value. It's a good source of complex carbohydrates, protein (it contains six of the eight essential amino acids), and minerals, but it's low in fat and calories. Dried pasta keeps almost indefinitely, so you can have a wide selection on hand for greater versatility. There's nothing better than pasta when it comes to feeding unexpected guests or putting on a last-minute dinner for the kids (who will almost always eat pasta eagerly). It can be a no-fuss meal for one, an elegant late-night supper after the theater, or an ordinary "Is there anything good to eat?" meal.

Although fresh pasta is currently in the limelight of popularity, we find that the so-called fresh pastas available in supermarkets are not really fresh enough to be worth their premium prices. Good fresh pasta should be locally, or at the very least recently, made. That said, we actually prefer the texture and taste of a good dried pasta made from durum semolina. Dried pasta has a nice bite that complements our favorite vegetable sauces.

In general, imported Italian dried pastas are superior to those made by the domestic manufacturers. Because of the rigid standards imposed by the Italian government (as well as the demands of an extremely discerning body of consumers), Italian pastas are made better and contain finer ingredients, resulting in a firmer, tastier, more nutritious product. We recommend that you spend a little more for Italian pastas and enjoy an effortless, built-in improvement to your meals. At Moosewood we use DeCecco brand, a fine pasta that is widely available in this country.

Combine pasta with leftovers for sometimes surprising, occasionally inspired, almost always pleasing results. Other possible pasta toppings found elsewhere in this book are:

Beans and Greens (see page 120)
The gorgonzola and hazelnut mix from Pears with Gorgonzola
 (see page 319)
Hazelnut – Red Peppers Sauce (see page 112)
Olivada (see page 49)
Peperonata (see page 83)
Pesto (see page 362)
Salsa Verde (see page 105)
White Bean and Tomato Salad (see page 137)

CAVATELLI WITH BROCCOLI RABE

1 pound fresh broccoli rabe
1 pound frozen cavatelli made with ricotta cheese *
3 tablespoons olive oil
5 garlic cloves, minced or pressed
juice of ½ lemon, or 2 teaspoons vinegar (optional)
salt and ground black pepper to taste
red pepper flakes (optional)

≈

grated Romano or Parmesan cheese (optional)

Found in the frozen pasta section of many supermarkets.

Bring a large covered pot of water to a rapid boil.

While the water heats, rinse the broccoli rabe and remove any tough or wilted outer leaves as well as the tough bottom part of the stems. Chop the remaining stems, florets, and leaves into 2-inch pieces, about the same size as the cavatelli. Place the chopped broccoli rabe in a steamer basket or colander that will fit into the pasta pot. When the water boils, submerge the colander in the water for about 3 minutes, until the broccoli rabe turns bright green. Remove the colander and set aside to drain.

Stir the cavatelli into the boiling water and re-cover the pot until the water comes back to a boil. Then uncover it. In a large nonreactive skillet, heat the oil and sauté the garlic for a minute, taking care not to let it brown. Stir in the drained broccoli rabe, the lemon juice or vinegar, and the salt and black pepper. Add the red pepper flakes, if you wish. Sauté until the greens are tender. Cover and set aside.

When the cavatelli are al dente, drain and toss them in a large warmed bowl with the sautéed greens. Sprinkle with cheese if you wish, and serve immediately.

PER 8-OZ SERVING: 333 CALORIES, 13 G PROTEIN, 14.2 G FAT, 40.1 G CARBOHYDRATE, 504 MG SODIUM, 0 MG CHOLESTEROL.

TOTAL TIME
25 minutes
SERVINGS
4
MENU
Cavatelli with Broccoli Rabe should be balanced by other strong flavors. We might place this dish in a menu that begins with Olivada Crostini (see page 262) and ends with Baked Peaches with Marsala (see page 306).

Broccoli rabe (also called rapini, broccoli rape, rappi, Italian broccoli, and Chinese broccoli) is somewhat bitter and is an acquired taste — but once the taste is acquired, it's addictive. Here it is paired with mild dumpling-like ricotta cavatelli to mitigate the bitterness. Both broccoli rabe and cavatelli come from a southern Italian tradition.

ORECCHIETTI WITH PEAS AND ONIONS

TOTAL TIME

25 minutes

SERVINGS

4 to 6

MENU

Serve with Fresh
Mozzarella and Tomato
Salad (see page 68),
Mushrooms in Lemon
Marinade (see page 81),
or a salad of slightly bitter
greens such as watercress,
endive, or arugula.

*The natural
sweetness of peas
and onions
contrasts nicely with the
sharpness of the
Pecorino cheese in this
dish. It can show off
freshly shelled peas in
the spring, but it is also
delicious with frozen
peas any time of year.
Orecchietti ("little
ears") is a good shape of
pasta to use because it
catches and holds the
peas.*

4 medium onions (about 4 cups sliced)
1 tablespoon olive oil
4 cups fresh or frozen tiny green peas (about 1 pound)
salt and freshly ground black pepper
1 pound orecchietti (little ear-shaped pasta) or other small
    shell pasta
freshly grated Pecorino cheese (about 1 cup) *

** We highly recommend Pecorino, a sheep's-milk cheese, because it is
sharper-tasting (so you get more flavor with less cheese) and about half
the price of a good Parmesan. However, Parmesan is an acceptable
substitute.*

Bring a large covered pot of water to a rapid boil. While the water
heats, cut the onions in half lengthwise and then cut crosswise into
thin slices. Cut the slices in half lengthwise. Heat the olive oil in a skillet or saucepan and add the onions. Cook on medium heat, stirring
occasionally, until the onions begin to brown. Add the peas and salt
and pepper to taste, and cook a few minutes longer. Add 2 tablespoons of the hot water to the skillet, stir, reduce the heat, and cover.

When the pot of water boils, add the pasta, stir, and cover until
the water boils again. Uncover the pot. As soon as the pasta is al
dente, drain it and toss it with some of the grated Pecorino, so that
the cheese will melt on the pasta. Top with the peas and onions, and
serve immediately. Serve extra grated cheese at the table.

PER 8-OZ SERVING: 329 CALORIES, 17.9 G PROTEIN, 10.2 G FAT, 41.6 G CARBOHYDRATE, 525 MG
SODIUM, 57 MG CHOLESTEROL.

PASTA VALENZANA

Excellent — ~~make more linguini~~

1 red or green bell pepper, cut into long thin strips
2 large garlic cloves, minced or pressed
pinch of crushed red pepper flakes or cayenne
2 tablespoons olive oil
½ cup dry sherry
⅔ cup chopped scallions
1 large ripe tomato, diced, or 1 cup drained chopped
    canned tomatoes
½ pound linguini
⅛ teaspoon crumbled saffron threads
¼ cup boiling water
⅔ cup frozen green peas
½ pound shelled shrimp, rinsed
salt to taste

≈

grated Parmesan cheese (optional)

TOTAL TIME

30 minutes

SERVINGS

2

MENU

Begin a relaxed meal with crudités and Black Bean Dip (see page 46) or a selection of olives to nibble while the pasta cooks. Follow Pasta Valenzana with refreshing Fennel and Orange Salad (see page 67), and end the meal with Goat Cheese with Honey and Walnuts (see page 313).

Bring a large covered pot of water to a rapid boil. While the water heats, in a large nonreactive skillet sauté the bell peppers, garlic, and crushed red pepper flakes or cayenne in the oil for about 5 minutes. Add the sherry. Stir the scallions and tomatoes into the peppers. When the water boils, cook the linguini for about 10 minutes, until al dente.

While the pasta cooks, stir the saffron into the ¼ cup of boiling water and add it to the skillet. Reduce the sauce on high heat for a minute, stir in the peas and lower to a simmer. Add the shrimp and cook until they are pink and just tender, about 4 minutes. Taste the sauce and add salt if needed. If the shrimp are done before the pasta, remove the skillet from the heat. Drain the cooked pasta and serve it immediately in warmed pasta bowls, with the sauce ladled over it. Top with grated Parmesan, if desired.

PER 8-OZ SERVING: 243 CALORIES, 11.8 G PROTEIN, 6.7 G FAT, 30.9 G CARBOHYDRATE, 185 MG SODIUM, 85 MG CHOLESTEROL.

Sherry and saffron each adds its distinctive bouquet to this dish, named for the Spanish port city of Valencia, the center of a saffron-growing region.

Excellent
I used more
garlic – probably 3-4 cloves

PASTA FRESCA

Serve this pasta dish outdoors if possible, with Bruschetta (see page 262) and Beans and Greens (see page 120), or with steamed or marinated green beans or Broiled Eggplant (see page 74).

This dish couldn't be easier. It is strictly for summertime, however, when the tomatoes are vine-ripened and the basil is fresh. Pasta Fresca so perfectly captures the fresh tastes of the season that we crave it again and again in hot weather, and we dream about it all winter.

4 cups chopped ripe tomatoes
6 – 8 large fresh basil leaves
1 large garlic clove, minced or pressed
1 tablespoon extra-virgin olive oil
salt and freshly ground pepper to taste

≈

1 pound butterfly (bow-tie) or fusilli pasta

≈

½ pound fresh mozzarella cheese, cut into ½-inch cubes
grated Parmesan or Pecorino cheese (optional)

Bring a large covered pot of water to a rapid boil.

Set aside 1 cup of the chopped tomatoes and 2 of the basil leaves. In a blender or food processor, purée the remaining tomatoes and basil with the garlic and olive oil until smooth. Add salt and pepper to taste.

When the water comes to a rolling boil, stir in the pasta, re-cover the pot, and return to a boil. Uncover and cook the pasta until al dente, about 8 to 10 minutes. Cut the reserved basil leaves into thin strips.

Drain the cooked pasta and toss it immediately with the mozzarella cubes. Add the sauce and mix well. Top with the reserved tomatoes and basil, and grated cheese if desired. Serve immediately.

PER 8-OZ SERVING: 273 CALORIES, 11.7 G PROTEIN, 9.2 G FAT, 36.2 G CARBOHYDRATE, 173 MG SODIUM, 63 MG CHOLESTEROL.

PASTA WITH BEANS AND ENDIVE

1 pound short, chunky pasta, such as orecchietti, fusilli,
    or penne

3 tablespoons minced garlic (5 or 6 large cloves)
3 onions, diced (about 3 cups)
3 tablespoons olive oil
1 pound curly endive (about 10 cups shredded) *
dash of salt and ground black pepper
3 cups undrained canned Italian plum tomatoes
    (28-ounce can)
3 – 4 cups drained cooked white beans, such as cannellini
    (two 16-ounce cans)
juice of 1 lemon

grated Pecorino or Parmesan cheese (optional)

Chard, escarole, or spinach may be substituted for the curly endive.

Bring a large covered pot of water to a rapid boil.

While the pasta water heats, in a large saucepan sauté the garlic and onions in the olive oil until translucent. Wash and coarsely shred the endive. Stir the endive, salt, and pepper into the onions and cook for several minutes, covered, until the endive is bright green and reduced by at least half.

When the pasta water boils, stir in the pasta, cover, and return to a boil. Then uncover the pot and cook the pasta until al dente. While the pasta cooks, add the juice from the tomatoes to the endive, and then either coarsely chop the tomatoes with a knife right in the can or crush them with your hand. Stir the tomatoes and the beans into the endive, and bring the sauce to a simmer. Add the lemon juice to the sauce just before you drain the pasta.

Serve the sauce immediately, ladled onto bowls of hot pasta. Top with grated cheese, if desired.

PER 8-OZ SERVING: 220 CALORIES, 8.3 G PROTEIN, 3.7 G FAT, 39 G CARBOHYDRATE, 107 MG SODIUM, 0 MG CHOLESTEROL.

MENU

Serve after Bruschetta (see page 262) and a platter of roasted peppers, sliced fresh mozzarella cheese, and ripe olives, all drizzled with extra-virgin olive oil. Finish this effortless meal with chewy sweet dried figs, small chunks of a good chocolate, and a few sips of your favorite dessert wine.

There are hundreds of variations of pasta e fagioli *all over Italy and in Italian-American communities. Our version of this hearty comfort food is rather simple and features the tonic sharpness of bitter greens and lemon.*

Excellent

PASTA TUTTO GIARDINO

TOTAL TIME
35 minutes

SERVINGS
4 to 6

MENU

Use this sauce on broad noodles like fettuccine or tagliatelle, or on shells, ziti, or orecchietti. You might choose a spinach pasta for additional flavor and color. The rest of the meal should be simple and light — perhaps a crisp green salad or chilled Easiest Artichokes (see page 77), with fresh fruit for dessert. This sauce also makes a luscious topping for simple broiled or baked fish.

Tutto giardino means "the whole garden" in Italian. This creamy sauce studded with a variety of colorful vegetables is our tribute to the bounty of the vegetable garden.

1½ cups chopped onions
2 garlic cloves, minced or pressed
1 medium carrot, diced
2 tablespoons olive oil
1 red or green bell pepper, diced
3 cups sliced mushrooms
1 medium zucchini or yellow squash, diced
1 tablespoon chopped fresh basil (1 teaspoon dried)
1 tablespoon chopped fresh marjoram (1 teaspoon dried)
pinch of oregano
salt and ground black pepper to taste
⅔ cup dry white wine

ROUX
3 tablespoons butter
¼ cup unbleached white flour
1½ cups milk (whole or 2%)

≈

1 pound broad pasta noodles, such as fettuccine or
      tagliatelle, or shells, ziti, or orecchietti

≈

1 cup diced tomatoes
½ cup fresh or frozen green peas
2 teaspoons fresh lemon juice (optional)

≈

grated Parmesan cheese

In a nonreactive saucepan, sauté the onions, garlic, and carrots in the olive oil. Stir occasionally. When the onions are translucent, add the bell peppers, mushrooms, zucchini or yellow squash, basil, marjoram, oregano, and salt and pepper, and cook for a minute or two. Stir in the wine, cover, and simmer for 8 to 10 minutes, until the vegetables are just tender.

While the vegetables are cooking, bring a large covered pot of water to a rapid boil.

To make the roux, melt the butter in a small heavy saucepan or skillet. Whisk in the flour and cook for 1 to 2 minutes. Slowly add the milk, whisking constantly until the sauce thickens. Cover and set the roux aside.

When the pasta water boils, stir in the pasta, and cover until the water returns to a boil. Uncover the pot and cook until al dente, about 8 to 10 minutes.

While the pasta cooks, stir the tomatoes and peas into the simmering vegetables, cook for about 2 minutes, and then stir in the roux. Adjust the seasonings. For a little more tang, add the lemon juice.

Drain the cooked pasta and place it in a warmed serving bowl. Ladle the sauce on the pasta and serve with grated Parmesan cheese.

PER 8-OZ SERVING: 208 CALORIES, 6.3 G PROTEIN, 5.4 G FAT, 32.5 G CARBOHYDRATE, 85 MG SODIUM, 8 MG CHOLESTEROL.

PASTA WITH GREENS AND RICOTTA

TOTAL TIME

20 minutes

SERVINGS

4 to 6

MENU

Begin a meal of Pasta
with Greens and Ricotta
with Antipasto Salad
(see page 118) or Greek
Diced Vegetable Salad
(see page 127). End with
Fresh Orange Compote
(see page 309) served with
biscotti and espresso.

Pansoti is a classic
greens-filled
pasta from
Genoa, which is served
with a mild ricotta and
walnut sauce. It is
exquisite, but you could
spend half a day
preparing it. Here we
combine those same
flavors in a sauce that
can be prepared while
plain pasta cooks.
Watercress and chard
are our current
favorites, but almost
any green will do.

1 bunch watercress (about 1 cup chopped), tough stems
    removed
1 bunch Swiss chard, tough stalks removed (about 4 cups
    chopped)
2 garlic cloves, minced or pressed
1 tablespoon olive oil
dash of salt and ground black pepper
¼ teaspoon nutmeg
¾ cup ricotta cheese
≈
1 pound pasta (fettuccine, penne, macaroni, fusilli,
    butterflies, or shells)
≈
grated Parmesan cheese or crumbled ricotta salata
chopped fresh tomatoes
toasted walnuts or pine nuts (see page 354)

Bring a large covered pot of water to a rapid boil.

While the water heats, rinse the watercress and chard well, shake
off any excess water, and chop coarsely. Sauté the garlic in the oil for a
minute, until soft and golden, taking care not to scorch it. Add the
damp greens and sauté, stirring often, until they are wilted but still
bright green. Sprinkle with the salt, pepper, and nutmeg, and remove
from the heat. In a blender, purée the cooked greens with the ricotta
until smooth and evenly colored. Add more salt and pepper to taste.

When the water boils, stir in the pasta, cover, and return to a boil.
Then uncover the pot and cook the pasta until al dente. Drain the
pasta and immediately toss it with the sauce in a warmed serving
bowl. Top with Parmesan or crumbled ricotta salata, tomatoes,
and/or toasted walnuts or pine nuts.

PER 8-OZ SERVING: 313 CALORIES, 12.2 G PROTEIN, 7.5 G FAT, 49.3 G CARBOHYDRATE, 200 MG SODIUM,
12 MG CHOLESTEROL.

PASTA WITH SPICY CAULIFLOWER

1 large onion, finely chopped (about 2 cups)
2 tablespoons olive oil
¼ cup red wine
2 cups undrained canned Italian plum tomatoes
    (16-ounce can)
¼ – ½ teaspoon crushed red pepper flakes
1½ teaspoons chopped fresh oregano (½ teaspoon dried)
1 cup black olives, pitted

½ cup bread crumbs
1 tablespoon olive oil

1 small head cauliflower
1 pound short, chunky pasta (shells, ziti, or fusilli)
chopped fresh parsley (optional)

Bring a large covered pot of water to a rapid boil.

While the water heats, sauté the onions in the oil until translucent. Add the wine and the juice from the tomatoes. Squeeze the tomatoes with your hand to crush them, and add them to the saucepan. Stir in the red pepper flakes and oregano. Slice each olive in half lengthwise, and add it to the sauce. Simmer gently, covered.

In a small heavy skillet, sauté the bread crumbs in the 1 tablespoon of olive oil, stirring constantly until crisp. Set aside.

Chop the cauliflower florets into bite-sized pieces. When the pot of water comes to a boil, ease in the cauliflower and cook for 5 minutes. Remove the cauliflower from the water with a slotted spoon or sieve, and add it to the simmering sauce. Stir well.

Cook the pasta in the same boiling water until al dente. Drain and divide it among warmed individual dishes. Top with the sauce. Sprinkle each serving with toasted bread crumbs, and parsley if desired, and serve immediately.

PER 8-OZ SERVING: 282 CALORIES, 7.7 G PROTEIN, 8.4 G FAT, 43.7 G CARBOHYDRATE, 410 MG SODIUM, 0 MG CHOLESTEROL.

TOTAL TIME
30 minutes

SERVINGS
4 to 6

MENU
A simple salad of mild fresh mozzarella sliced onto a platter of shredded arugula makes a good starter course for this pasta. Lemon Date Bars (see page 315) would be a pleasing dessert, served with hot mint tea.

A light pasta dish with a piquant, full-bodied flavor. For a Sicilian flavor, add some currants, pinenuts, and capers.

Toss any leftover pasta and sauce with a little Provolone, Pecorino, or ricotta salata cheese, and bake it in an oiled dish for about 20 to 25 minutes for an interesting twist on macaroni and cheese.

PENNE WITH SUN-DRIED TOMATOES AND CAPERS

TOTAL TIME
25 minutes

SERVINGS
4 to 6

MENU

A crisp green salad and a glass of red wine complement this pasta well. Coffee Ricotta Mousse (see page 307) is a good choice for a dessert.

This is a tangy pasta with complex flavors that can be served hot, at room temperature, or chilled.

15 sun-dried tomatoes (not packed in oil), minced
½ cup very hot water

≈

3 tablespoons olive oil
2 medium onions, thinly sliced (about 2 cups)
4 medium tomatoes
6 garlic cloves, minced or pressed
3 tablespoons capers, rinsed and drained
1½ teaspoons minced fresh thyme (¾ teaspoon dried) *
1 tablespoon minced fresh tarragon (1½ teaspoons dried) *
1 cup fresh or frozen green peas (optional)
salt and ground black pepper

≈

1 pound penne

≈

½ cup chopped fresh parsley
grated Parmesan cheese

If you prefer, substitute ½ cup chopped fresh basil for the thyme and tarragon.

Bring a large covered pot of water to a rapid boil. Place the minced sun-dried tomatoes in a small bowl and cover them with the ½ cup of very hot water. Set aside.

In a nonreactive skillet or heavy saucepan, heat the oil and sauté the onions on medium heat, covered, for 3 minutes. Chop the fresh tomatoes and set them aside. Drain the sun-dried tomatoes, reserving their liquid, and add them to the onions. Stir in the garlic, capers, thyme, and tarragon. Add the chopped fresh tomatoes, optional peas, and the reserved sun-dried tomato soaking liquid. Sauté, covered, until the tomatoes soften and lose their shape. Add salt and pepper to taste.

As soon as the pasta water boils, stir in the penne, cover, and return to a boil. Then uncover, and cook the pasta until al dente. Drain well.

In a large warmed serving bowl, toss the hot pasta with the sauce, and stir in the chopped parsley. Top with Parmesan and serve immediately.

PER 8-OZ SERVING: 279 CALORIES, 9.5 G PROTEIN, 5.9 G FAT, 48.9 G CARBOHYDRATE, 198 MG SODIUM, 1 MG CHOLESTEROL.

PASTA WITH PORCINI MUSHROOM SAUCE

Serve with crusty French bread and Caesar Salad (see page 122), Easiest Artichokes (see page 77), or steamed green beans. Pears with Gorgonzola (see page 319) is an ideal dessert.

This is an earthy, rich-tasting pasta for a hearty fall or winter meal.

The mushroom sauce is also good over Polenta (see page 150), mashed potatoes, or Bulghur Burgers (see page 144).

3 tablespoons crumbled dried porcini mushrooms
1½ cups boiling water

≈

1 cup chopped onions
2 tablespoons olive oil
2 cups sliced fresh mushrooms
1 tablespoon chopped fresh marjoram (1 teaspoon dried)
4 teaspoons thinly sliced fresh sage (2 teaspoons dried)
dash of salt

≈

½ pound linguini or spaghetti

≈

1 tablespoon unbleached white flour
⅔ cup dry red wine
1 tablespoon soy sauce

≈

grated Parmesan or Romano cheese
ground black pepper to taste

In a small heatproof bowl, cover the porcini mushrooms with the boiling water and set aside.

Bring a large covered pot of water to a rapid boil. While the water heats, sauté the onions in the olive oil in a heavy nonreactive skillet or saucepan for 10 minutes or until translucent. Add the fresh mushrooms and the marjoram, sage, and a dash of salt. Continue to sauté, stirring often.

When the water boils, stir in the pasta, cover, and return to a boil. Then uncover the pot, and cook until the pasta is al dente.

Meanwhile, drain the porcini mushrooms, reserving the liquid. Thoroughly rinse the porcini to remove any grit. Strain the reserved liquid through a paper coffee filter or cheesecloth. When the sautéing mushrooms begin to soften, add the porcini. Stir in the flour and then the strained porcini liquid, the wine, and the soy sauce. Simmer on medium-high heat, stirring, until the sauce thickens.

Serve the drained pasta in warmed bowls, topped with the sauce, Parmesan or Romano cheese, and black pepper.

PER 8-OZ SERVING: 285 CALORIES, 7.8 G PROTEIN, 6.9 G FAT, 43.5 G CARBOHYDRATE, 229 MG SODIUM, 0 MG CHOLESTEROL.

SPAGHETTI WITH PECORINO AND BLACK PEPPER

TOTAL TIME

20 minutes

SERVINGS

2

MENU

Serve with sliced tomatoes and a few olives, a steamed green vegetable, or a crisp green salad. Stir a beaten raw egg into any leftovers and fry them into a pasta frittata.

T*his Roman specialty is the easiest-to-prepare pasta we know, and yet we never tire of it. It's perfect for feeding an unexpected crowd, the kids love it, and it's a delicious no-fuss dish for one.*

½ pound spaghetti
¼ pound Pecorino cheese (about ¾ cup grated)
2 teaspoons extra-virgin olive oil (optional)
freshly ground black pepper to taste

Bring a large covered pot of water to a rapid boil. Add the spaghetti, stir, and cover the pot until the water returns to a boil. Uncover the pot. While the pasta cooks, grate the Pecorino. When the pasta is just al dente, drain it, and immediately transfer it to a warmed serving bowl. Sprinkle the pasta with the optional olive oil and the Pecorino. Toss well, add plenty of black pepper, toss again, and serve immediately.

PER 8-OZ SERVING: 501 CALORIES, 25.9 G PROTEIN, 15.9 G FAT, 62 G CARBOHYDRATE, 706 MG SODIUM, 30 MG CHOLESTEROL.

Spaghetti with Zucchini and Lemon

1 pound spaghetti or linguini

≈

1 tablespoon olive oil
4 garlic cloves, minced or pressed
6 – 8 small, tender young zucchini, sliced (4 cups)
dash of salt and ground black pepper
juice of 1 lemon
6 large fresh basil leaves, cut into thin strips
1 – 2 cups grated Pecorino cheese (3 – 6 ounces)

Bring a large covered pot of water to a rapid boil. Add the pasta, stir briefly, and cover the pot until the water boils again. Uncover the pot.

While the pasta cooks, heat the olive oil in a large heavy nonreactive skillet. Add the garlic and zucchini, and sauté on medium-high heat until the zucchini begins to brown. Sprinkle with salt and pepper. Add the lemon juice and basil, stir, and remove from the heat. The zucchini should be done just before the pasta is ready. When the pasta is al dente, drain it and then toss the hot pasta in a large warmed serving bowl with about a cup of the cheese. Top with the zucchini and serve immediately. Offer more cheese at the table, if desired.

PER 8-OZ SERVING: 294 CALORIES, 13.3 G PROTEIN, 6.9 G FAT, 44.4 G CARBOHYDRATE, 291 MG SODIUM, 11 MG CHOLESTEROL.

TOTAL TIME
25 minutes

SERVINGS
4 to 6

MENU
We suggest this spaghetti be served after Bruschetta (see page 262) and Gigondes (see page 69), with a salad of fresh tomatoes, followed by Peach Parfait with Amaretto Cream (see page 318) for a taste of *la dolce vita*.

Although adding lemon juice to certain pasta dishes is common practice in Italian cuisine, it's still something of a novelty in this country. Here it tastes just right. For best results, use small, firm zucchini without seeds and a good Italian brand of spaghetti, such as DeCecco.

STEWS

OVER THE PAST TWENTY YEARS at Moosewood Restaurant, we have satisfied the appetites of our customers by featuring one appealing vegetable stew or another at nearly every meal. Particularly well suited to vegetarian cuisine, stews highlight the endless variety of fresh vegetables and are enhanced by a delightful range of herbs, spices, legumes, grains, and garnishes.

Stews are not restricted to any season; there are hearty warming choices like Winter Vegetable Stew or African Pineapple Peanut Stew and fresh summery ones like Caribbean Vegetable Stew. All of these colorful stews can be made ahead and are impressive company fare.

Making stews at home need not be a lengthy or laborious process. Simply chop and sauté the vegetables, stir in the seasonings, then add liquid and simmer the stew for about half an hour, while you relax and await your delicious one-dish meal. Or if you feel more ambitious, you could use this time to prepare an accompanying grain, bake a quick bread, toss together a salad, or make one of our nearly instant desserts.

Here's a special tip for using leftover stew: simply thin the leftovers with juice, stock, or water to make a delicious soup. Now you have the effortless beginning of another meal!

AFRICAN PINEAPPLE PEANUT STEW

TOTAL TIME

35 minutes

SERVINGS

4

MENU

Serve on rice, millet, or couscous, topped with crushed peanuts and chopped scallions. Complete this meal with Creamy Banana Ice (see page 308) or Banana Shakes (see page 311).

West African–inspired, this is a rich and very fresh-tasting stew, eclectic and surprising in its combination of ingredients. If you have a few extra leaves of kale, put them in; this stew can absorb lots of greens. Any leftovers will make a good soup when thinned with tomato juice or water.

1 cup chopped onions
2 garlic cloves, minced or pressed
1 tablespoon vegetable oil
1 bunch kale or Swiss chard (4 cups sliced)
2 cups undrained canned crushed pineapple
        (20-ounce can)
½ cup peanut butter
1 tablespoon Tabasco or other hot pepper sauce
½ cup chopped fresh cilantro
salt to taste

≈

crushed skinless peanuts *
chopped scallions

To crush peanuts, whirl whole peanuts in a food processor or blender until chopped into pieces and "crumbles," or use a rolling pin to crush the peanuts in a folded piece of waxed paper.

In a covered saucepan, sauté the onions and garlic in the oil for about 10 minutes, stirring frequently, until the onions are lightly browned. While the onions sauté, wash the kale or Swiss chard. Remove and discard the large stems and any blemished leaves. Stack the leaves on a cutting surface and slice crosswise into 1-inch-thick slices.

Add the pineapple and its juice to the onions and bring to a simmer. Stir in the kale or chard, cover, and simmer for about 5 minutes, stirring a couple of times, until just tender. Mix in the peanut butter, Tabasco, and cilantro and simmer for 5 minutes. Add salt to taste, and serve.

PER 8-OZ SERVING: 225 CALORIES, 7.4 G PROTEIN, 12 G FAT, 25.7 G CARBOHYDRATE, 169 MG SODIUM, 0 MG CHOLESTEROL.

CARIBBEAN VEGETABLE STEW

2 cups chopped onions
2 tablespoons vegetable oil
3 cups chopped cabbage
1 fresh chile, minced (seeded for a milder "hot"), or
    ¼ teaspoon cayenne

≈

1 tablespoon grated fresh ginger root
2 cups water
3 cups diced sweet potatoes, cut into ½- to ¾-inch cubes
salt to taste
2 cups undrained chopped fresh or canned tomatoes
2 cups fresh or frozen sliced okra
3 tablespoons fresh lime juice
2 tablespoons chopped fresh cilantro

≈

chopped peanuts
sprigs of cilantro (optional)

In a nonreactive soup pot, sauté the onions in the oil on medium heat for 4 or 5 minutes. Add the cabbage and the chile or cayenne and continue to sauté, stirring often, until the onions are translucent, about 8 minutes.

Add the grated ginger and the water, cover the pot, and bring to a boil. Stir in the sweet potatoes, sprinkle with salt, and simmer for 5 or 6 minutes, until the potatoes are barely tender. Add the tomatoes, okra, and lime juice. Simmer until all of the vegetables are tender, about 15 minutes. Stir in the cilantro and add more salt to taste.

Sprinkle the stew with chopped peanuts. Top with a few sprigs of cilantro, if you like.

PER 8-OZ SERVING: 117 CALORIES, 2.5 G PROTEIN, 3.3 G FAT, 21.2 G CARBOHYDRATE, 33 MG SODIUM, 0 MG CHOLESTEROL.

TOTAL TIME
35 minutes

SERVINGS
4

MENU
Finish the meal with a Tropical Fruit Salad (see page 324). If you have the time, sautéed tempeh cubes make an excellent garnish. For a richer flavor, add ½ cup of coconut milk (see page 360).

Lime, ginger, and cilantro lend vibrancy to this unusual stew. Serve the stew on rice or with a fresh crusty bread.

CAULIFLOWER PAPRIKASH

PAPRIKASH ONLY
25 minutes

WITH SPÄTZLE
40 minutes

SERVINGS
4

MENU
This dish needs only a simple green salad to make a satisfying meal.

This paprikash is fine served on egg noodles, but with a little extra effort you can also prepare spätzle, a traditional dumpling. Our instructions for spätzle tell you how to prepare it while making the paprikash, so they'll be done about the same time.

1 medium onion, finely chopped (about 1 cup)
1 red or green bell pepper, finely chopped (about 1 cup)
3 tablespoons vegetable oil
2 tablespoons sweet paprika
½ cup dry sherry
½ cup water
10 ounces mushrooms, sliced (about 5 cups)
pinch of salt
1 large head cauliflower
1 cup sour cream
salt and ground black pepper to taste

In a large saucepan or soup pot, sauté the onions and peppers in the oil for 2 or 3 minutes. Stir in the paprika, sherry, and water and cook on high heat for a minute. Add the mushrooms and a pinch of salt to draw out the juices. Lower the heat to medium, cover, and cook for about 5 minutes, while you cut the cauliflower into florets. Mix in the florets and simmer until the cauliflower is tender but still firm, about 5 to 7 minutes. Remove the pan from the heat and stir in the sour cream. Add salt and pepper to taste. Cover the paprikash and keep it warm until ready to serve, but prevent it from simmering or it may curdle.

SPÄTZLE

1½ cups unbleached white flour
½ teaspoon salt
pinch of freshly grated nutmeg
pinch of ground black pepper
2 large eggs, beaten
½ cup milk

≈

4 quarts salted water

≈

2 tablespoons butter

Before you begin the paprikash, prepare the spätzle batter: Combine the flour, salt, nutmeg, pepper, eggs, and milk in a bowl, and stir well. When you begin to sauté the onions and bell peppers for the paprikash, bring the water to a boil in a large covered pot. After you add the cauliflower to the paprikash, place the thick spätzle batter in a colander with large holes. Set the colander on the rim of the pot of boiling water, and using the back of a sturdy wooden spoon, push the batter through the holes into the boiling water. Lower the heat to a simmer and cook the spätzle for about 5 minutes, until firm but light. Remove the spätzle with a mesh strainer or a large slotted spoon, and place in a warmed serving dish. Add the butter. Serve immediately.

PER 8-OZ SERVING PAPRIKASH WITH SPÄTZLE: 156 CALORIES, 3.1 G PROTEIN, 11 G FAT, 10.7 G CARBOHYDRATE, 108 MG SODIUM, 12 MG CHOLESTEROL.

SPÄTZLE PER SERVING: 58 CALORIES, 1.9 G PROTEIN, 2.2 G FAT, 7.6 G CARBOHYDRATE, 8.6 MG SODIUM, 28 MG CHOLESTEROL.

To prepare these little dumplings, you will need a colander with large holes.

Chick Pea and Artichoke Heart Stew

TOTAL TIME
25 minutes

SERVINGS
4 to 6

MENU
We suggest Crostini
with Olivada
(see pages 262, 49),
Fennel and Orange Salad
(see page 67), and big
bunches of black grapes to
complete the meal.

*T*his golden-
colored Spanish
peasant stew is
permeated with the
wonderful pungency of
rosemary and sage. It is
satisfying, not too heavy,
and good any time of
year.

4 cups water or vegetable stock
2 medium onions, chopped (about 1½ cups)
2 garlic cloves, minced or pressed
2 tablespoons olive oil
1 teaspoon turmeric
1 teaspoon sweet paprika
4 medium red or white potatoes, cut into ½-inch cubes
(about 4 cups)
1 sprig fresh rosemary (1 teaspoon ground dried)
5 leaves fresh sage, minced (½ teaspoon dried)
½ cup puréed winter squash or sweet potatoes *
3 cups drained cooked chick peas (two 15-ounce cans)
1½ cups drained quartered artichoke hearts (14-ounce can)
salt and ground black pepper to taste

≈

lemon wedges (optional)
grated Pecorino or Parmesan cheese (optional)

** We have found that a 4.5-ounce jar of puréed squash baby food works
very well in this recipe and is just the right size.*

In a saucepan, bring the water or vegetable stock to a simmer.
While the water heats, sauté the onions and garlic in the oil for about
8 minutes, until soft. Stir the turmeric and paprika into the onions
and sauté for a minute. Add the potatoes, rosemary, sage, and the
simmering water or stock. Cook for about 12 minutes, until the pota-

toes are tender. Stir in the puréed squash or sweet potatoes, and add the drained chick peas and artichoke hearts. Remove the rosemary sprig, add salt and pepper to taste, and return to a simmer.

Serve with lemon wedges and top with grated Pecorino or Parmesan cheese, if you wish.

PER 8-OZ SERVING: 157 CALORIES, 4.6 G PROTEIN, 3 G FAT, 29.2 G CARBOHYDRATE, 171 MG SODIUM, 0 MG CHOLESTEROL.

CURRIED VEGETABLES WITH DAHL

TOTAL TIME

40 minutes

SERVINGS

4 to 6

MENU

Serve with Coconut Basmati Rice (see page 155) or another simple grain.

*D*ahl *is the Indian word for any dried legume—lentils, beans, or peas. Yellow split peas or red lentils provide a rich golden base for this appealing mild curry.*

TIME-SAVING TIP: To further reduce cooking time (to 15 to 20 minutes), soak rinsed split peas in an equal volume of water for a few hours before beginning.

1½ cups red lentils or yellow split peas
4 or 5 cups hot water

≈

1 onion, chopped (about 1 cup)
1 fresh green chile, minced
3 tablespoons vegetable oil or ghee (clarified butter)
2 sweet potatoes, peeled and diced (about 4 cups)
1 tablespoon mild curry powder
1 teaspoon ground cumin
2 tablespoons grated fresh ginger root
2 cups water
½ head cauliflower (about 4 cups florets)
2 green or red bell peppers, chopped (about 2 cups)
10 ounces fresh spinach
2–3 tablespoons fresh lemon juice
salt to taste

Rinse the lentils or split peas. Lentils cook faster and absorb less water than split peas, so use 4 cups of water for lentils, 5 cups of water for split peas. In a covered saucepan, bring the water and lentils or peas to a boil. Reduce the heat, uncover, and simmer for about 30 minutes, until tender.

In a large soup pot, sauté the onion and chile in the oil for several minutes. Add the sweet potatoes, curry powder, cumin, and ginger and continue to sauté for 2 to 3 minutes, stirring often. Pour in the

2 cups of water. Cut the cauliflower into florets and add to the pot. Add the bell peppers, cover, and simmer for 10 minutes.

While the vegetables simmer, rinse, stem, and coarsely chop the spinach. Pour the lentils or peas and their cooking liquid into a blender or food processor, and purée for 2 to 3 minutes to make a smooth dahl. When the cauliflower is tender, stir in the spinach, the dahl, and the lemon juice. Simmer just until the spinach has wilted. Add salt to taste, and serve immediately.

PER 8-OZ SERVING: 162 CALORIES, 8.1 G PROTEIN, 4.2 G FAT, 25.2 G CARBOHYDRATE, 401 MG SODIUM, 0 MG CHOLESTEROL.

EGGPLANT MYKONOS

TOTAL TIME

35 minutes

SERVINGS

4

MENU

This tangy stew is delicious over rice or couscous, or served with bread to dip in the savory juices.

Eggplant has a way of making a dish rich and satisfying. Here it combines naturally with olive oil, dill, fennel, and tomato. If you expect to have leftover stew, set some aside before adding the spinach, because the spinach will lose its fresh color. Rewarm the leftover stew, and stir in the spinach just before serving.

2 medium onions, chopped (about 2 cups)
2 garlic cloves, minced or pressed
2 tablespoons olive oil
1 medium-large eggplant (6 cups cubed)
1 large red or green bell pepper
3 cups undrained canned tomatoes (28-ounce can)
½ cup unsweetened apple juice or water
½ teaspoon salt
1 teaspoon ground fennel
2 tablespoons chopped fresh dill (2 teaspoons dried)
2 tablespoons fresh lemon juice
3 cups chopped rinsed fresh spinach, packed (about ½ pound)
salt and ground black pepper to taste

≈

1 cup grated feta cheese (optional)

In a nonreactive stewpot, sauté the onions and garlic in the olive oil until translucent. Cut the eggplant into 1-inch cubes and add them to the pot. Slice the pepper into 1-inch-square pieces. Crush the tomatoes. Add the peppers, tomatoes, apple juice or water, salt, and fennel to the pot. If using dried dill, add it now. Cover the pot and simmer, stirring frequently, until the eggplant is completely tender, about 15 minutes. Stir in the fresh dill, if used, and add the lemon juice and spinach. Simmer for another minute or two until the spinach wilts but is still bright green. Add salt and pepper to taste.

Serve topped with grated feta cheese, if desired.

PER 8-OZ SERVING: 107 CALORIES, 2.3 G PROTEIN, 3.7 G FAT, 18.2 G CARBOHYDRATE, 258 MG SODIUM, 0 MG CHOLESTEROL.

GREEN BEANS AND FENNEL RAGOUT

3 garlic cloves, minced or pressed
1½ cups chopped onions
3 tablespoons olive oil
3 large potatoes, cut into ½-inch cubes (about 3½ cups)
3 cups undrained chopped fresh or canned tomatoes
    (28-ounce can)
1 teaspoon dried thyme
1 cup water
1 pound green beans
2 cups sliced fresh fennel bulb (¼-inch-thick slices)
2 pinches of saffron threads
1½ teaspoons freshly grated orange peel
juice of ½ lemon
salt and ground black pepper to taste

In a soup pot, sauté the garlic and onions in the olive oil, stirring occasionally, until the onions are translucent. Add the potatoes and tomatoes. Stir in the thyme and water. Cover and bring to a boil, then reduce the heat to a simmer. Stem the green beans and cut them into 1-inch pieces. Add the beans and sliced fennel bulb to the pot. Stir in the saffron, orange peel, and lemon juice. Simmer, covered, for 15 to 20 minutes, stirring occasionally, until the potatoes and green beans are tender. Add salt and pepper to taste.

PER 8-OZ SERVING: 138 CALORIES, 3 G PROTEIN, 5.2 G FAT, 22.6 G CARBOHYDRATE, 37 MG SODIUM, 0 MG CHOLESTEROL.

PREPARATION TIME
20 minutes

TOTAL TIME
40 minutes

SERVINGS
4 to 6

MENU
Serve with crusty bread and chèvre or brie.

I nspired by the cooking of southern France, this stew is enlivened by fragrant seasonings. Since the flavors meld nicely over time, it makes an appealing leftover.

MENESTRA

Accompany this with garlic bread or another crusty loaf.

A Spanish vegetable stew, delicately seasoned with sherry and paprika. We recommend using sweet Hungarian paprika for the best flavor. Seasonal vegetables, such as asparagus, fresh tomatoes, or green beans can be added or substituted for some of those suggested here. If you intend to use hard-boiled eggs as a garnish, put them on the stove to cook when you begin the recipe.

1 – 2 onions (1½ – 2 cups sliced)
3 garlic cloves
3 tablespoons olive oil
2 medium carrots (about 1½ cups sliced)
1 large potato (about 2 cups diced)
1 tablespoon sweet paprika
2 bay leaves
pinch of cayenne
2 cups hot water *
½ cup dry sherry
½ teaspoon salt
½ pound mushrooms
1 red bell pepper
5 artichoke hearts (14-ounce can)
1 cup fresh or frozen green peas
salt to taste

≈

chopped Spanish olives
4 hard-boiled eggs, cut into quarters (optional)

* Or use the liquid from the canned artichoke hearts plus enough water to make a total of 2 cups.

Halve and thinly slice the onion, then cut the slices in half. Mince or press the garlic. In a pot, sauté the onions and garlic in the oil on medium heat until tender. Peel the carrots, cut them in half lengthwise, and then slice them crosswise into half circles, and add them to the pot. Peel the potato if you like, and cut it into ½-inch cubes. Add the potato, paprika, bay leaves, and cayenne and sauté for a minute or so, stirring to prevent sticking. Pour in the water, sherry, and salt. Cover the pot and bring to a boil. Reduce the heat to a simmer.

Wash the mushrooms and cut off and discard the stems. Leave any small mushrooms whole, but cut the larger ones into halves or quarters. Chop the pepper into 1-inch pieces. Add the mushrooms and peppers to the pot. Cut the artichoke hearts into halves. When the vegetables are just tender, stir in the artichokes and peas. Simmer for 3 to 4 minutes. Add salt to taste.

Serve topped with chopped olives, and wedges of hard-boiled egg if you like.

PER 8-OZ SERVING: 145 CALORIES, 4.3 G PROTEIN, 5.8 G FAT, 19.2 G CARBOHYDRATE, 238 MG SODIUM, 0 MG CHOLESTEROL.

PERUVIAN QUINOA STEW

TOTAL TIME
35 minutes

SERVINGS
4

MENU
Serve with Inside-Out Mango (see page 314) for dessert.

According to Moosewood worker *Faustino Cutipa, this is one way quinoa is eaten in his homeland.*

½ cup quinoa
1 cup water

≈

2 cups chopped onions
2 garlic cloves, minced or pressed
2 tablespoons vegetable oil
1 celery stalk, chopped
1 carrot, cut on the diagonal into ¼-inch-thick slices
1 bell pepper, cut into 1-inch pieces
1 cup cubed zucchini
2 cups undrained chopped fresh or canned tomatoes
1 cup water or vegetable stock
2 teaspoons ground cumin
½ teaspoon chili powder
1 teaspoon ground coriander
pinch of cayenne (or more to taste)
2 teaspoons fresh oregano (1 teaspoon dried)
salt to taste

≈

chopped fresh cilantro (optional)
grated cheddar or Monterey Jack cheese (optional)

Using a fine sieve, rinse the quinoa well. Place it in a pot with the water and cook, covered, on medium-low heat for about 15 minutes, until soft. Set aside.

While the quinoa cooks, in a covered soup pot sauté the onions and garlic in the oil for about 5 minutes on medium heat. Add the celery and carrots, and continue to cook for 5 minutes, stirring often.

Add the bell pepper, zucchini, tomatoes, and water or stock. Stir in the cumin, chili powder, coriander, cayenne, and oregano, and simmer, covered, for 10 to 15 minutes, until the vegetables are tender. Stir the cooked quinoa into the stew and add salt to taste. Top with cilantro and grated cheese, if you wish. Serve immediately.

PER 8-OZ SERVING: 140 CALORIES, 2.8 G PROTEIN, 4.7 G FAT, 22.9 G CARBOHYDRATE, 52 MG SODIUM, 0 MG CHOLESTEROL.

SICILIAN SEAFOOD STEW

TOTAL TIME

35 minutes

SERVINGS

6

MENU

Accompany this stew with a thick slice of your favorite bread or with Bruschetta (see page 262).

An assertive stew with aromatic Mediterranean seasonings. If you have the time to clean them, mussels can be used instead of the scallops and shrimp.

1 cup chopped onions
¼ cup olive oil
1 cup chopped celery
1 green bell pepper, chopped
1 red bell pepper, chopped
3 garlic cloves, minced or pressed
pinch of crushed red pepper flakes or cayenne
1 teaspoon dried oregano (2 teaspoons fresh)
1 teaspoon dried basil (1 tablespoon fresh)
1 teaspoon dried marjoram (2 teaspoons fresh)
2 cups bottled clam juice
3 cups undrained canned tomatoes, chopped or crushed (28-ounce can), or 4 cups undrained chopped fresh tomatoes
½ cup red wine

≈

½ pound scallops, rinsed
½ pound fresh or frozen shelled shrimp
juice of 1 lemon (about 2 tablespoons)
ground black pepper to taste

≈

lemon wedges
capers (optional), rinsed and drained
chopped black olives (optional)

In a soup pot, sauté the onions in the olive oil on high heat for 2 minutes, stirring constantly. Add the celery and bell peppers and sauté, stirring, for 2 minutes. Stir in the garlic, crushed red pepper flakes or cayenne, oregano, basil, and marjoram. Lower the heat, cover, and cook for 2 minutes. Add the clam juice, tomatoes, and wine. Cover and simmer for 15 minutes.

Add the scallops and shrimp, and cook until the scallops are no longer opaque and the shrimp are just pink, about 4 minutes. Stir in the lemon juice and season with pepper to taste.

Serve with lemon wedges, and top each serving with a sprinkling of capers and/or chopped black olives if desired.

PER 8-OZ SERVING: 138 CALORIES, 11.4 G PROTEIN, 6.6 G FAT, 8.1 G CARBOHYDRATE, 224 MG SODIUM, 58 MG CHOLESTEROL.

NOTE: This recipe can be partially prepared a day or two ahead, to the point just before the scallops and shrimp are added. Cover and refrigerate. Shortly before you plan to serve the meal, bring the stew to a full simmer, then add the seafood. Continue the recipe as described above.

TOMATICAN

TOTAL TIME
30 minutes

SERVINGS
4

MENU
Serve on rice, polenta, or
quinoa, or with warm
tortillas or cornbread.

*A*n easy, colorful
Chilean stew
that can be as
spicy or as mild as you
like. Our version is
quickly assembled from
vegetables in the freezer
or cupboard, but you
can also use fresh
vegetables: green beans
could replace the limas;
zucchini or yellow
squash could be added
for variety.

2 cups chopped onions
1 fresh chile, minced, or ¼ teaspoon cayenne
2 tablespoons olive oil
2 teaspoons ground cumin
2 cups frozen lima beans
3 cups undrained canned tomatoes (28-ounce can)
2 cups fresh or frozen cut corn
¼ cup chopped fresh cilantro
salt to taste

OPTIONAL GARNISHES
avocado cubes or slices
Seasoned Tempeh (see page 85)
grated Monterey Jack or cheddar cheese

In a heavy nonreactive soup pot or saucepan, sauté the onions and
chile or cayenne in the oil for about 5 minutes, until the onions begin
to soften. Add the cumin and lima beans and sauté, stirring, for a
couple of minutes. Add the juice from the tomatoes, cover, and simmer for 5 minutes.

Chop the whole tomatoes right in the can. Stir the chopped tomatoes, corn, and cilantro into the pan. Cover and simmer for about
10 minutes, until the vegetables are tender. Add salt to taste.

Serve plain or topped with any or all of the suggested garnishes.

PER 8-OZ SERVING: 142 CALORIES, 3.6 G PROTEIN, 5.8 G FAT, 22.3 G CARBOHYDRATE, 189 MG SODIUM,
0 MG CHOLESTEROL.

Tunisian Vegetable Stew

1½ cups thinly sliced onions
2 tablespoons olive oil
3 cups thinly sliced cabbage
dash of salt
1 large green bell pepper, cut into thin strips
2 teaspoons ground coriander
½ teaspoon turmeric
¼ teaspoon cinnamon
⅛ teaspoon cayenne (or to taste)
3 cups undrained canned tomatoes, chopped
(28-ounce can)
1½ cups drained cooked chick peas (16-ounce can)
⅓ cup currants or raisins (optional)
1 tablespoon fresh lemon juice
salt to taste

≈

grated feta cheese
toasted slivered almonds (see page 354) (optional)

In a large skillet, sauté the onions in the olive oil for 5 minutes, or until softened. Add the cabbage, sprinkle with salt, and continue to sauté for at least 5 minutes, stirring occasionally. Add the bell pepper, coriander, turmeric, cinnamon, and cayenne to the skillet and sauté for another minute or so. Stir in the tomatoes, chick peas, and optional currants or raisins, and simmer, covered, for about 15 minutes, until the vegetables are just tender. Add the lemon juice and salt to taste.

Top with feta, and toasted almonds if you like.

PER 8-OZ SERVING: 150 CALORIES, 4.8 G PROTEIN, 5.1 G FAT, 23 G CARBOHYDRATE, 354 MG SODIUM, 0 MG CHOLESTEROL.

TOTAL TIME
30 minutes

SERVINGS
4

MENU
Serve on couscous or another grain of your choice.

This lovely stew makes an ideal quick meal that is flavorful, healthful, and economical.

VEGETABLE STIFADO

TOTAL TIME

40 minutes

SERVINGS

4 to 6

MENU

Finish the meal with a selection from Strawberries Three Ways (see page 321).

A rustic Mediterranean-style stew, good on rice or served with pita or a hearty bread. If you are serving it on rice, start cooking the rice just before you begin to cut up the vegetables for the stew.

1 medium onion, chopped
3 garlic cloves, minced or pressed
2 tablespoons olive oil
1 large potato (about 2 cups cubed)
1 medium eggplant
3 cups undrained canned tomatoes (28-ounce can)
1½ cups water
1 teaspoon salt
1 sprig fresh rosemary (1 scant teaspoon dried)

≈

1 medium zucchini or yellow squash
1 bell pepper
1 cup frozen sliced okra (optional)
juice of 1 lemon (or to taste)
1 tablespoon chopped fresh dill (1 teaspoon dried)
ground black pepper to taste

≈

grated feta cheese

In a large stewpot, sauté the onions and garlic in the oil over medium heat until just softened. Cut the potato into ½-inch cubes and add to the pot. Cut the eggplant into 1-inch cubes. Add the eggplant and the juice from the tomatoes, setting aside the tomatoes. Stir in the water, salt, and rosemary. Bring the stew to a boil, reduce the heat, and simmer, covered, for about 10 minutes. After the first 10 minutes, the stew can be simmered uncovered.

While the stew simmers, cut the squash into 1-inch cubes and the bell pepper into 1-inch pieces. When the potatoes are just beginning to soften, add the squash and bell pepper and continue to cook for 5 minutes. Coarsely chop the reserved tomatoes and add them to the pot, along with the okra, lemon juice, and dill. Simmer for about 5 minutes, until the vegetables are tender. Add black pepper to taste, and remove the rosemary sprig if you used the fresh herb.

Serve topped with feta cheese.

PER 8-OZ SERVING: 83 CALORIES, 2 G PROTEIN, 3.2 G FAT, 13.4 G CARBOHYDRATE, 322 MG SODIUM, 0 MG CHOLESTEROL.

WINTER VEGETABLE STEW

TOTAL TIME
35 minutes

SERVINGS
4

MENU
Serve with a dark bread
and a strong cheese such
as Fontina, Camembert,
cheddar, or chèvre.

*A n earthy,
warming stew
that juxtaposes
the sweetness of root
vegetables with the tang
of Dijon mustard and
beer.*

2 onions, chopped (about 2 cups)
2 celery stalks, chopped
2 tablespoons olive oil or vegetable oil
2 medium carrots
2 parsnips
2 large potatoes
10 ounces green beans (about 2 cups trimmed and halved)
1 tablespoon chopped fresh dill (1 teaspoon dried)
1 tablespoon chopped fresh marjoram (1 teaspoon dried)
1 cup beer or vegetable stock
1½ cups water
1 green or red bell pepper
2 cups sliced mushrooms (about 6 ounces)
1 tablespoon Dijon mustard (or more to taste)
1 tablespoon molasses
salt and ground black pepper to taste

In a heavy pot, sauté the onions and celery in the oil until the onions are translucent. While the onions sauté, peel and coarsely chop the carrots and parsnips. Stir them into the pot. Cut the potatoes into 1-inch cubes, and stem and halve the green beans. Add them to the sautéing vegetables along with the dill, marjoram, beer or stock, and water. Bring the stew to a low boil. Coarsely chop the bell pepper, and stem and slice the mushrooms; stir them into the pot. Add the mustard and molasses and continue to simmer for about 10 minutes, until the potatoes are tender. Add salt and pepper to taste, and serve.

PER 8-OZ SERVING: 126 CALORIES, 2.8 G PROTEIN, 3.6 G FAT, 22.5 G CARBOHYDRATE, 62 MG SODIUM, 0 MG CHOLESTEROL.

STIR-FRIES
AND SAUTÉS

STIR-FRYING AND SAUTÉING are two cooking techniques that are by nature quick and straightforward. Both involve the rapid cooking of food over high heat, with sautéing proceeding at a somewhat slower pace than stir-frying. For a brief discussion of this technique see page 353.

The recipes that follow are simple combinations for fast meals. Feel free to mix and match—add a carrot, or substitute cauliflower. Once the basic technique is mastered, create your own stir-fries or sautés by varying the seasonings and other ingredients.

ASPARAGUS, TOMATO, AND GREEN PEA SAUTÉ

TOTAL TIME
25 minutes

SERVINGS
2

MENU
Serve on rice, orzo,
or couscous, accompanied
by Carrot and Parsley
Salad (see page 65) or
Mushrooms in Lemon
Marinade (see page 81).

*Lovely to
behold, fresh and
colorful.*

6 sun-dried tomatoes (not packed in oil)
½ cup boiling water
≈
1½ tablespoons olive oil
2 garlic cloves, minced or pressed
¾ pound fresh asparagus spears, trimmed and cut into
       2-inch pieces
¼ cup dry white wine
1 large tomato, diced (about 1 cup)
1 generous tablespoon finely chopped fresh tarragon
       (1½ teaspoons dried)
½ cup fresh or frozen tiny green peas
ground black pepper to taste
≈
crumbled mild (not aged) chèvre *

* Parmesan, feta, or Fontina cheese could be used in place of the chèvre.

In a small heatproof bowl, cover the sun-dried tomatoes with the boiling water; set aside.

Prepare all of the ingredients and have them within easy reach before you begin to stir-fry.

Heat the oil in a large skillet or a wok on high heat. Swirl the garlic in the oil for just a moment and then add the asparagus. Stir-fry for half a minute. Add the wine, cover, and let steam for a couple of minutes. Uncover and add the tomatoes and tarragon. Cook on high heat for 2 to 3 minutes to reduce the liquid. Drain and chop the sun-dried tomatoes, and then add them along with the peas. Stir-fry until the asparagus is crisp but tender and the liquid is reduced to a sauce. Add black pepper to taste.

Serve immediately, topped with crumbled chèvre.

PER 8-OZ SERVING: 222 CALORIES, 9.5 G PROTEIN, 12.4 G FAT, 19.6 G CARBOHYDRATE, 362 MG SODIUM, 25 MG CHOLESTEROL.

BROCCOLI-TOFU STIR-FRY

Very good

SAUCE

3 tablespoons hoisin sauce (see page 336)

⅔ cup water

3 tablespoons rice vinegar or white vinegar

3 tablespoons soy sauce

1 tablespoon cornstarch

≈

3 – 4 tablespoons vegetable oil

2 garlic cloves, minced or pressed

1 small fresh chile, seeded and minced

1½ cakes tofu (about 18 ounces), cut into 1-inch cubes

1 large head broccoli, cut into 1-inch florets, stems peeled and sliced ¼ inch thick (about 5 cups)

⅓ cup dry sherry

1 bunch scallions, cut into 1-inch pieces (about 1½ cups)

1 red bell pepper, cut into strips (optional)

≈

unsalted peanuts

Combine the sauce ingredients in a small bowl. Before beginning to stir-fry, prepare the vegetables and have all the ingredients at hand.

In a wok or large skillet, heat 2 tablespoons of the oil on medium-high heat. Add the garlic and chile and stir-fry for just 30 seconds before adding the tofu. Continue to stir-fry for 3 to 4 minutes, until the tofu is lightly browned. Remove the tofu and set it aside. Add another tablespoon of oil to the wok, heat for a few seconds, and then add the broccoli. Stir-fry for a minute and pour in the sherry. Stir-fry for 3 minutes. If the broccoli begins to scorch, add a tablespoon of water. Add the scallions and optional bell pepper, continue to stir-fry for a minute, and then the tofu and the sauce. Stir carefully and bring to a simmer. Simmer for 3 or 4 minutes, until the sauce thickens.

Top with peanuts and serve immediately.

PER 8-OZ SERVING: 156 CALORIES, 9 G PROTEIN, 9.3 G FAT, 10.9 G CARBOHYDRATE, 690 MG SODIUM, 0 MG CHOLESTEROL.

TOTAL TIME

35 minutes

SERVINGS

4

MENU

Serve on rice or pasta; udon noodles, linguini, and whole wheat noodles are all good. Finish the meal with Inside-Out Mango (see page 314).

This satisfying sauté is enriched by the sweet, spicy flavor of Chinese hoisin sauce.

CURRIED FRIED RICE

TOTAL TIME

25 minutes

SERVINGS

4 as a main dish,
6 as a side dish

MENU

Tropical Fruit Salad
(see page 324) is a
refreshing dessert that
complements this spicy
entrée.

W*hen leftover
rice is on
hand, this is
one of our favorite
quick lunches. Garnish
the rice with lime
wedges, mung bean
sprouts, chopped toasted
nuts, and scallions.*

1 tablespoon vegetable oil
4 large eggs, lightly beaten with a pinch of salt

≈

2 tablespoons vegetable oil
2 garlic cloves, minced or pressed
1 tablespoon curry paste * or curry powder
2 medium tomatoes, diced
generous handful fresh spinach, rinsed, large stems
     removed, and large leaves torn (about ¼ pound)
4 cups cooked brown rice
1½ cups fresh or frozen green peas
2 tablespoons soy sauce (or more to taste)
2 teaspoons fresh lime or lemon juice

** Patak's medium-hot curry paste is a widely available brand. There are
also a variety of Thai curry pastes at Asian or other well-stocked markets.*

Prepare all of the ingredients and have them within easy reach before beginning to stir-fry. In a large skillet or a wok, heat the oil, add
the beaten eggs, and cook on moderately high heat. When the edges
of the eggs begin to set, lift them with a spatula and tilt the pan to
allow the uncooked eggs to run under, onto the hot skillet. After 2 or
3 minutes, when the bottom is set, flip the omelet over. You may
need to cut it into sections to flip it. As soon as the omelet is well
cooked, transfer it from the skillet to a plate. Cut it into long ½-inch-
wide strips and set aside.

    Wipe out the skillet and heat the 2 tablespoons of oil on medium
heat. Add the garlic and curry paste or powder; cook for a minute,
stirring constantly to prevent scorching. Add the tomatoes and

spinach. Stir-fry on high heat until the spinach just wilts. Add the rice and peas and cook until heated through. Stir in the egg strips, soy sauce, and lime or lemon juice.

Adjust the soy sauce to taste, and serve at once.

PER 8-OZ SERVING: 244 CALORIES, 8.5 G PROTEIN, 9.1 G FAT, 32.8 G CARBOHYDRATE, 420 MG SODIUM, 103 MG CHOLESTEROL.

FRAGRANT RICE NOODLES WITH VEGETABLES

A *Southeast Asian–inspired sauté with colorful strips of leeks and squash in a creamy, peanut-lime sauce.*

1½ quarts water

SAUCE
2 tablespoons fresh lime juice
1 tablespoon freshly grated lime peel
½ cup peanut butter (preferably smooth)
2 teaspoons brown sugar
1 cup vegetable stock (see page 359)
½ teaspoon salt
3 garlic cloves, minced or pressed

≈

6 ounces ¼-inch-wide rice noodles (or linguini if
    rice noodles are unavailable)

≈

2 leeks, well rinsed
2 small zucchini
2 small yellow squash
3 tablespoons vegetable oil
¼ cup water

In a covered pot, bring the water to a rapid boil.

Combine the sauce ingredients and mix them by hand or purée them in a blender until smooth.

When the water boils, add the noodles and cook for 3 to 5 minutes, until just tender. Drain, rinse briefly under cool water, drain again, and set aside.

Cut the leeks, zucchini, and yellow squash into sticks 5 to 6 inches long and ¼ to ½ inch wide. Heat the oil in a wok or large skillet. Stir-fry the leek sticks on medium-high heat for 2 to 3 minutes. Add the zucchini and yellow squash and continue to stir-fry for about 3 to 4 minutes, until the vegetables are just tender. To prevent scorching or sticking, add about ¼ cup water while stir-frying. Add the noodles and the sauce and toss well until heated through. Serve at once.

PER 8-OZ SERVING: 294 CALORIES, 9 G PROTEIN, 16.9 G FAT, 30.8 G CARBOHYDRATE, 270 MG SODIUM, 21 MG CHOLESTEROL.

FRIED RICE

TOTAL TIME

25 minutes

SERVINGS

4

MENU

Finish with melon wedges
for a simple but complete
meal.

A basic Chinese-style fried rice. This recipe invites variation: use whatever vegetables are at their seasonal peak and cook until tender-crisp.

TOFU MARINADE

1 tablespoon grated fresh ginger root
4 garlic cloves, minced or pressed
¼ cup soy sauce
2 tablespoons rice vinegar or cider vinegar
2 teaspoons molasses or brown sugar
2 tablespoons dark sesame oil
½ teaspoon chili paste, or splash of chili oil (optional)

≈

1 cake tofu (about ¾ pound)

≈

3 tablespoons peanut oil or vegetable oil
2 medium red or green bell peppers, cut into thin strips
6 ounces snow peas, stemmed (about 2 cups)
¼ cup water
4 cups cooked brown rice
⅔ cup chopped scallions

≈

chopped toasted almonds (see page 354) (optional)

In a shallow nonreactive bowl, mix together the marinade ingredients. Cut the tofu into strips 1 inch long, ½ inch wide, and about ½ inch thick. Add the tofu strips to the marinade and stir gently, using a rubber spatula to avoid breaking the tofu. Marinate for about 10 minutes.

Prepare all of the remaining ingredients and have them at hand before starting to stir-fry.

Heat a wok or large skillet. Swirl the oil around the wok, add the peppers, and stir-fry for 3 to 5 minutes on medium-high heat. Add the snow peas and water and continue to stir-fry, uncovered, until the water evaporates and the snow peas are crisp and beginning to puff up. Using a slotted spoon, remove the tofu from the marinade and add it to the wok. Stir for a moment, then add the rice and heat thoroughly. Pour on the marinade, add the scallions, and stir.

Serve immediately, garnished with chopped almonds if you like.

PER 8-OZ SERVING: 266 CALORIES, 7.8 G PROTEIN, 12 G FAT, 33 G CARBOHYDRATE, 479 MG SODIUM, 0 MG CHOLESTEROL.

GINGERED GREENS AND TOFU

TOTAL TIME
30 minutes

SERVINGS
4

MENU
**Serve with Coconut
Basmati Rice
(see page 155).**

A classic stir-fry with the fresh, clean nip of ginger and cilantro and highly nutritious greens.

TOFU MARINADE*
½ cup soy sauce
½ cup dry sherry
¼ cup rice vinegar
3 tablespoons brown sugar

≈

2 cakes tofu (about 1½ pounds)

≈

¼ cup peanut oil or vegetable oil
2 tablespoons grated fresh ginger root
6 cups coarsely shredded bok choy, kale, Chinese cabbage,
    or Swiss chard, packed
3 tablespoons fresh lime juice
2 tablespoons chopped fresh cilantro
pinch of cayenne or splash of chili oil

≈

toasted cashews or peanuts (see page 354) (optional)

* If you have Asian Marinade (see page 108) on hand, use 1 cup of it as the marinade here.

In a small saucepan, bring the marinade ingredients to a boil. Simmer for 1 minute and remove from the heat. Cut the blocks of tofu into ½-inch slices, then cut the slices into 1-inch squares. Place the squares in a single layer in a nonreactive heatproof pan. Pour the marinade over the tofu squares, sprinkle on 2 tablespoons of the oil, and set aside for about 5 minutes.

Preheat the broiler. Prepare the remaining ingredients and have them at hand before beginning to stir-fry.

Broil the tofu for 7 to 8 minutes, until lightly browned; then turn it over with a spatula and brown the other side.

While the tofu broils, heat the remaining 2 tablespoons of oil in a wok or large skillet. Stir in the ginger, add the greens, and stir constantly on high heat until the greens wilt. When the greens are just tender, add the lime juice, cilantro, and cayenne or chili oil, and remove from the heat. When the tofu is browned, gently toss it with the marinade and the cooked greens, and reheat if necessary. Top with toasted nuts if you like, and serve immediately.

PER 8-OZ SERVING: 200 CALORIES, 9.7 G PROTEIN, 11.7 G FAT, 15.4 G CARBOHYDRATE, 595 MG SODIUM, 0 MG CHOLESTEROL.

MUSHROOMS WITH CHINESE BLACK BEAN SAUCE

TOTAL TIME

40 minutes

SERVINGS

4

MENU

Serve with Sesame Spinach (see page 86) and rice.

*C*hinese black beans contribute a rich fragrance and pungent flavor to this home-style stir-fry.

2 cups water
10 dried shiitake mushrooms

≈

¼ cup vegetable oil
2 cakes tofu (about 1½ pounds), cut into 1-inch cubes

SAUCE
¼ cup rice wine or dry sherry
1 tablespoon molasses
1½ tablespoons rice vinegar or white vinegar
1 tablespoon soy sauce
1 teaspoon cornstarch
1 cup soaking liquid from shiitake mushrooms

≈

3 garlic cloves, minced or pressed
3 tablespoons Chinese fermented black beans, rinsed and
    chopped (see page 332)
1½ pounds fresh mushrooms, sliced
1 red or green bell pepper, thinly sliced

≈

chopped scallions

Bring the water to a boil. Place the shiitake in a heatproof bowl, cover with the boiling water, and set aside for about 10 minutes. Prepare all of the remaining ingredients and have them within easy reach before beginning to stir-fry.

Heat the oil in a wok or skillet. Add about a third of the tofu cubes and stir-fry for about 3 minutes, until tofu is lightly golden. Drain on paper towels. Stir-fry and drain the remaining tofu in two batches. Remove the wok from the heat.

Drain the shiitake, reserving the liquid. Cut off and discard the tough stems of the shiitake, and thinly slice the caps. In a small bowl, combine the sauce ingredients.

Return the wok to the heat. Add the garlic and black beans to the remaining oil in the wok, and stir-fry for a minute. Add the fresh mushrooms, peppers, and shiitake, and continue to stir-fry until the mushrooms are tender, about 5 minutes. Add ¼ cup shiitake soaking liquid or water if necessary to prevent scorching. Stir in the sauce and heat to a simmer. Add the cooked tofu and gently reheat to a simmer.

Serve immediately, topping each portion with chopped scallions.

PER 8-OZ SERVING: 178 CALORIES, 8.8 G PROTEIN, 11.9 G FAT, 10.7 G CARBOHYDRATE, 225 MG SODIUM, 0 MG CHOLESTEROL.

PAD THAI

TOTAL TIME
40 minutes

SERVINGS
4

MENU
Serve with tossed salad
with Japanese Carrot
Dressing (see page 125)
and Creamy Banana Ice
(see page 308) for a
simple yet lavish meal.

A spicy Thai
noodle dish
that is
authentically seasoned
with fish sauce (soy
sauce is an acceptable
substitute).

2 quarts water
¾ pound mung bean sprouts
6 ounces rice noodles (¼ inch wide)

SAUCE
3 tablespoons fresh lime juice
3 tablespoons catsup
1 tablespoon brown sugar
¼ cup fish sauce (see page 334) or soy sauce
≈
3 tablespoons peanut oil or vegetable oil
3–4 garlic cloves, minced or pressed
1 tablespoon minced fresh chile, or 1½ teaspoons crushed
    red pepper flakes
2 cups grated carrots
4 large eggs, lightly beaten with a pinch of salt
⅔ cup chopped peanuts
6–8 scallions, chopped (about 1 cup)

In a covered pot, bring the water to a rolling boil. Blanch the
mung bean sprouts by placing them in a strainer or small colander
and dipping it into the boiling water for 30 seconds. Set aside to drain
well. When the water returns to a boil, stir in the rice noodles and
cook for 3 to 5 minutes, until tender but firm. Drain the cooked
noodles, rinse them under cool water, and set them aside to drain
well. Meanwhile, in a small bowl, mix together the sauce ingredients.

Prepare the remaining ingredients and have them near at hand before you begin to stir-fry. Heat the oil in a wok or large skillet. Add
the garlic and chile, swirl them in the oil for a moment, and stir in the

grated carrots. Stir-fry for 1 minute. Push the carrots to the sides to make a hollow in the center. Pour the beaten eggs into the center and quickly scramble them. When the eggs have just set, pour in the sauce mixture and stir everything together. Add the drained rice noodles and mung sprouts, and toss to distribute evenly. Stir in the peanuts and scallions, and serve at once.

PER 8-OZ SERVING: 296 CALORIES, 11.3 G PROTEIN, 15 G FAT, 31 G CARBOHYDRATE, 712 MG SODIUM, 142 MG CHOLESTEROL.

Seitan – Green Bean Curry

TOTAL TIME

35 minutes

SERVINGS

4 to 6

MENU

Serve on rice with Carrot
and Parsley Salad
(see page 65) or
Vegetables in Mint
Vinaigrette (see page 72),
followed by Inside-Out
Mango (see page 314).

*S*eitan is a low-fat
wheat protein
source that adds
a chewy texture to this
well-spiced curry.
Reheat any leftover
curry in a corn or
wheat tortilla for an
easy enchilada or
burrito.

3 tablespoons vegetable oil
2 medium onions, finely chopped (about 2 cups)
3 garlic cloves, minced or pressed
2 teaspoons minced fresh chile, or ¼ teaspoon cayenne
4 teaspoon garam masala (see page 334)
1 teaspoon ground cumin
1 pound green beans, cut into 1-inch pieces
    (about 3 – 3½ cups)
1 pound seitan (wheat gluten), finely chopped or coarsely
    grated
2½ cups chopped fresh tomatoes
⅔ cup coconut milk (see page 360)
¾ cup water
salt and ground black pepper to taste

≈

toasted unsalted cashews (see page 354) (optional)

Prepare the vegetables and have all of the ingredients near at hand
before beginning to sauté.

Heat the oil in a large skillet or wok and add the onions and garlic.
Sauté for 2 to 3 minutes before adding the chile or cayenne, garam
masala, and cumin. Stirring, sauté for another 2 or 3 minutes. Add
the green beans, then the seitan, and mix well. Stir in the tomatoes,
coconut milk, and water. Cover and bring to a simmer. Cook, covered, for about 10 minutes, until the beans are firm-tender.

Add salt and pepper to taste, and serve topped with toasted
cashews for a nice contrast in texture.

PER 8-OZ SERVING: 167 CALORIES, 10.2 G PROTEIN, 10.3 G FAT, 11.2 G CARBOHYDRATE, 84 MG SODIUM,
0 MG CHOLESTEROL.

SWEET AND SOUR PEPPERS

SAUCE

¼ cup catsup

¼ cup soy sauce

⅓ cup cider vinegar

¼ cup packed brown sugar

¾ cup water

1 tablespoon cornstarch dissolved in 2 tablespoons water

≈

3 tablespoons vegetable oil

2 garlic cloves, minced or pressed

2 cups very thinly sliced onions

2 large red bell peppers, cut into thin strips

2 large green bell peppers, cut into thin strips

15 ounces canned baby corn, drained

1½ cups raw or toasted cashews, whole or half pieces
     (see page 354)

TOTAL TIME

35 minutes

SERVINGS

4

MENU

Serve on rice or noodles, with Miso Soup (see page 31) or Broiled Tofu (see page 261).

A colorful stir-fry with zesty flavor.

Combine the sauce ingredients in a bowl. Have the remaining ingredients at hand before beginning to stir-fry.

In a wok or large skillet, heat the oil. Add the garlic and onions, and stir-fry for 3 or 4 minutes. Add the pepper strips and continue to stir-fry. Add a couple of tablespoons of water if necessary to prevent scorching. When the peppers and onions are beginning to soften, add the baby corn and cashews. Stir-fry for a minute, then add the sauce mixture and simmer for another minute. Remove from the heat and serve immediately.

PER 8-OZ SERVING: 338 CALORIES, 7.8 G PROTEIN, 18.2 G FAT, 42.6 G CARBOHYDRATE, 705 MG SODIUM, 0 MG CHOLESTEROL.

FISH

Those of us who include fish in our diets appreciate its low fat, high protein, and ease of preparation. Baking, grilling, broiling, and braising are healthful preparations for fish that are well suited to the challenge of a last-minute meal. The recipes in this chapter combine flavorful toppings and seasonings with these simple cooking methods to produce meals that are exotic and satisfying. Many of the recipes create an entrée, vegetable, and tasty sauce all in one pan, or an entire meal in a foil packet.

Buy the freshest fish you can (the eyes should be convex and clear, and if you press your finger into the flesh it should not leave a lasting indentation) and plan on about 6 ounces per serving. We suggest using firm fillets, such as scrod, flounder, haddock, cod, turbot, monkfish, catfish, and bluefish. Fish steaks, such as salmon, tuna, and swordfish, are particularly suited to grilling or broiling. When we don't give a suggestion for a specific type of fish, use whatever suits your taste.

You will find other good suggestions for preparing fish in the Dressings, Salsas, and Sauces chapter. Coat the fish with the dressing, marinade, or sauce of your choice, and either bake, grill, or broil it. Or top the cooked fish with a salsa.

ASIAN FISH IN A PACKET

TOTAL TIME
30 minutes

SERVINGS
2

This recipe and the three that follow it are delicious main dishes that can be prepared and baked to serve at once, or can be put together a few hours ahead of time, refrigerated, and then popped into the oven when you're ready. Everything goes into the foil packet, so there are no pots to clean! Use just about any fish: scrod, turbot, haddock or other firm fillets, or fish steaks such as salmon.

2 firm fish fillets or steaks (5 – 6 ounces each), or 1 larger fillet (10 – 12 ounces), cut in half
1 cup cooked rice
2 cups coarsely chopped mustard greens or bok choy
2 scallions, chopped
1 tablespoon vegetable oil
1 teaspoon grated fresh ginger root
1 garlic clove, minced or pressed
2 tablespoons soy sauce
2 teaspoons dark sesame oil
chili oil (optional)

Preheat the oven to 450°.

Take two 12 x 24-inch sheets of aluminum foil, and fold each sheet of foil over to make a double-thick square. Brush a little oil the center part of each square. Rinse the fish and prepare all of the ingredients.

Spread half of the rice on the center of each foil square and then layer the greens, fish, and scallions on top of the rice. In a small bowl, combine the vegetable oil, grated ginger, garlic, soy sauce, sesame oil, and a few drops of the optional chili oil. Pour half of the sauce over each serving. Fold the foil into airtight packets. Bake for 20 minutes. Carefully avoiding the steam that will be released, open a packet and check that the fish is cooked.

To serve, carefully open the foil and transfer the contents to plates or bowls.

PER 6-OZ SERVING: 183 CALORIES, 15.5 G PROTEIN, 5.4 G FAT, 17.7 G CARBOHYDRATE, 432 MG SODIUM, 31 MG CHOLESTEROL.

NOTE: Water chestnuts, julienned daikon or turnips, or slices of fresh shiitake placed on the greens beneath the fish make a nice addition to this recipe.

CARIBBEAN FISH IN A PACKET

2 sheets aluminum foil, 12 x 24 inches
2 5- or 6-ounce firm fish fillets or steaks, or 1 10-ounce
      fillet, cut in half
1 small tomato or bell pepper, thinly sliced
2 tablespoons olive oil
3 scallions, chopped
2 tablespoons chopped fresh cilantro
juice of 1 lime
½ fresh chile, minced, or a few dashes of Tabasco or
      other hot pepper sauce
dash of salt and ground black pepper

TOTAL TIME
30 minutes
SERVINGS
2
MENU
Serve with steamed cabbage and baked or mashed sweet potatoes, or include parboiled sliced sweet potatoes and cabbage in the packets as the bottom layer. Finish the meal with a tropical flair: Sautéed Bananas (see page 320) or Tropical Fruit Salad (see page 324).

Preheat the oven to 450°.

Fold each sheet of foil over to make a square of double thickness. Brush a little oil on the center portion of each square. Rinse the fish and prepare all of the ingredients.

Place half of the fish on each square. Top with the tomato or bell pepper slices, and sprinkle with the olive oil, scallions, cilantro, lime juice, chiles or hot pepper sauce, salt, and black pepper. Fold the foil into airtight packets. Bake for 20 minutes. Carefully avoiding the steam that will be released, open a packet and check that the fish is cooked.

Transfer the fish, vegetables, and juices to serving plates.

PER 6-OZ SERVING: 212 CALORIES, 22.4 G PROTEIN, 10.5 G FAT, 6.9 G CARBOHYDRATE, 273 MG SODIUM, 52 MG CHOLESTEROL.

French Fish in a Packet

TOTAL TIME
30 minutes

SERVINGS
2

MENU
Try a potato side dish,
such as Mediterranean
Potato Salad
(see page 132), or a grain,
such as Couscous with
Sun-Dried Tomatoes
(see page 145), to
complete this meal.

2 sheets aluminum foil, 12 x 24 inches
2 5- or 6-ounce firm fish fillets or steaks, or 1 10-ounce
    fillet, cut in half
1 small zucchini, thinly sliced
1 cup sliced mushrooms
½ red onion, thinly sliced
2 tablespoons olive oil
juice of 1 lemon
¼ cup dry white wine
dash of salt and ground black pepper
1 tablespoon chopped fresh marjoram or basil
    (1 teaspoon dried)
6 black olives, halved and pitted

Preheat the oven to 450°.

Fold each sheet of foil in half to form a double-thick square. Brush a little oil on the center portion of each square. Rinse the fish and prepare all of the ingredients.

Layer half of the following ingredients in the middle of each square in this order: zucchini, mushrooms, fish, and onion slices. Sprinkle with the olive oil, lemon juice, wine, salt and black pepper, and marjoram or basil. Top with the black olive halves. Fold the foil into airtight packets. Bake for 20 minutes. Carefully avoiding the steam that will be released, open a packet and check that the fish is cooked.

To serve, lift the fish and vegetables with a spatula or large spoon onto individual serving dishes and pour the liquid left in the foil over each serving.

PER 6-OZ SERVING: 151 CALORIES, 13.8 G PROTEIN, 8 G FAT, 4.6 G CARBOHYDRATE, 320 MG SODIUM, 31 MG CHOLESTEROL.

GREEK FISH IN A PACKET

Be sure Very good fish is thawed

2 sheets aluminum foil, 12 x 24 inches
2 5- or 6-ounce firm fish fillets, or 1 10-ounce fillet,
    cut in half
1 cup thinly sliced fennel bulb
1 small tomato, sliced
8 thin slices red onion
2 tablespoons olive oil
juice of 1 lemon or lime
1 tablespoon chopped fresh dill (1 teaspoon dried)
dash of salt and ground black pepper

TOTAL TIME
30 minutes
SERVINGS
2

We like to serve this dish with rice, couscous, or orzo and to top it with some grated or crumbled feta cheese.

Preheat the oven to 450°.

Fold each sheet of foil over to make a double-thick square. Brush a little oil on the center of each square. Rinse the fish and prepare all of the ingredients.

Layer half of the sliced fennel, tomatoes, and onions on each square. Top each with half of the fish. In a cup, combine the olive oil, lemon or lime juice, and dill and pour it over the fish. Sprinkle on salt and pepper. Fold the foil into an airtight packet. Bake for 20 minutes. Place the foil packets on a plate and, being careful to avoid the steam that will be released, open the foil and check that the fish is cooked.

With a spatula, transfer the fish and vegetables to individual serving dishes, and pour the liquid remaining in the foil over each serving.

PER 6-OZ SERVING: 226 CALORIES, 20.1 G PROTEIN, 11 G FAT, 14.8 G CARBOHYDRATE, 223 MG SODIUM, 39 MG CHOLESTEROL.

Braised Fish with Artichoke Hearts and Red Peppers

TOTAL TIME
20 minutes

SERVINGS
4 to 6

MENU
Serve with Herbed Lemon Pilaf with Almonds (see page 158) or on couscous.

The beauty of this recipe is that you create a vegetable/fish entrée with a tasty sauce all in one pan.

1½ pounds firm fish fillets

≈

1 cup thinly sliced onions
3 tablespoons olive oil
1 red bell pepper
5 artichoke hearts (14-ounce can)
1 teaspoon sweet paprika
1 tablespoon chopped fresh dill (1 teaspoon dried)
2 tablespoons chopped fresh parsley
½ cup dry white wine
dash of salt and ground black pepper
1 tablespoon unbleached white flour

Rinse the fish fillets and set aside.

In a large nonreactive skillet, sauté the onions in the olive oil for 3 minutes. Thinly slice the bell pepper lengthwise, add it to the onions, and continue to sauté for 3 more minutes. Drain the artichoke hearts, reserving the brine. Quarter the artichoke hearts and add them to the skillet along with the paprika, dill, and chopped parsley. Sauté for 1 minute, stirring to prevent sticking. Add the wine and ½ cup of the reserved artichoke brine. Lay the fish fillets, skin side down, on top of the simmering vegetables and sprinkle with salt and pepper. Cover the skillet and cook for 5 to 10 minutes on low heat until the fish flakes easily with a fork.

With a slotted spatula or large spoon, transfer the fish and vegetables to a warmed serving dish. Turn up the heat until the juices remaining in the skillet are very hot. Whisk the flour into the pan juices and stir until thickened and smooth. Pour the sauce over the fish and serve immediately.

PER 6-OZ SERVING: 165 CALORIES, 18 G PROTEIN, 6.1 G FAT, 7.8 G CARBOHYDRATE, 168 MG SODIUM, 39 MG CHOLESTEROL.

CHESAPEAKE CATFISH

1½ pounds catfish fillets
¼ cup fresh lemon juice
¼ cup Old Bay Seasoning or other brand Chesapeake
     seasoning (see page 331)
2 tablespoons butter, cut into thin pats

Preheat the oven to 350°.

Rinse the catfish fillets and place them in an oiled 8 x 12-inch baking dish. Sprinkle the lemon juice over the fillets and then cover them with a thin coating of Old Bay Seasoning. Dot with pats of butter. Bake, covered, for 25 minutes, until the fish is hot and tender.

PER 6-OZ SERVING: 277 CALORIES, 31.7 G PROTEIN, 15.8 G FAT, 1 G CARBOHYDRATE, 2,294 MG SODIUM, 131 MG CHOLESTEROL.

TOTAL TIME
30 minutes

SERVINGS
4

MENU
**Mashed sweet potatoes
and Spicy Kale
(see page 88) are the
perfect accompaniments;
they can be cooked while
the fish bakes. Corn on
the cob and Asian
Cabbage Slaw
(see page 64) wouldn't
be bad either.**

Old Bay Seasoning is a favorite blend of spices used in Maryland seafood cooking. Here it tops catfish, which are plentiful in the tributaries of the Chesapeake Bay. If you are concerned about your salt intake, reduce the amount of Old Bay Seasoning to 3 tablespoons and use unsalted butter.

FISH ALGIERS

TOTAL TIME

30 minutes

SERVINGS

4

MENU

Accompany with
Marinated Zucchini
(see page 71) or Not Your
Mother's Green Beans
(see page 82) and rice or
couscous.

B *aked fillets with the spicy aroma of a North African port.*

1½ pounds firm fish fillets
dash of salt

≈

1 tablespoon cumin seeds
3 tablespoons olive oil
juice of 2 lemons
2 garlic cloves, minced or pressed
¼ teaspoon cayenne (optional)
1 large tomato, sliced, each slice cut into quarters

≈

lemon wedges
chopped fresh parsley (optional)

Preheat the oven to 375°.

Rinse and dry the fish fillets and place them in a single layer, skin side down, in an oiled 9 x 12-inch baking pan. Sprinkle with salt and set aside.

Toast the whole cumin seeds in a dry skillet for a few minutes. Grind them in a spice grinder or with a mortar and pestle. In a cup, whisk together the toasted cumin, olive oil, lemon juice, garlic, and optional cayenne. Layer the quartered tomato slices on top of the fish, evenly pour on the marinade, cover, and bake for about 20 minutes, until the fish is white and flakes easily with a fork. Serve topped with lemon wedges, and chopped parsley if you like.

PER 6-OZ SERVING: 209 CALORIES, 26.4 G PROTEIN, 9.9 G FAT, 3.2 G CARBOHYDRATE, 209 MG SODIUM, 62 MG CHOLESTEROL.

Excellent
used plain ~~plain~~ *yogurt* *fat free or low fat – It was vanilla*
used white onion

FISH OTIS

10 – 12 ounces firm fish fillets

≈

4 teaspoons fresh lemon juice
2 teaspoons chopped fresh dill (¾ teaspoon dried)
dash of salt and ground black pepper
⅓ – ½ cup sour cream
2 – 3 thick slices red onion

Preheat the oven to 375°.

Rinse and dry the fish fillets and place them, skin side down, in an oiled baking pan. Sprinkle with the lemon juice, dill, and salt and pepper. Spread the sour cream evenly over the fillets. Break the onion slices into rings, and press them into the sour cream.

Cover the pan and bake until the fish is no longer translucent and flakes easily with a fork. The amount of time varies with the thickness of the fish, but it usually takes 25 to 30 minutes.

PER 6-OZ SERVING: 248 CALORIES, 28.4 G PROTEIN, 12.1 G FAT, 5.2 G CARBOHYDRATE, 440 MG SODIUM, 65 MG CHOLESTEROL.

TOTAL TIME

35 minutes

SERVINGS

2

MENU

Serve on egg noodles, rice, or parsleyed potatoes with your favorite vegetable.

S our cream and dill are happily paired as seasonings for this luscious fish dish. For an attractive garnish, top with thin lemon slices, a sprig of fresh dill, and/or a strip of pimiento.

Excellent

FISH WITH SAFFRON AND GARLIC

Serve with couscous and a vegetable side dish such as Shredded Zucchini (see page 87).

S affron imparts a golden hue and distinctive taste to this richly scented baked fish. Garnish it with a chopped fresh green herb such as chives, mint, or parsley.

¾ pound firm fish fillets

≈

pinch of saffron threads
1 tablespoon boiling water

≈

2 tablespoons butter
3 garlic cloves, minced or pressed
1 tablespoon fresh lemon juice
¼ teaspoon ground fennel
1 tomato, diced
dash of salt and ground black pepper

≈

lemon wedges

Rinse the fish and set aside.

Crumble the saffron threads into a small heatproof bowl, add the tablespoon of boiling water, and set aside.

Prepare the remaining ingredients. Melt the butter in a nonreactive skillet. Add the garlic and sauté for a minute or two, until the garlic is just golden but not brown. Stir in the lemon juice, fennel, tomatoes, and saffron solution. Add the fish fillets, spoon a little of the sauce over the fish, and sprinkle with salt and pepper. Cover the skillet and cook on low heat for 5 to 10 minutes, until the fish flakes easily with a fork.

Serve immediately, garnished with lemon wedges.

PER 6-OZ SERVING: 202 CALORIES, 23.2 G PROTEIN, 10.3 G FAT, 4.1 G CARBOHYDRATE, 408 MG SODIUM, 79 MG CHOLESTEROL.

FISH WITH TOMATO-ORANGE SALSA

4 swordfish or tuna steaks (about 6 ounces each),
  or 1½ pounds firm fish fillets

MARINADE
3 tablespoons orange juice
juice of 1 lemon
1 garlic clove, minced or pressed
1 tablespoon olive oil
dash of Tabasco or other hot pepper sauce, or ⅛ teaspoon
  crushed red pepper flakes

≈

Tomato-Orange Salsa (see page 106)

Rinse the fish and set aside.

Combine all of the marinade ingredients in a shallow nonreactive bowl. Add the fish to the bowl, spoon the marinade over it, and set aside.

Prepare the Tomato-Orange Salsa and set aside.

Broil or grill the fish for about 10 minutes, basting with the marinade several times while cooking. When the fish flakes easily with a fork but is still moist, serve immediately, topped with a generous amount of the salsa.

PER 6-OZ SERVING: 166 CALORIES, 22.8 G PROTEIN, 6.7 G FAT, 2.5 G CARBOHYDRATE, 126 MG SODIUM, 64 MG CHOLESTEROL.

TOTAL TIME
30 minutes

SERVINGS
4

MENU
Serve with Sweet Potato Salad (see page 135) and avocado slices.

This vibrant dish brings to mind the ease and pleasure of the tropics.

GREEK SCAMPI

TOTAL TIME

20 minutes

SERVINGS

2

MENU

Serve the scampi on rice, couscous, or orzo, with steamed broccoli or asparagus.

This Greek version of a classic shrimp dish is especially easy to prepare and is superbly flavored. Decorate each serving with a lemon wedge.

½ **pound shrimp**

≈

2 **garlic cloves, minced or pressed**
2 **tablespoons olive oil**
1 **cup diced tomatoes**
½ **cup crumbled feta cheese**
juice of ½ lemon
2 **teaspoons chopped fresh dill (¾ teaspoon dried)**
dash of salt and ground black pepper

Shell and devein the shrimp, if necessary, rinse them, and set aside. Have all the ingredients prepared and at hand before beginning to sauté.

Sauté the garlic in the oil briefly, then add the shrimp. Cook on medium heat for a minute. Add the tomatoes, feta, lemon juice, and dill. Stir so that the shrimp cook on both sides. When the shrimp are pink and the tomatoes and feta have made a sauce, it's ready. Sprinkle with salt and pepper to taste and serve at once.

PER 6-OZ SERVING: 205 CALORIES, 14.7 G PROTEIN, 14.3 G FAT, 5.1 G CARBOHYDRATE, 531 MG SODIUM, 121 MG CHOLESTEROL.

SPICY CAJUN SHRIMP

1 – 1½ pounds unshelled shrimp

≈

⅓ cup olive oil
⅓ cup butter
1 medium onion, thinly sliced
4 garlic cloves, minced or pressed
1 teaspoon dried thyme
1 teaspoon crumbled dried rosemary
1 teaspoon ground black pepper
½ teaspoon cayenne (or to taste)
2 teaspoons sweet paprika
2 tablespoons Worcestershire Sauce (see page 344)
½ cup dry white wine
2 tablespoons fresh lemon juice

Rinse the shrimp and set aside.

Heat the oil and butter in a large heavy skillet until the butter has melted. Add the onions and garlic and sauté on medium heat for 4 to 5 minutes, until the onions are softened. Stir in the thyme, rosemary, black pepper, cayenne, paprika, and the shrimp, and sauté for another minute or so, stirring to turn the shrimp. Pour in the Worcestershire Sauce, wine, and lemon juice. Simmer for 3 or 4 minutes, until the shrimp are pink and tender, but be careful not to overcook them.

PER 6-OZ SERVING: 374 CALORIES, 21.1 G PROTEIN, 28.4 G FAT, 4.8 G CARBOHYDRATE, 405 MG SODIUM, 221 MG CHOLESTEROL.

TOTAL TIME
20 minutes

SERVINGS
3 or 4

MENU
Serve this in bowls with Caribbean Yellow Rice and Pigeon Peas (see page 154) or crusty bread.

For havin' some fun down on the bayou, try this shrimp dish sparked with cayenne and aromatic herbs.

Traditionally, the shrimp are cooked unpeeled and then shelled at the table. If this seems too messy, shelled shrimp may be used. The sauce is spicy, but you can reduce the amount of cayenne and the sauce will still be fine. And if the shrimp is going to be peeled at the table, don't forget the napkins.

TERIYAKI BROILED OR GRILLED FISH

TOTAL TIME
45 minutes

SERVINGS
6

MENU
Serve with rice and a fresh
spinach salad with Lemon
Sesame Dressing
(see page 98).

Our simple Asian marinade provides a tangy accent for this broiled or grilled fish. If you wish, use the remaining marinade as a condiment for topping the fish and rice: Briefly simmer it and serve it hot at the table.

6 salmon, monkfish, or tuna steaks (about ¼ pound each)

MARINADE
½ cup soy sauce
2 teaspoons grated fresh ginger root
½ cup Chinese cooking wine, rice wine, or dry sherry
1 tablespoon sugar
2 garlic cloves, minced or pressed

Rinse the fish and set it aside.

In a saucepan, bring the soy sauce and grated ginger to a boil. Strain it and discard the ginger. In a bowl, combine the gingered soy sauce, wine, sugar, and minced garlic. Place the fish in a bowl, pour the marinade over it, and let it sit for about 30 minutes in the refrigerator, turning once or twice.

Lift the fish out of the marinade, and broil it on a baking sheet covered with aluminum foil or grill it over medium-hot coals for 5 minutes. Turn the fish over, brush with more marinade, and broil for another 5 minutes, until the flesh is opaque and flakes with a fork.

PER 6-OZ SERVING: 316 CALORIES, 39.6 G PROTEIN, 15.9 G FAT, 0.5 G CARBOHYDRATE, 236 MG SODIUM, 126 MG CHOLESTEROL.

SANDWICHES, FILLED TORTILLAS, AND PIZZAS

The sandwich in its endless permutations stands out as the definitive fast and easy meal. Our broad definition of sandwiches embraces a wide variety of toppings and fillings and an eclectic array of mediums: French, Italian, or pita bread (always use the very best bread you can find), corn or wheat tortillas, and some very easy pizza crusts.

We love it that sandwiches are adaptable, casual, portable, and can even be made right at the table. One of our favorite childhood memories involves being called inside from play to eat lunch, quickly grabbing a sandwich, and returning to our friends within minutes. Not that sandwich-making need be a rushed affair; sandwiches can also be served to friends and family in a relaxed and sociable dining atmosphere.

SANDWICHES

BARBECUED TEMPEH AND PEPPERS

TOTAL TIME
25 minutes

SERVINGS
4

MENU

This is a hearty, high-protein lunch dish that can be served over toast, in a pita with crisp romaine or leaf lettuce, or on split Savory Scallion Biscuits (see page 58). Try Asian Cabbage Slaw (see page 64) as an accompaniment.

Several types of soy and mixed-grain tempehs are available in the markets now, so experiment and discover your own favorites. Tempeh can be stored frozen. To prevent crumbling, we dice it before it's completely thawed; it still heats quickly in a skillet.

2–3 tablespoons vegetable oil
2 medium onions, chopped (about 2 cups)
1 large garlic clove
1 bell pepper (red is nice)
½ pound soy or mixed-grain tempeh (1 package)

SAUCE
1 tablespoon soy sauce
3 tablespoons tomato paste
1 tablespoon molasses or brown sugar
⅔ cup water

≈

1 tablespoon ground coriander
1½ teaspoons ground fennel
1–2 teaspoons Tabasco or other hot pepper sauce
    (or to taste)
salt to taste

≈

4 pita breads
fresh lettuce leaves

Heat 2 tablespoons of the oil in a heavy skillet and sauté the chopped onions for 3 to 4 minutes, until they begin to soften. While the onions sauté, mince the garlic and chop the bell pepper; add them to the onions. Continue to cook another 5 minutes, stirring often. Cube the tempeh, add it to the skillet, and sauté for about 5 minutes, until it begins to brown. If necessary, add a little more oil to prevent sticking. While the tempeh browns, mix together the sauce ingredients in a small bowl and set aside.

Add the coriander and fennel to the tempeh and vegetables, and stir constantly for a minute. Pour on the sauce and simmer for about 5 minutes, until the sauce has thickened. Add Tabasco and salt to taste.

Serve in warmed pita pockets stuffed with crisp lettuce leaves.

PER 8-OZ SERVING: 276 CALORIES, 14.3 G PROTEIN, 11.8 G FAT, 31.6 G CARBOHYDRATE, 424 MG SODIUM, 0 MG CHOLESTEROL.

BROILED TOFU

1 cake tofu (¾ pound)
2 teaspoons vegetable oil
2 tablespoons soy sauce
dash of Tabasco or other hot pepper sauce
3 – 4 drops dark sesame oil

Place the tofu between two plates. Weight the top with a heavy object such as a small cast-iron skillet, heavy can, or large book, and press the tofu for 10 minutes.

Preheat the broiler.

While the tofu is being pressed, stir together the vegetable oil, soy sauce, Tabasco, and sesame oil, and set the marinade aside. Slice the tofu crosswise into thirds and place the square pieces in a flameproof dish. Pour the marinade over the tofu and broil for about 5 minutes on each side, until bubbly, browned, and crisp.

Serve immediately.

PER BURGER: 121 CALORIES, 9.8 G PROTEIN, 8.7 G FAT, 3.1 G CARBOHYDRATE, 635 MG SODIUM, 0 MG CHOLESTEROL.

NOTE: Although this dish is best served right away, it may be refrigerated and then reheated. Broiled Tofu is also good thinly sliced and added to soups or stews.

TOTAL TIME
20 minutes

SERVINGS
3

This could be the simplest tofu burger in the world! It's delicious and satisfying, and might instantly become a family favorite. Many toppings come to mind: mayonnaise, catsup, salsa, mustard, relish, red onion, tahini, sliced avocado, sprouts, tomato slices, and/or crisp greens. Prepare any condiments while the tofu is being pressed.

BRUSCHETTA AND CROSTINI

PREPARATION TIME
5 minutes

TOTAL TIME
20 minutes

SERVINGS
1 or 2 slices per person

*B*ruschetta *(pronounced bruce-ketta), a traditional shepherd's lunch, is a simple and succulent dish — grilled or toasted peasant bread, rubbed with raw garlic and drizzled with olive oil. This is perfect by itself or can easily become the base for Crostini. Crostini ("toast" in Italian) is sliced crisp bread with a savory topping.*

Bruschetta or Crostini are usually served as appetizers. An assortment of Crostini presented as cocktail party canapés looks quite spectacular, and party-goers always love

BRUSCHETTA

firm, crusty, coarse-textured bread (peasant-style, Italian
    bread, or French baguette)
fresh garlic cloves, peeled and cut in half
extra-virgin olive oil
salt and freshly ground black pepper (optional)

Cut the bread into slices ½ to ¾ inch thick. A baguette should be cut on a diagonal to produce long oval shapes. Grill the bread over hot coals or broil it in an oven broiler 4 or 5 inches from the heat, turning it once, until it is golden on both sides. The bread should be crisply toasted on the outside but still soft and chewy on the inside. How long this takes will depend on your oven; in some oven broilers it will take as little as a minute per side. Alternatively, the bread can be toasted in a preheated 400° oven, placed directly on the oven racks or on baking sheets (in which case the bread is turned once), for about 15 minutes.

While the toast is still hot, rub one side of it with the cut side of a garlic clove (about ½ clove per slice). Arrange the toast, garlicked side up, on a platter, and brush or drizzle with oil. Sprinkle with salt and pepper, if desired.

Serve immediately.

PER PIECE, APPROXIMATELY: 125 CALORIES, 3 G PROTEIN, 5 G FAT, 17 G CARBOHYDRATE, 750 MG SODIUM, 0 MG CHOLESTEROL.

BRUSCHETTA WITH TOMATO: Top the oiled toast with finely chopped fresh tomatoes (about ½ medium tomato per slice), or rub a cut tomato against the rough surface of the toast after rubbing with garlic. Then drizzle with oil and sprinkle with salt and pepper.

BRUSCHETTA WITH HERBS: Use one of the mixtures given here or mix herbs to your taste. Sprinkle fresh herbs over the oiled toast. Soak dried herbs in oil and then brush on the bread.

Fresh Herb Mix

1 tablespoon minced fresh parsley

1 tablespoon minced fresh basil

1 teaspoon fresh oregano or marjoram leaves

Dried Herb Mix

1 teaspoon dried thyme

1 teaspoon dried basil

½ teaspoon dried whole rosemary, crushed

freshly ground black pepper to taste

CROSTINI

Use one or several of these toppings on grilled or toasted bread cut ½ inch thick or on Bruschetta.

- Avocado mashed with lemon juice and salt
- Beans and Greens (see page 120) spread on toast, or the greens alone as a topping for Bruschetta
- Black Bean Dip (see page 46) alone or with sliced tomatoes or sliced avocado
- Cheese (Gruyère, mozzarella, Parmesan, Gorgonzola) melted under the broiler
- Olivada (see page 49) alone or with strips of roasted red pepper, tomato slices, or slices of fresh mozzarella
- Peperonata (see page 83)
- Pesto (see pages 362–63) with tomato slices and/or cheese
- Salsa Verde (see page 105) with fresh mozzarella
- Onion slices sautéed in oil
- Ricotta cheese (or a soft goat cheese) spread over Bruschetta with Herbs
- Roasted red peppers cut into strips or blended into a paste

cont. on next page

them. However, they aren't particularly well suited for stand-up eating; you'll probably be more comfortable eating Crostini while seated at the table. In fact, for the messier varieties, you may want both elbows on the table. To our way of thinking, many Crostini can be the centerpiece of a meal. A few Crostini, a jug of wine, and thou . . .

As always with a dish this straightforward, the quality of the ingredients makes all the difference. The oil should be a fruity extra-virgin olive oil. The best bread is a firm, coarse-textured peasant-style bread, but a thin Italian loaf or a French baguette will do. Your enjoyment of Bruschetta and Crostini will begin with the enticing fragrance of the freshly crisped bread (especially if it was grilled over the embers of a smoky wood fire), followed by the aroma of the garlic and the good green oil rubbed against the bread's hot rough surface.

The best and most glamorous method of cooking the bread is outdoors in the summer on a grill, right next to the grilled vegetables, but a few of us romantics have also improvised grills in the indoor fireplace during winter. Serve 1 or 2 slices per person as an appetizer; each slice requires ½ clove of garlic and 1 or 2 teaspoons of oil.

All of these toppings (except broiled melted cheese) can be made ahead of time and kept refrigerated, but they are best served at room temperature or briefly warmed under the broiler. However, Crostini should not be assembled very long before serving time. If last-minute preparation, spreading, and arranging is not convenient, simply serve the topping in a bowl surrounded by the crisp bread and let everyone put together their own Crostini. The bread can be crisped in quantity hours ahead, but be sure to allow it to cool completely before storing, so that it does not steam and soften.

For toppings that already contain sufficient garlic and oil, such as Olivada or Pesto, use plain grilled or toasted bread rather than Bruschetta as a base.

GREEK PITA

FILLING

5 artichoke hearts, cut into quarters (14-ounce can)

¼ cup roasted red peppers, drained and chopped (about
       3 ounces), or ½ cup chopped red bell pepper

2 celery stalks, chopped

1 medium tomato, chopped

1 garlic clove, minced or pressed

2 tablespoons olive oil

juice of ½ lemon

1 tablespoon chopped fresh dill (1 teaspoon dried)

2 tablespoons chopped fresh parsley

⅔ cup grated or crumbled feta cheese (about 5 ounces)

salt and ground black pepper to taste

1 – 2 tablespoons capers (optional), rinsed and drained

¾ cup pitted Calamata olives, sliced (optional)

≈

pita bread

romaine or leaf lettuce

Prepare all of the filling ingredients.

In a large bowl mix together the filling ingredients. Cut the pita breads in half and lightly toast them in a toaster oven. Fill each half with a lettuce leaf and about ½ cup of filling. Serve immediately, while the pita is still warm and soft.

PER 6-OZ SERVING OF FILLING: 178 CALORIES, 6.4 G PROTEIN, 9.2 G FAT, 19.8 G CARBOHYDRATE, 304 MG SODIUM, 14 MG CHOLESTEROL.

TOTAL TIME
15 minutes

SERVINGS
4 to 6

MENU
Serve with Broccoli Egg-Lemon Soup (see page 24) or North African Cauliflower Soup (see page 33) for lunch.

A lways a popular sandwich at Moosewood.

PAN BAGNAT

PREPARATION
TIME

15 minutes

TOTAL TIME

1 hour and 15 minutes

SERVINGS

4

*P*an Bagnat
(literally "bathed
bread" in
French) is great for
picnics or casual
suppers—it's like a
portable Salade Niçoise.
Here the sandwich is
pressed under a weight,
so that the inside of the
bread becomes
saturated with the
pungent, briny flavors
of the ingredients. If
you're going to take it
on a picnic, travel to
the park with the Pan
Bagnat in the trunk
under *the cooler.*

1 baguette or other long thin loaf of French bread
1 garlic clove, pressed
¼ cup olive oil
1 tomato, thinly sliced
1 cucumber, thinly sliced
½ red or Vidalia onion, thinly sliced
½ cup pitted and sliced Calamata or other ripe black olives
salt and ground black pepper to taste

OPTIONAL INGREDIENTS
4 ounces sliced mild provolone or other cheese
2 hard-boiled eggs, sliced
1 green or red bell pepper, thinly sliced
¼ cup capers, rinsed and drained
½ cup roasted red peppers, chopped or cut into strips
anchovies to taste
1 cup artichoke hearts, sliced into quarters
½ cup Pesto (see pages 362–63)
herbs, such as basil, marjoram, thyme, oregano

Slice the bread in half lengthwise, nearly all the way through.
Open the loaf and spread the garlic on one of the cut sides. Drizzle
the olive oil on both sides. Layer the tomato, cucumber, onion, olives,
and any optional ingredients on one half of the bread. Sprinkle with
salt and pepper to taste. Close the loaf and wrap it tightly with plastic
wrap or aluminum foil. Weight the full length of the Pan Bagnat with
a heavy book (or with a baking tray topped with bricks, a 25-pound
weight, a toddler, or whatever you can find) for 1 to 3 hours.

Slice and serve.

PER 7-OZ SERVING OF FILLING, NOT INCLUDING OPTIONAL INGREDIENTS: 278 CALORIES, 5 G PROTEIN,
11 G FAT, 30.2 G CARBOHYDRATE, 646 MG SODIUM, 1 MG CHOLESTEROL.

PISSALADIÈRE ON FRENCH BREAD

3 medium onions, thinly sliced (about 3 cups)
2 tablespoons olive oil
1 baguette
1 teaspoon fresh thyme (½ teaspoon dried)
generous amount of freshly ground black pepper
dash of salt
2 tablespoons brandy (optional)

≈

¼ cup Greek or Niçoise olives
1 cup freshly grated Romano or Parmesan cheese
2 tomatoes, thinly sliced
1 tin anchovies or sardines, rinsed and drained
    (about ¼ pound) (optional)

TOTAL TIME
25 minutes

SERVINGS
3

MENU
Serve with a green salad
or marinated vegetables
and a light soup, such as
Herbed Green Pea Soup
(see page 29).

This makes a satisfying meal that is fun to assemble at the table. The sweetness of the onions provides a counterpoint to the briny taste of the olives.

Preheat the oven to 300°.

Sauté the onions in the olive oil on medium-low heat for about 15 to 20 minutes, until the onions begin to brown. When the oven is warm, heat the baguette for about 10 minutes, until it is crusty on the outside. Add the thyme, pepper, salt, and optional brandy to the onions and sauté for another minute or so. Remove from the heat.

Crush the olives, using the flat side of a large knife and applying pressure with the palm of your free hand. Remove the pits and chop the olives coarsely.

To serve, slice the warm baguette in half lengthwise and then crosswise into thirds. Place a portion of bread on each plate and top it with cheese, the warm sautéed onion, olives, tomatoes, and anchovies or sardines if you like.

PER 6-OZ SERVING OF FILLING: 680 CALORIES, 29 G PROTEIN, 32.6 G FAT, 69.6 G CARBOHYDRATE, 2,054 MG SODIUM, 36 MG CHOLESTEROL.

FILLED TORTILLAS

SIMPLE QUESADILLAS

COOKING TIME
6 minutes

SERVINGS
2 quesadillas per person

Width a crisp wheat or corn tortilla shell and a melting interior, quesadillas are like a Mexican grilled cheese sandwich. Traditional quesadillas are unbaked tortillas or specially prepared dough wrapped around a filling and fried in oil or lard. Here we give you our simple method for preparing quick quesadillas. The filling can be whatever combination of ingredients you think will taste good or have on hand. We don't limit ourselves to ingredients that are traditionally Mexican. Many

8- or 10-inch wheat or corn tortillas
grated cheese (Monterey Jack, Muenster, cheddar, feta, Jarlsberg, Swiss, smoked cheeses)

CHOOSE ANY OF THE FOLLOWING:
chopped olives (black or green)
chopped scallions, red onions, or sweet Spanish onions
finely chopped red or green bell peppers
sliced roasted red peppers or pimientos
thinly sliced chiles (fresh or canned)
avocado slices or guacamole
sliced hard-boiled eggs
fresh herbs (such as cilantro, dill, chives, basil, oregano, or sage)
refried beans
salsa
leftovers (such as spicy beans, vegetables, or mashed potatoes)

Before beginning to assemble the quesadillas, have all of the filling ingredients of your choice prepared and at hand. Lightly oil a heavy skillet (see notes). Warm the skillet on medium heat. Sprinkle or spread the filling ingredients on one half of each tortilla, leaving a ½-inch border along the edge. Don't pile it on too thick or the filling will ooze into the skillet; about ½ inch deep is good. Fold the plain half of the tortilla over the filling (see note below). Place the quesadillas (as many as you're cooking or as many as will fit) in the heated skillet and cook each side for 2 or 3 minutes, until the cheese is melted and the filling is hot. Add more oil to the skillet if necessary, and cook the remaining quesadillas.

PER QUESADILLA: 286 CALORIES, 13 G PROTEIN, 14.7 G FAT, 26.5 G CARBOHYDRATE, 666 MG SODIUM, 40 MG CHOLESTEROL.

NOTES

- If you have two large skillets, you can reduce the total cooking time by heating several quesadillas at once.
- A heavy cast-iron skillet will not need repeated oiling. In fact, it is possible to cook the quesadillas without using any oil, but the result will be a less crisp tortilla.
- If the tortilla cracks when you fold it over the filling, briefly heat each tortilla in the warm skillet, to make it more pliable, before topping it with the filling.
- If you cook the quesadillas in batches, keep the first ones warm in a low oven while you cook the remaining batches.

quesadillas are especially good topped with salsa and/or sour cream.

Make-your-own quesadillas are great for an informal gathering of friends or family. Leftover Easy Refritos (see page 79), Borani (see page 47), and Black Bean Dip (see page 46) can be used as fillings for quesadillas for a quickly prepared lunch.

CHILE AND BELL PEPPER QUESADILLAS

FILLING
PREPARATION TIME
12 minutes

SERVINGS
2

MENU
Throw the quesadillas together while you reheat some Spanish Potato Onion Soup (see page 40) or Mexican Tomato Lime Soup (see page 30). Or serve Chile and Bell Pepper Quesadillas with Mexican Seitan (see page 80) and a salad of shredded jicama. Sip a soothing cup of hot chocolate for dessert.

This sweet and spicy quesadilla can really spark up a simple meal and takes only a moment's work.

2 tablespoons vegetable oil
1 fresh chile (about 2 inches long), minced
2 cups diced bell peppers (a mixture of green, red, and/or yellow is nice)
¼ cup chopped fresh basil, or 2 tablespoons each chopped fresh parsley and cilantro
8 cherry tomatoes, cut in half, or 1 large tomato, sliced
1 cup grated sharp cheddar cheese

≈

4 tortillas (8- or 10-inch)

Heat the oil in a skillet and add the minced chile and diced peppers. Sauté for 5 minutes on medium-high heat, stirring often. When the peppers are tender-crisp, remove them from the heat. Spread one-fourth of the sautéed pepper mixture, 1 tablespoon of the chopped herbs, 4 cherry tomato halves or 2 tomato slices, and ¼ cup of the grated cheese on each tortilla. Cook the filled tortillas by following the procedure for Simple Quesadillas (see page 268).

PER QUESADILLA: 334 CALORIES, 12.3 G PROTEIN, 19 G FAT, 32.4 G CARBOHYDRATE, 233 MG SODIUM, 30 MG CHOLESTEROL.

Spicy Corn Quesadillas

2 tablespoons vegetable oil
1 medium onion, chopped (about 1 cup)
2 garlic cloves, minced or pressed
1 medium carrot, grated (about ½ cup)
1 fresh chile, minced (seeded for a milder "hot"),
    or ⅛ teaspoon cayenne or to taste *
3 cups fresh, frozen, or canned cut corn
2 teaspoons ground cumin
1 teaspoon ground coriander
1–2 teaspoons chopped fresh cilantro (optional)
salt and ground black pepper to taste
1½ cups grated Monterey Jack or cheddar cheese, or
    cubed cream cheese

≈

8 tortillas (8- to 10-inch)

If topping with salsa, a less spicy filling may be desirable.

FILLING
PREPARATION TIME
20 minutes

SERVINGS
4

MENU

Not just a snack, this quesadilla is a substantial meal needing only some shredded lettuce and avocado to complement it.

Heat the oil in a skillet and add the onion and garlic. Sauté on medium heat for about 5 minutes, until the onions begin to soften. Stir in the grated carrot and sauté for 2 more minutes. Add the chile or cayenne, corn, cumin, coriander, and optional cilantro and cook, covered, for 3 or 4 minutes, stirring often. Add salt and pepper to taste and remove from the heat. Stir the cheese into the hot vegetables. Cover and let stand for a few minutes, until the cheese partially melts. Spread one-eighth of the filling on each tortilla. Cook the filled tortillas by following the procedure for Simple Quesadillas (see page 268).

PER QUESADILLA: 565 CALORIES, 19.9 G PROTEIN, 26.5 G FAT, 67.3 G CARBOHYDRATE, 435 MG SODIUM, 45 MG CHOLESTEROL.

SWEET POTATO QUESADILLAS

FILLING
PREPARATION TIME
20–25 minutes

SERVINGS
4

MENU
When served with a green
salad, these make a
delectable meal.

*S*weet potato
quesadillas are
colorful as well as
tasty and unusual.

1½ cups finely chopped onion
2 garlic cloves, minced or pressed
3 tablespoons vegetable oil
4 cups grated peeled sweet potato (about 3 potatoes)
½ teaspoon dried oregano
1 teaspoon chili powder
2 teaspoons ground cumin
generous pinch of cayenne
salt and ground black pepper to taste
1 cup grated sharp cheddar cheese

≈

8 tortillas (8- to 10-inch)
commercial Mexican-style tomato salsa
sour cream

Sauté the onions and garlic in the vegetable oil until the onions are translucent. Add the grated sweet potatoes, oregano, chili powder, cumin, and cayenne and cook, covered, for about 10 minutes, stirring frequently to prevent sticking. When the sweet potato is tender, add salt and pepper to taste and remove the filling from the heat. Spread one-eighth of the filling and 2 tablespoons of the cheese on each tortilla. Cook the filled tortillas by following the procedure for Simple Quesadillas (see page 268).

Serve immediately, topped with salsa and sour cream.

PER QUESADILLA: 486 CALORIES, 12.8 G PROTEIN, 19.5 G FAT, 66.7 G CARBOHYDRATE, 275 MG SODIUM, 24 MG CHOLESTEROL.

TOFU BURRITOS

3 tablespoons vegetable oil
3 garlic cloves, minced or pressed
1 fresh chile, minced, or ¼–½ teaspoon cayenne
2 medium onions, finely chopped (about 2 cups)
1 red or green bell pepper, diced
2 teaspoons paprika
1 tablespoon ground cumin
1 teaspoon ground coriander
1 teaspoon dried oregano
½ cup fresh or frozen cut corn
2 cakes firm tofu (about 1½ pounds), crumbled or mashed
¼ cup tomato paste
2 tablespoons soy sauce
¼ cup chopped green olives (optional)
salt and ground black pepper to taste
≈
6 wheat tortillas (10-inch)
≈
your favorite salsa (optional)

PREPARATION TIME
30 minutes

TOTAL TIME
50 minutes

SERVINGS
4 to 6

These are well-seasoned burritos with a low-fat, high-protein filling. This appetizing tofu dish can also be made without the tortillas and served on rice, or combined with cooked seasoned beans to make a rich chili. Covered in the refrigerator, this filling will keep for 2 to 3 days.

Heat the oil in a large skillet and sauté the garlic, chile or cayenne, and onions for a minute or two. Stir in the bell peppers and continue to sauté on medium heat. When the onions begin to soften, add the paprika, cumin, coriander, oregano, corn, and crumbled tofu and continue to sauté.

Preheat the oven to 350°.

When the vegetables are tender, mix in the tomato paste, soy sauce, and the olives if you wish. Add salt and pepper to taste.

Lightly oil a baking pan or shallow casserole dish. Fill each tortilla with about ¾ cup of the tofu-vegetable filling and roll it up. Place the burritos in the oiled pan, cover tightly with aluminum foil, and bake for 20 minutes. Serve topped with salsa, if desired.

PER BURRITO: 338 CALORIES, 15.9 G PROTEIN, 17.8 G FAT, 32.9 G CARBOHYDRATE, 578 MG SODIUM, 0 MG CHOLESTEROL.

PIZZAS

PIZZA CRUSTS

Pizzas can be made with any number of tasty savory toppings, and several sorts of bread can serve as pizza crusts. On the pages following are recipes for six of our favorite pizzas. Other recipes in this book that gladly do double duty as pizza toppings are Pestos (see pages 362–63), Pasta with Greens and Ricotta (see page 188), Peperonata (see page 83), Mexican Seitan (see page 80), and Borani (see page 47).

PITA BREAD

BAKING TIME

15 minutes

Halved pita bread makes a thin pizza crust for a light meal, snack, or appetizer. We prefer the flavor and texture of whole wheat pita.

Preheat the oven to 450°.
Prepare the topping and set it aside.
Lightly toast the whole pita bread in a toaster oven or bake it in a conventional oven at 450° for 3 minutes. Remove the pita from the oven, and carefully slice it in half around its outer edge to yield two equal rounds. Spread on the topping and bake at 450° for about 10 minutes, until the cheese is bubbling and the topping is hot.

WHOLE WHEAT TORTILLAS

BROILING TIME

2 minutes

Tortillas make crisp, thin crusts for pizzas that can be quickly prepared. For tortilla crusts, choose a thick topping that is not too juicy.

Preheat the broiler.
Prepare the topping and set it aside.
Place the plain tortillas on an unoiled baking sheet and broil for a few seconds about 3 or 4 inches from the heat, until several brown spots develop. Flip the tortillas over and quickly brown the other side. Remove the tortillas from the broiler and spread on the topping. Broil the tortilla pizzas for about a minute, until the cheese is just melted and hot.

French Bread

Preheat the oven to 450°.

Prepare the topping and set it aside.

Cut the loaves of bread in half lengthwise. Spread on the topping and bake for 10 to 15 minutes, until the cheese is bubbling and the bread is crusty.

BAKING TIME

15 minutes

Traditional, sourdough, or whole wheat French bread makes a chewy, substantial crust. Juicy savory toppings soak luxuriously into the thick layer of bread.

Prebaked Pizza Shells

Preheat the oven to 450°.

Prepare the topping and set it aside. If using a frozen crust, allow it to thaw to room temperature while preparing the topping.

Place the crust on an unoiled baking sheet. (Using a pizza pan or screen, or a baking stone, rather than a simple baking sheet will produce a more evenly baked crust.) Spread on the topping and bake for 10 to 15 minutes, until the cheese is bubbling and the crust is crisp.

BAKING TIME

15 minutes

Seasoned prebaked pizza shells are instantly ready to be topped and baked. We have tried Boboli, Platina, and Pitza brands, which all have ample crusts that readily absorb sauces, juices, and herb seasonings. Pitza brand has the advantage of using no preservatives, containing whole-grain ingredients, and being available refrigerated or frozen; it's found at natural food stores.

FETA SPINACH PIZZA

TOPPING
PREPARATION TIME

15 minutes

SERVINGS

2 or 3 as a main dish,
4 to 8 as an appetizer

One of our most popular dishes at the restaurant is spanakopita, a spinach-cheese filo pastry. This pizza recipe is an easier-to-make rendition with the same flavors.

CHOOSE A PIZZA CRUST (SEE PAGE 274)
6 pita bread halves (6-inch size)
1 loaf French bread (16–20 inches long)
1 prebaked pizza shell (15-inch size)

TOPPING
10 ounces fresh spinach, rinsed, stemmed, and coarsely
    chopped
1 tablespoon olive oil
½ cup chopped scallions
1 tablespoon chopped fresh dill (1 teaspoon dried)
1 cup crumbled or grated feta cheese
1 cup ricotta cheese
dash of ground black pepper
2 tomatoes, thinly sliced, or 6 cherry tomatoes, cut in half
    (optional)

Preheat the oven according to the directions for the pizza crust you are using (see page 274).

Sauté the spinach in the oil on high heat for several minutes until just wilted. Drain the cooked spinach in a colander or sieve, and press out any excess moisture with the back of a large serving spoon. In a large bowl, combine the spinach, scallions, dill, feta, and ricotta. Add a dash of pepper.

Spread the feta-spinach topping on the pizza crust, and top with the sliced tomatoes. Bake following the instructions given for the crust you are using.

PER SERVING, USING 1/6 LOAF FRENCH BREAD: 288 CALORIES, 12.7 G PROTEIN, 12.8 G FAT, 30.9 G CARBOHYDRATE, 545 MG SODIUM, 37 MG CHOLESTEROL.

GARLIC AND GREENS PIZZA

CHOOSE A PIZZA CRUST (SEE PAGE 274)

6 pita bread halves (6-inch size)
3 whole wheat tortillas (10-inch size)
1 loaf French bread (16–20 inches long)
1 prebaked pizza shell (15-inch size)

TOPPING

⅓ cup sun-dried tomatoes (not packed in oil) (optional)
½ cup boiling water (optional)
≈
4 large garlic cloves, minced or pressed
3 tablespoons olive oil
4 packed cups coarsely chopped rinsed and stemmed kale
¼ teaspoon salt
¼ cup chopped fresh basil (2 tablespoons dried)
1½ cups grated mozzarella cheese
¼ cup grated Pecorino cheese

TOPPING
PREPARATION TIME
20 minutes

SERVINGS
2 or 3 as a main dish,
4 to 8 as an appetizer

A very tasty pizza recipe that will have kids "eating their greens" with no coaxing necessary.

Preheat the oven according to the directions for the pizza crust you are using (see page 274).

If you are using the sun-dried tomatoes, place them in a heatproof bowl, cover with the boiling water, and set aside.

In a large skillet, sauté the minced garlic in the oil for about a minute. Add the kale to the skillet along with the salt, and sauté on medium-high heat for 5 to 10 minutes, stirring frequently, until just tender. The cooking time will vary with the age and freshness of the kale. While the kale cooks, drain and chop the optional sun-dried tomatoes. Add the chopped basil and sun-dried tomatoes to the kale and remove the skillet from the heat.

Spread the kale topping on the pizza crust using a slotted spoon, and sprinkle the cheeses on top. Bake following the instructions given for the crust you are using.

PER SERVING, USING 1/6 LOAF FRENCH BREAD: 358 CALORIES, 17.4 G PROTEIN, 15.9 G FAT, 37 G
CARBOHYDRATE, 653 MG SODIUM, 24 MG CHOLESTEROL.

HERBED CHÈVRE AND TOMATO PIZZA

TOPPING
PREPARATION TIME
10 minutes

SERVINGS
**2 or 3 as a main dish,
4 to 8 as an appetizer**

This au courant topping, without the tomatoes, could double as a spread for crackers or crusty bread; or you could toss it with pasta for a quick meal.

CHOOSE A PIZZA CRUST (SEE PAGE 274)
6 pita bread halves (6-inch size)
1 loaf French bread (16–20 inches long)
1 prebaked pizza shell (15-inch size)

TOPPING
8 ounces chèvre
1½ cups ricotta cheese
**2 tablespoons chopped fresh basil or tarragon, or a
   combination (2 teaspoons dried)**
2 tablespoons chopped fresh parsley
2–3 garlic cloves, minced or pressed
½ cup chopped black olives (optional)
2 tomatoes, thinly sliced
freshly ground black pepper to taste

Preheat the oven according to the directions for the pizza crust you are using (see page 274).

In a large bowl, combine the chèvre, ricotta, basil and/or tarragon, parsley, garlic, and optional olives.

Spread the herbed cheese topping on the pizza crust and top with the sliced tomatoes and black pepper. Bake following the instructions given for the crust you are using.

PER SERVING, USING ⅙ LOAF FRENCH BREAD: 348 CALORIES, 16.6 G PROTEIN, 17 G FAT, 32.4 G CARBOHYDRATE, 748 MG SODIUM, 64 MG CHOLESTEROL.

ITALIAN-STYLE TOFU PIZZA

CHOOSE A PIZZA CRUST (SEE PAGE 274)

6 pita bread halves (6-inch size)
1 loaf French bread (16–20 inches long)
1 prebaked pizza shell (15-inch size)

TOPPING
1½ cakes firm tofu (18 ounces)
2 tablespoons olive oil
2 teaspoons ground fennel
2 garlic cloves, minced or pressed
¼–½ teaspoon cayenne
1½ tablespoons soy sauce
1 tablespoon tomato paste
1 tablespoon chopped fresh oregano (1 teaspoon dried)
2 cups prepared tomato sauce
salt and ground black pepper to taste

TOPPING
PREPARATION TIME
15 minutes

SERVINGS
2 or 3 as a main dish,
4 to 8 as an appetizer

A high-protein dairy-free pizza topping. If you like, top it with some grated soy cheese or other cheeses.

Preheat the oven according to the directions for the pizza crust you are using (see page 274).

Grate the tofu by hand or in a food processor, or chop it into small pea-sized pieces. Heat the oil in a large skillet and sauté the grated tofu, fennel, garlic, and cayenne for 2 to 3 minutes. Stir in the soy sauce, tomato paste, and oregano and continue to sauté for another minute. Add the tomato sauce, remove from the heat, and add salt and pepper to taste.

Spread the tofu topping on the pizza crust. Bake following the instructions given for the crust you are using.

VARIATIONS

• Substitute Seasoned Tempeh (see page 85) for the tofu.
• For a topping with firmer texture, use frozen tofu that has been thawed, squeezed of its excess water, and grated.

PER SERVING, USING ⅙ LOAF FRENCH BREAD: 392 CALORIES, 19.9 G PROTEIN, 19.9 G FAT, 36 G CARBOHYDRATE, 1,256 MG SODIUM, 31 MG CHOLESTEROL.

MUSHROOM AND SMOKED-CHEESE PIZZA

TOPPING
PREPARATION TIME
20 minutes

SERVINGS
**2 or 3 as a main dish,
4 to 8 as an appetizer**

*R*ich, flavorful,
and hearty, this
pizza will bring
warmth to a chilly fall
or winter evening.

CHOOSE A PIZZA CRUST (SEE PAGE 274)

6 pita bread halves (6-inch size)
3 whole wheat tortillas (10-inch size)
1 loaf French bread (16–20 inches long)
1 prebaked pizza shell (15-inch size)

TOPPING

1 pound mushrooms, rinsed and sliced
1 tablespoon vegetable oil
dash of salt and ground black pepper
1 tablespoon chopped fresh sage or dill (1 teaspoon dried)
1 teaspoon Dijon mustard
1 cup grated smoked cheese, such as cheddar, Provolone,
     or Swiss
1 cup grated mild cheese, such as Muenster or mozzarella
½ cup chopped scallions

Preheat the oven according to the directions for the pizza crust you are using (see page 274).

In a heavy skillet, sauté the mushrooms in the oil on high heat, stirring often, until they begin to release their juice. Add the salt and pepper, sage or dill, and mustard, and continue to cook until the excess juice has evaporated. Remove from the heat. Stir the cheeses and scallions into the mushroom mixture.

Spread the topping on the pizza crust. Bake following the instructions given for the crust you are using.

PER SERVING, USING ⅙ LOAF FRENCH BREAD: 270 CALORIES, 14.6 G PROTEIN, 13.4 G FAT, 23.5 G CARBOHYDRATE, 450 MG SODIUM, 33 MG CHOLESTEROL.

Zucchini Fontina Pizza

CHOOSE A PIZZA CRUST (SEE PAGE 274)

6 pita bread halves (6-inch size)
3 whole wheat tortillas (10-inch size)
1 loaf French bread (16 – 20 inches long)
1 prebaked pizza shell (15-inch size)

TOPPING

2 tablespoons olive oil
1 cup finely chopped onions
1 tablespoon chopped fresh thyme (1 teaspoon dried)
2 cups grated zucchini (about 1 medium)
¼ teaspoon salt
1 large tomato, diced
1¾ cups grated Fontina cheese

TOPPING
PREPARATION TIME
15 minutes
SERVINGS
2 or 3 as a main dish,
4 to 8 as an appetizer

Onions and thyme have a wonderful affinity; here they combine with zucchini for a delicately aromatic pizza.

Preheat the oven according to the directions for the pizza crust you are using (see page 274).

In a large skillet, heat the oil and sauté the onions and thyme on medium heat for about 5 minutes, until the onions soften. Add the zucchini and stir in the salt. Continue to cook for 2 minutes. Increase the heat and add the tomatoes, stirring for another 1 to 2 minutes. Remove from the heat.

Spread the zucchini mixture on the pizza crust and sprinkle the cheese on top. Bake following the instructions given for the crust you are using.

PER SERVING, USING ⅙ LOAF FRENCH BREAD: 259 CALORIES, 8.8 G PROTEIN, 11.2 G FAT, 31.1 G CARBOHYDRATE, 476 MG SODIUM, 17 MG CHOLESTEROL.

EGGS AND PANCAKES

MOST OF US don't make time for eggs or pancakes at weekday breakfasts, but for a special weekend brunch or an easy supper at home, we find them quite welcome — pancakes provide an especially homey and soothing evening meal. Egg dishes are an essential part of a vegetarian cook's repertoire. Eggs are nutritious, economical, and amazingly adaptable both to the occasion and to the sundry ingredients in the pantry. They are also a convenient choice for a solitary diner.

In this chapter eggs are combined with grains, vegetables, and cheeses for simple, quick, and hearty one-dish entrées. The most common dishes of this type are omelets and frittatas. Omelets, cooked eggs folded around a filling, can be topped with almost any kind of sauce, salsa, or vegetable relish. In frittatas the eggs hold the filling together. Beaten eggs are poured over cheese and/or cooked vegetables and grains and then cooked on top of the stove or in the oven.

The choice of fillings and toppings is endless. Leftovers from many recipes in this book are deliciously suitable for omelets and frittatas. Try Peperonata, Salsa Verde, Pesto, Borani, sautées, tortilla fillings, or toppings for pasta and pizza. Use leftover potatoes, roasted vegetables, pilafs, and risottos. Try cubes of leftover Polenta or Cheese Grits. Sun-ripened tomatoes, fresh herbs, and smoked fish are other possibilities. Stir a beaten egg into leftover pasta and fry it up as a pasta frittata. Any vegetables in your refrigerator that are going nowhere special can be quickly and easily sautéed and elegantly incorporated into an omelet or frittata.

Eggs provide protein, iron, and the essential vitamins A, D, and B_{12}, but they have a high cholesterol content in the yolk. The American Heart Association recommends a maximum of 4 whole eggs per week per person, but allows unlimited egg whites. This allowance gives most people plenty of freedom to indulge in at least occasional egg dishes. If you are on a cholesterol-restricted diet you may wish to decrease the number of yolks used, adding more whites, or to replace whole eggs with egg whites alone; substitute 2 egg whites for each whole egg called for in a recipe. There are also several good cholesterol-free egg substitutes on the market (but check the labels for fat content). You can't make a fried egg with these, of course, but they are fine for omelets, frittatas, or pancakes.

ASPARAGUS WITH FRIED EGGS AND CHEESE

1 pound fresh asparagus

≈

½ tablespoon butter
½ tablespoon olive oil
4 large eggs *
salt and freshly ground black pepper to taste
¼ – ½ cup grated Parmesan or Pecorino cheese

Depending on your appetite and your cholesterol-consciousness, you may wish to use only 1 egg per serving.

In a wide pot, bring several inches of water to a boil. While the water heats, snap off the fibrous tough ends of the asparagus spears. Cook the asparagus in the boiling water for 5 to 8 minutes, until just tender.

While the asparagus cook, heat the butter and olive oil in a heavy skillet. Crack the eggs into the skillet. Cover and cook until the whites are firm and crisp around the edges and the yolks are partially cooked but not hard-set. Arrange the hot asparagus on warmed serving plates, top with the fried eggs, and sprinkle with salt, pepper, and grated cheese. Serve immediately.

PER SERVING: 169 CALORIES, 12.4 G PROTEIN, 11.3 G FAT, 5.6 G CARBOHYDRATE, 275 MG SODIUM, 222 MG CHOLESTEROL.

TOTAL TIME
15 minutes

SERVINGS
2

MENU
Serve with Lemon Tomato Salad (see page 70) or after Herbed Green Pea Soup (see page 29).

This is a classic Italian dish and perfect for a spontaneous celebration of the first asparagus that appear in your garden or market in the spring. The eggs and finely grated cheese combine deliciously with the asparagus, almost like a sauce.

CHAKCHOUKA

TOTAL TIME
20 minutes

SERVINGS
2

MENU

A sliced cucumber salad with Roasted Garlic Dressing (see page 99) or Easiest Artichokes (see page 77) would be enticing accompaniments. Or serve Chakchouka with warm pita bread and top with feta cheese.

Chakchouka is a spicy dish of eggs poached in juicy sautéed bell peppers and tomatoes. Traditionally it is fiery in flavoring, but adjust the cayenne or hot pepper sauce to your taste.

2 tablespoons olive oil
1 cup chopped onions
2 red bell peppers (or 1 red and 1 green pepper)
2 or 3 garlic cloves
1 teaspoon ground cumin
½ teaspoon ground coriander
pinch of cayenne, or dash of Tabasco or other hot pepper
    sauce
2 cups undrained canned peeled tomatoes (16-ounce can)
salt and ground black pepper to taste
4 large eggs

In a large skillet, heat the olive oil and sauté the onions for about 5 minutes. While the onions sauté, slice the bell peppers into strips and mince the garlic. Add the peppers and garlic to the skillet and stir in the cumin, coriander, and cayenne or Tabasco. Continue to sauté for 5 minutes more, until the peppers begin to soften. While the vegetables and spices cook, drain the tomatoes, reserving the juice. Chop the tomatoes and stir them in with about ½ cup of the reserved juice. Add salt and pepper to taste.

When the vegetables are hot and simmering, make four evenly spaced indentations in them and carefully crack one egg into each hollow. Lower the heat, cover the skillet, and gently cook for several minutes until the whites are set and the yolks are soft-cooked.

Serve in shallow bowls.

PER SERVING: 105 CALORIES, 4.5 G PROTEIN, 6.5 G FAT, 8 G CARBOHYDRATE, 130 MG SODIUM, 106 MG CHOLESTEROL.

Chèvre and Red Peppers Omelet

TIME-SAVING TIP: About ½ cup of pimientos or roasted red peppers can be substituted for the sautéed red pepper.

1 – 1½ tablespoons butter
1 small red bell pepper, sliced
4 large eggs
1 tablespoon water
2 – 3 ounces chèvre
salt and ground black pepper to taste

Heat 1 tablespoon of the butter in a large skillet and sauté the sliced bell pepper for 3 to 4 minutes, until tender and warm. Remove from the skillet and set aside.

If the skillet is dry, add another ½ tablespoon of butter. In a small bowl, beat together the eggs and water with a fork and pour the mixture into the skillet. When the eggs begin to set, spread the sautéed peppers over half of the omelet and drop the chèvre by teaspoonfuls on top of the peppers. With a spatula, fold the plain half of the omelet over the peppers and chèvre, and cook for about 2 more minutes, while the cheese melts.

Cut the omelet into two pieces and serve immediately.

PER SERVING: 315 CALORIES, 15.1 G PROTEIN, 26.3 G FAT, 4.4 G CARBOHYDRATE, 355 MG SODIUM, 470 MG CHOLESTEROL.

TOTAL TIME
20 minutes

SERVINGS
2

MENU
Chèvre and Red Pepper Omelet might be accompanied by Sugar Snaps in Lemon Butter (see page 90), Dilly Beans (see page 66), or Easy Elegant Asparagus (see page 78).

This gorgeous omelet is enhanced by chèvre, a creamy goat's milk cheese. Many brands of chèvre are prepared with herbs such as chives, thyme, or dill, or with combinations like herbes de Provence. Any kind would work here.

EGG WHITE OMELET

TOTAL TIME
15 minutes

SERVINGS
2

MENU
Serve with Lemon
Tomato Salad
(see page 70) or Carrot
and Parsley Salad
(see page 65).

Egg whites make a light, delicate omelet that won't overwhelm the flavors of the vegetables and herbs, which can really shine.

We used mushrooms in this omelet, but bell peppers would also work well.

1 – 2 teaspoons vegetable oil
1 small onion, chopped (about ½ cup)
½ cup sliced mushrooms
pinch of dried or minced fresh marjoram, thyme, or basil
dash of salt and ground black pepper
6 egg whites
1 tablespoon water
¼ cup grated cheddar, Swiss, Jarlsberg, Monterey Jack, or
    mozzarella cheese

Heat the oil in an 8-inch skillet and sauté the onion for about 5 minutes, until softened. Add the mushrooms and the herb of your choice and continue to sauté, stirring frequently. In a small bowl, beat together the salt, pepper, egg whites and water with a fork until frothy. Pour evenly over the sautéed vegetables and cook on low heat until the egg whites are opaque and almost firm. Sprinkle the grated cheese on top. When the cheese begins to melt, fold the omelet in half and cook for another minute.

Slice the folded omelet into two pieces and serve immediately.

PER SERVING: 262 CALORIES, 17.4 G PROTEIN, 17.9 G FAT, 7.7 G CARBOHYDRATE, 302 MG SODIUM, 440 MG CHOLESTEROL.

N O T E : Less oil will be necessary if a nonstick skillet is used. Also, using a "lite" or low-fat cheese will further reduce the fat and cholesterol of this dish.

GREEK SPINACH FRITTATA

2 tablespoons olive oil
1 medium potato, cut into quarters and thinly sliced
1 medium onion, thinly sliced
4 cups chopped rinsed, stemmed spinach (about 5 ounces)
1 tablespoon chopped fresh dill (1 teaspoon dried)
salt * and ground black pepper to taste
4 large eggs, beaten
½ cup grated feta or Swiss cheese

If you use feta cheese, very little, if any, additional salt will be necessary.

Follow the procedure for the Simple Frittata (see page 292). Add the spinach when the onions have softened and the potatoes are partially tender. When the spinach wilts, stir in the dill, salt if needed, and pepper. Add the eggs and sprinkle on the cheese. Continue to follow the basic instructions. Serve piping hot.

PER SERVING: 295 CALORIES, 13 G PROTEIN, 16.6 G FAT, 23.9 G CARBOHYDRATE, 124 MG SODIUM, 212 MG CHOLESTEROL.

TOTAL TIME
25 minutes

SERVINGS
2

MENU
Try this frittata with Carrot and Parsley Salad (see page 65) or Lemon Tomato Salad (see page 70), and maybe a small bowl of ripe olives to nibble.

This is a fairly substantial frittata with a strong character.

SIMPLE FRITTATA

Teamed with a side salad such as Marinated Zucchini (see page 71) or a cooked vegetable, some chewy bread, and a piece of fruit, a frittata provides a substantial, satisfying meal.

A frittata is a dish combining *eggs, vegetables, herbs, and sometimes cheese. Unlike an omelet, which is folded over, a frittata is lightly browned, often on both sides, and not folded at all. Using an ovenproof nonstick skillet produces the most reliable results.*

2 tablespoons vegetable oil or butter (or a combination)
1 medium potato, cut into quarters and thinly sliced
1 medium onion, thinly sliced
1½ teaspoons chopped fresh marjoram, basil, tarragon, rosemary, or oregano
1 garlic clove, minced or pressed (optional)
4 large eggs, beaten
½ cup grated cheese (optional)
salt and ground black pepper

Heat the oil in a large skillet. Sauté the potatoes and onions covered, stirring frequently, for about 8 minutes, until they are tender and golden. Stir in the herb and the optional garlic. Pour the beaten eggs over the sautéed vegetables, tilting the pan to distribute them evenly. Sprinkle on the cheese, and salt and pepper to taste. Cover the pan and cook on low heat for 10 minutes, until the eggs are set and golden on the bottom.

To brown the top of the frittata: If your skillet is flameproof, simply place the frittata under a preheated broiler for about 2 minutes. Otherwise, carefully slide the frittata onto a plate and then flip it over, back into the skillet, to brown the other side. To serve, cut the frittata in half.

PER SERVING: 316 CALORIES, 11.3 G PROTEIN, 16.7 G FAT, 30.6 G CARBOHYDRATE, 149 MG SODIUM, 282 MG CHOLESTEROL.

VARIATION
For a pepper-potato frittata, add 1 red bell pepper, sliced, and a sprinkling of red pepper flakes to the sautéing potato and onion. Use marjoram and mozzarella cheese.

NOTE: If you plan to cook for 4 or more people and are increasing this or another frittata recipe, you may find it easier to finish cooking the frittata in the oven. Although this method takes longer, it requires less attention. Add ½ cup of milk for every 4 eggs, and beat the milk and eggs together. Spoon the cooked vegetables into a lightly oiled shallow baking dish and pour the egg mixture over them. Sprinkle on the cheese and salt and pepper, and bake at 350° for about 25 minutes, until puffed and golden.

Almost any vegetable can be added to a frittata. This recipe can serve as a point of departure for your own flights of fancy or for the final journey for some of those vegetables in your refrigerator.

ASIAN-STYLE FRITTATA

TOTAL TIME
25 minutes

SERVINGS
2

MENU
Serve Asian-Style Frittata with rice, hot tea, and a slice of fresh orange or pineapple.

This is a great recipe for using up lots of vegetables. Feel free to make substitutions for the vegetables listed: Replace the broccoli with thinly sliced cabbage or bok choy. Add some green peas or sliced snow peas for color. Mung sprouts or chopped water chestnuts would add crunch. Use anything that pleases you for a combined total of approximately 4 cups of vegetables.

1 medium onion, thinly sliced (about 1 cup)
2 tablespoons vegetable oil
1 garlic clove, minced or pressed (optional)
1 stalk broccoli, peeled and diced (about 1 cup)
1 cup sliced mushrooms
1 medium red or green bell pepper, finely sliced
4 large eggs
1 teaspoon soy sauce
1 teaspoon grated fresh ginger root

SAUCE
½ cup water or vegetable stock
1 tablespoon soy sauce
1 tablespoon sherry or rice wine
¼ teaspoon dark sesame oil
1 scallion, finely chopped (about 2 tablespoons)
2 teaspoons cornstarch
2 teaspoons cool water

In a large skillet on medium heat, sauté the onions in the oil for 3 or 4 minutes. Stir the optional garlic and the broccoli into the onions and continue to sauté for 3 to 4 minutes. Add the mushrooms and peppers to the skillet. In a bowl, whisk the eggs with the soy sauce and ginger. When the vegetables are crisp-tender, pour the eggs over them and cook on low heat, covered, until the eggs are set, about 6 minutes.

While the eggs cook, make the sauce. In a small saucepan, bring the ½ cup water, soy sauce, sherry or rice wine, dark sesame oil, and scallions to a boil. Dissolve the cornstarch in the cool water and stir it into the simmering sauce. Stir until the sauce thickens and then remove it from the heat.

Serve the frittata drizzled with the sauce.

PER SERVING: 119 CALORIES, 5.5 G PROTEIN, 8.6 G FAT, 5.3 G CARBOHYDRATE, 188 MG SODIUM, 141 MG CHOLESTEROL.

VARIATION

Make several small pancakes instead of a larger frittata: Prepare the sauce while the vegetables sauté. Stir the sautéed vegetables into the whisked eggs. Spoon about one-sixth of this mixture into the oiled skillet for each pancake. When set, flip each pancake over to brown the other side.

Good

LIGHT BROCCOLI FRITTATA

TOTAL TIME

20 minutes

SERVNGS

2

MENU

Serve with Bruschetta (see page 262) or a dark crusty bread and sliced tomatoes or any tangy light salad.

T*his good-looking frittata provides an enjoyable contrast in texture, with just enough creamy-smooth eggs to hold together the still slightly crisp broccoli.*

1 tablespoon olive oil
1 cup chopped onions
2 cups chopped fresh or frozen broccoli (½-inch pieces)
2 garlic cloves, minced or pressed
2 teaspoons chopped fresh basil (1 teaspoon dried)
dash of salt and ground black pepper
6 egg whites — *whole eggs*
¼ cup grated sharp cheddar, Pecorino, or ricotta salata
        cheese (optional)

Preheat the broiler.

Heat the oil in a large flameproof skillet and sauté the onions for about 5 minutes, until softened. Add the broccoli, garlic, and basil to the onions and continue to sauté for another 5 minutes, stirring occasionally, until the broccoli is bright green and crisp-tender. Add the salt and pepper to the egg whites and beat with a fork until frothy. Pour the beaten egg whites over the broccoli, tilting the skillet so that the eggs will flow evenly throughout the broccoli. Cook on low heat for 3 to 4 minutes, until the egg whites are opaque and almost firm. Sprinkle grated cheese on top, if you like, and place the skillet under the broiler for 2 to 3 minutes, until the cheese melts and begins to brown.

Cut the frittata in half and serve.

PER SERVING: 201 CALORIES, 12.4 G PROTEIN, 12.3 G FAT, 12.2 G CARBOHYDRATE, 170 MG SODIUM, 284 MG CHOLESTEROL.

FRUIT-FILLED FRENCH TOAST

4 slices Italian, French, or challah bread (about 4 inches in diameter, sliced 1 inch thick)

4 generous tablespoons fruit spread (see page 334)

≈

2 large eggs, lightly beaten

½ cup milk

1 teaspoon pure vanilla extract

¼ teaspoon cinnamon

2 teaspoons butter

2 teaspoons vegetable oil

≈

plain yogurt (optional)

TOTAL TIME

20 minutes

SERVINGS

2

*F*olks find Fruit-Filled French Toast as much fun to eat as it is to say—more, even. We like it for Sunday brunch or a casual late-night supper.

With a sharp serrated knife, cut lengthwise through each slice of bread to within ½ inch of the bottom and side crusts to make a pocket. Using a butter knife, fill each pocket with a generous tablespoon of fruit spread.

In a shallow bowl that is large enough to hold the four bread slices in one layer, mix together the eggs, milk, vanilla, and cinnamon. Soak the bread slices for 2 or 3 minutes, turning them over once.

Warm a large skillet on medium-low heat. Coat the bottom of the skillet with 1 teaspoon each of the butter and oil. Cook two slices of bread at a time for about 6 minutes, turning the slices over several times, until both sides are nicely browned and crisp. Add the remaining teaspoon of butter and oil to the skillet and cook the final two slices of bread.

Serve hot, either plain or topped with yogurt.

PER SERVING: 410 CALORIES, 13.5 G PROTEIN, 16.2 G FAT, 52.2 G CARBOHYDRATE, 463 MG SODIUM, 230 MG CHOLESTEROL.

Cornmeal Pancakes

TOTAL TIME

25 minutes

SERVINGS

**4 to 6 (about twenty
4-inch pancakes)**

MENU

There's no finer side dish than Cornmeal Pancakes for savory beans or a stew.

Pancakes need not be limited to breakfast! These beautiful, lacy, crisp-edged crêpes make a satisfying light dinner. Fill them with grated Monterey Jack cheese, roll them up, and serve them with salsa and slices of avocado. Or simply top them with sour cream, yogurt, applesauce, or maple syrup.

1¼ cups milk
2 teaspoons baking powder
½ teaspoon baking soda
¾ teaspoon salt
2 large eggs
1¼ cups cornmeal
½ cup unbleached white flour
2 tablespoons butter or margarine
1 tablespoon maple syrup

≈

1 – 2 tablespoons vegetable oil

Combine the milk, baking powder, baking soda, salt, eggs, cornmeal, flour, butter or margarine, and maple syrup in a blender or food processor and whirl for about 30 seconds, until well blended. You may need to stop the blender or processor and scrape the sides of the container with a rubber spatula to be sure no dry ingredients are sticking.

Heat about a tablespoon of oil in a large nonstick skillet. Pour the batter onto the skillet to make several pancakes about 4 inches in diameter. When the pancakes puff up and begin to form bubbles, flip them over and brown the other side. Remove them to a plate and keep them warm in a low oven while you cook the remaining batches. You may need to add a little oil to the skillet with subsequent batches. Serve hot.

PER 6.2 OZ (4–5 PANCAKES): 396 CALORIES, 11.1 G PROTEIN, 14.2 G FAT, 55 G CARBOHYDRATE, 997 MG SODIUM, 127 MG CHOLESTEROL.

VARIATIONS

• Stir 1 cup of cut corn and 1 teaspoon ground cumin into the batter.
• Stir 1 cup of fresh fruit into the blended batter.

NOTE: If you prefer to mix the batter with a whisk or electric mixer, melt the butter or margarine first.

COTTAGE CHEESE APPLE PANCAKES

1 large or 2 small apples (about ¾ cup grated)

½ cup small-curd cottage cheese

2 large eggs

¼ teaspoon cinnamon

⅛ teaspoon nutmeg (optional)

1 tablespoon maple syrup

¼ teaspoon salt

¼ cup unbleached white flour

1 teaspoon baking powder, sifted

≈

1 tablespoon butter or vegetable oil

≈

maple syrup

Peel, core, and grate the apple into a mixing bowl. Thoroughly mix in the cottage cheese, eggs, cinnamon, nutmeg, maple syrup, and salt. Sprinkle in the flour and sifted baking powder, and stir well.

Butter or oil a heavy griddle or nonstick skillet and place it on medium heat. For each pancake, ladle ¼ cup of the batter onto the hot skillet. When bubbles form on the tops and the bottoms are browned, flip the pancakes over and brown them on the other side.

Serve immediately, topped with maple syrup.

PER SERVING: 320 CALORIES, 15 G PROTEIN, 15.4 G FAT, 30.8 G CARBOHYDRATE, 978 MG SODIUM, 220 MG CHOLESTEROL.

NOTE: The butter is not necessary in a non-stick pan, but it enhances the flavor of the pancakes.

TOTAL TIME

20 minutes

SERVINGS

2 (eight 4-inch pancakes)

Try these charming, delicate pancakes for breakfast, brunch, or lunch. They are particularly delightful with a dollop of sour cream and a sprinkling of fresh berries.

DESSERTS

O N FIRST CONSIDERATION, dessert might seem to have little place in a quick and easy cuisine. If we scarcely have time to make dinner, then dessert is probably the first thing we deem inessential enough to forgo. The problem is that we love it so. Dessert can sweeten the day and bring radiant smiles to the faces of our children.

Dessert doesn't have to be something you do without because you're pressed for time. You can have dessert without a big fuss and without reliance on expensive commercial products. Many desserts actually add to the nutritional value of a meal rather than detract from it, while still providing sweet satisfaction. Almost all of the desserts in this book require no more than 15 minutes preparation time. Many can be ready to serve in 5 minutes. Some require no labor at all. The secret is to broaden the idea of what a dessert should be.

For starters, we recommend serving fresh fruit for dessert on a daily basis. It's an attractive, light, healthful offering that certainly takes no effort. There's something wonderful about observing the natural seasonal progression, from the first strawberries in the spring, through the lush melons and fragrant raspberries of summer, to crisp apples and perfect ripe pears in the fall. You'll have to wait and wonder when you'll find beautiful bright tangerines in the market in winter. One learns to anticipate and appreciate each succulent fruit as it appears on the table. It can be an adventure to try unfamiliar fruits too. The inside of a papaya is a marvel. And don't miss the opportunity to try Asian pear apples.

But however much we admire a cuisine in which fresh, unadorned fruits are prized, we are not always this enlightened about dessert in our own culture. Maybe dessert is too often declared the reward or the bribe for eating all our turnips. Children (and many adults) want to know what's for dessert even before beginning dinner. Too often, chocolate cake may be more what we had in mind than a healthful piece of raw fruit.

Happily, we find that the smallest effort can sometimes transform even ordinary ingredients into a bona fide dessert. Sautéed Bananas (see page 320) is very simple and takes only a few minutes to make but yields a warm, fragrant dessert with an intriguing flavor. Coffee Ricotta Mousse (see page 307) is a rich indulgence that can speedily and conveniently be made ahead. Peach Parfait with Amaretto Cream (see page 318) is elegant and lush but requires only a quick assembly. Don't hesitate to make an occasional baked treat, such as Six-Minute Chocolate Cake (see page 322) or Lemon Date Bars (see page 315). While the dessert is in the oven, you can prepare the rest of the meal. You can dress up purchased frozen yogurt or ice cream and easily turn it into a homemade confection. Many desserts in this book can be blended, broiled, or assembled at the last minute, in the amount of time required to clear the dinner dishes from the table.

Whether it takes 2 minutes or 15, each dessert will make your family and friends feel pampered and appreciated, and you can relax and reap praise quite out of proportion to your labors.

SOME NO-LABOR DESSERTS

• Fresh ripe fruit in season
• A basket of whole nuts and a fine liqueur or sherry
• Pears and Pecorino cheese
• A good imported chocolate and dried figs
• Fresh table grapes, brie cheese, and crackers
• Fruit lightly dressed with flavored yogurt. Try peach slices with raspberry yogurt, raspberries with coffee yogurt, or seedless grapes with lemon yogurt.

- Stir in cherries and chocolate chips.
- Stir in peach slices and crumbled sugar cookies or amaretti.
- Stir in coarsely ground hazelnuts and a little Frangelico liqueur.
- Stir in ground ginger, chopped ginger in syrup, or crumbled ginger snaps and a little brandy.
- Stir in a ribbon of partially defrosted orange juice or limeade concentrate.
- Stir in the frozen crumbs of that last leftover piece of cake or brownie.
- Top with Fresh Orange Compote (see page 309), Gingered Plum Sauce (see page 312), Maple Walnut Sauce (see page 316), Sautéed Bananas (see page 320), or Strawberries Three Ways (see page 321).

DESSERTS THAT CAN BE PREPARED
IN 5 MINUTES

- Fruit Shakes (see page 311)
- Goat Cheese with Honey and Walnuts (see page 313)
- Inside-Out Mango (see page 314)
- Sautéed Bananas (see page 320)

BAKED PEACHES WITH MARSALA

Good

PREPARATION TIME
5 minutes

TOTAL TIME
15 minutes

SERVINGS
4

MENU
Baked Peaches with
Marsala is a particularly
well-suited ending for any
Mediterranean-style meal
from a French omelet, to
an Italian pasta, to a
North African stew.

This traditional Italian dessert makes the most of its flavors in a simple, elegant way. Use firm but ripe peaches, when the fruit is in its peak season. A dollop of whipped cream is a delicious accompaniment but not essential.

4 firm, ripe freestone peaches
8 amaretti cookies, crumbled, or ½ cup sugar cookie
   crumbs
2 tablespoons butter
¼ cup Marsala

Preheat the oven to 375°.

Cut the peaches in half, remove the pits, and place the halves, cut side up, in a baking dish. Sprinkle the cookie crumbs on top of the peaches and dot them with the butter. Pour the Marsala over the peaches. Bake for 7 to 10 minutes, until the topping is bubbling and lightly toasted. Serve immediately.

PER SERVING: 158 CALORIES, 1.6 G PROTEIN, 8 G FAT, 19.2 G CARBOHYDRATE, 126 MG SODIUM, 26 MG CHOLESTEROL.

COFFEE RICOTTA MOUSSE

1 pound ricotta cheese
½ cup confectioners' sugar
2 tablespoons instant coffee granules
½ teaspoon pure vanilla extract
1 tablespoon brandy (optional)

In the bowl of a food processor or using an electric mixer, whip all of the ingredients together until smooth and evenly colored. Serve immediately in individual dessert cups, or make a day or two ahead and keep covered and refrigerated.

PER 4-OZ SERVING: 227 CALORIES, 11.4 G PROTEIN, 13.1 G FAT, 16.5 G CARBOHYDRATE, 85 MG SODIUM, 51 MG CHOLESTEROL.

TOTAL TIME
5 minutes
SERVINGS
4
MENU
The high protein content of this dessert makes it especially nice after a light meal of vegetables or salad.

Thick and creamy, this pudding by itself is a rich indulgence, but you still may wish to add a dusting of cocoa or shaved chocolate, a dollop of whipped cream, or some fresh fruit, such as raspberries or peaches.

CREAMY BANANA ICE

PREPARATION TIME
5 minutes

FREEZING TIME
1 hour

SERVINGS
4

MENU

The perfect sweet cold dessert to top off a spicy hot meal such as Pad Thai (see page 236) or African Pineapple Peanut Stew (see page 200).

Whor we found this recipe in Food & Wine *magazine a couple of years ago, we enjoyed the intensely flavored ice cream—like confection and were surprised and delighted by the ingredients list. We've had fun with it ever since.*

4 large very ripe bananas *

* For the best flavor, use well-ripened bananas whose skins are no longer tinged with green. Bananas are at their sweetest just as the skin becomes speckled with brown. If your bananas are not ripe enough for this dish, they may be perfect for Sautéed Bananas (see page 320).

Peel the bananas and slice them into ½-inch-thick rounds. Place the slices on a baking sheet or a large plate lined with waxed paper. Freeze the bananas for at least 1 hour (see note).

In a food processor or blender, purée the frozen banana slices, stopping the machine occasionally to scrape the sides of the container. As the bananas thaw slightly, the texture will become smooth and creamy. Serve immediately.

PER SERVING: 104 CALORIES, 1.2 G PROTEIN, 0.5 G FAT, 26.5 G CARBOHYDRATE, 1 MG SODIUM, 0 MG CHOLESTEROL.

NOTE: The uncovered frozen banana slices can be kept in the freezer for 2 days before puréeing. Or, when the bananas are frozen, transfer them to a freezer bag or covered container, where they will keep for several weeks.

FRESH ORANGE COMPOTE

8 seedless oranges (at least 2 cups peeled and sectioned)
¼ cup orange marmalade
2 tablespoons orange liqueur, such as Grand Marnier

Peel and section the oranges (see below) into a serving bowl. In another, smaller bowl, mix together the orange marmalade and liqueur to make a sauce. If necessary, add the juice from a few orange sections to the marmalade to reach a pourable consistency. Stir the sauce into the oranges. Refrigerate at least 20 minutes, and serve chilled.

TO SECTION AN ORANGE QUICKLY: Cut both of the ends from the orange and place it cut side down on a cutting board. Slice down the sides of the orange with wide strokes, just deep enough to remove the peel and all of the white pith. Hold the peeled orange over the serving bowl to catch any dripping juice, and with a paring knife, carefully cut between the membrane and one side of each orange section and back out the other side to release it from the membrane. This can be done with one smooth in-and-out motion. When all of the sections are removed, squeeze any remaining juice from the membrane into the bowl.

PER 1-CUP SERVING: 68 CALORIES, 2.6 G PROTEIN, 0.4 G FAT, 55.8 G CARBOHYDRATE, 8 MG SODIUM, 0 MG CHOLESTEROL.

PREPARATION TIME
15 minutes

TOTAL TIME
35 minutes

SERVINGS
4

MENU
Fresh Orange Compote is an especially refreshing dessert after a North African meal such as Tunisian Vegetable Stew (see page 217) and Couscous with Sun-Dried Tomatoes (see page 145), or North African Couscous Paella (see page 146).

Attractive, refreshing, and not too sweet, *Fresh Orange Compote may be served alone or with shortbread or chocolate wafer cookies on the side. Leftovers, should you have any, can be served the next day on vanilla ice cream or stirred into yogurt.*

FRUIT RICOTTA MOUSSE

10 minutes

TOTAL TIME
30 minutes

SERVINGS
8

This fluffy pudding is a perennial favorite at Moosewood Restaurant.

We think this mousse is most welcome as a dessert after a light, dairy-free meal. Fruit Ricotta Mousse is also wonderful mounded in a melon half for brunch.

TIP: When choice fruits are plentiful, freeze some for out-of-season enjoyment. To prevent soft fruits—such as berries, pitted cherries, or sliced peaches—from clumping together, spread them on trays with each piece separate and not touching its neighbor. Freeze for 24 hours. Then, working quickly, pack the fruit into tightly sealed bags.

1 pound ricotta cheese
1 pint strawberries, cherries, blueberries, or raspberries *
½ cup fruit spread (see page 334) †
1 cup heavy cream

In the winter we might use frozen blueberries, raspberries, or pitted sweet cherries. We don't recommend using frozen strawberries because they don't retain their texture well. Look for frozen fruit that contains no added sugar or syrup.

† Use a spread made of the same fruit as the fresh fruit you are using.

In the bowl of a food processor or with an electric mixer, whip the ricotta for about 2 minutes, or until very smooth and slightly fluffed up. Rinse and stem the fresh fruit. Cut large strawberries into smaller pieces, and pit cherries. Set aside several pieces of fruit for garnishing the finished mousse. Fold the fresh fruit and the fruit spread into the ricotta. Whip the cream until quite stiff, and fold it in.

Refrigerate for at least 20 minutes, and then serve in individual dessert cups, topped with the reserved fruit garnish.

PER 4-OZ SERVING: 194 CALORIES, 5.9 G PROTEIN, 14.4 G FAT, 11.4 G CARBOHYDRATE, 48 MG SODIUM, 54 MG CHOLESTEROL.

NOTE: If you make Fruit Ricotta Mousse ahead of time, wait until just before serving to fold in the whipped cream.

FRUIT SHAKES

PEACH SHAKE

2 – 3 fresh peaches, peeled and sliced, or
    1 cup frozen peach slices
1 cup plain or vanilla nonfat yogurt
½ cup peach juice or apricot nectar

STRAWBERRY SHAKE

1 pint fresh strawberries, cleaned and stemmed, or
    1 pint frozen strawberries
1 cup plain, vanilla, or lemon nonfat yogurt
3 – 4 tablespoons orange juice, apple juice, or
    apple-strawberry juice
2 – 3 tablespoons maple syrup (optional)

MANGO SHAKE

1 ripe mango, pitted and peeled (see page 351)
1 tablespoon frozen limeade concentrate
1 cup milk or pineapple juice

BANANA SHAKE

1 ripe banana, peeled and sliced
1 cup plain or vanilla nonfat yogurt
½ cup orange juice
1 teaspoon honey or sugar (optional)

For any fruit shake, purée all of the ingredients in a blender until smooth. Serve chilled, topped with a dollop of freshly whipped cream if you're feeling indulgent.

1 BANANA SHAKE: 143 CALORIES, 6.5 G PROTEIN, 2 G FAT, 26.2 G CARBOHYDRATE, 83 MG SODIUM, 7 MG CHOLESTEROL.

TOTAL TIME

5 minutes

SERVINGS

2

MENU

A Fruit Shake is especially refreshing after a spicy Indian, Mexican, or Caribbean meal. It's also good for breakfast with a muffin.

These simple, healthful drinks make a pleasant dessert that kids will love and adults will enjoy sipping leisurely. Serve in stemmed glasses garnished with whole berries or fresh mint leaves, or orange, lime, or peach slices. You might like to serve gingersnap cookies on the side.

GINGERED PLUM SAUCE

TOTAL TIME

15 minutes

SERVINGS

2 cups

MENU

Serve warm or cold on vanilla ice cream, frozen yogurt, or lemon sherbet, or serve as a kissel topped with whipped cream. Gingered Plum Sauce is also excellent at breakfast on oatmeal or pancakes. Try it on Cornmeal Pancakes (see page 298).

This chunky tart-sweet sauce is a brilliant burgundy color. Gingered Plum Sauce fits well into many cuisines: Eastern European, New England, Chinese, and Scandinavian among others.

1 pound firm fresh plums (6 – 7 large purple plums, 10 – 12 prune plums)
¼ cup maple syrup
¼ teaspoon ground ginger
1 teaspoon cornstarch
juice of ½ lemon (about 2 tablespoons)

Cut the plums along the midlines, twist apart, and remove the pits. Slice each half into 3 or 4 wedges. In a nonreactive saucepan, heat the plums, maple syrup, and ginger, stirring frequently. In a small bowl or cup, stir the cornstarch into the lemon juice until dissolved. When the plums begin to release their juice but are still firm, add the lemon juice mixture and bring to a boil. Cook, stirring frequently, until the liquid thickens and clears.

This will keep for 1 week, covered and refrigerated. Serve warm or cold.

PER 2-OZ SERVING: 35 CALORIES, 0.5 G PROTEIN, 0.1 G FAT, 9.8 G CARBOHYDRATE, 1 MG SODIUM, 0 MG CHOLESTEROL.

Goat Cheese with Honey and Walnuts

12 shelled walnuts, or about ⅓ cup walnut pieces
1 log fresh mild chèvre (about 9 ounces)
1 tablespoon honey, or to taste

≈

fresh fruit slices (optional)
plain crackers or water biscuits (optional)

Toast the walnuts (see page 354). Slice the log of chèvre into 12 rounds, and arrange them either on four small dessert plates or on a larger platter. Scatter the walnuts over the cheese and drizzle with the honey. Serve plain or garnished with fresh fruit, such as cherries, strawberries, or sliced apples or pears. Plain creackers, such as water biscuits, are another tasty accompaniment.

PER SERVING: 247 CALORIES, 10.6 G PROTEIN, 20.2 G FAT, 7.5 G CARBOHYDRATE, 713 MG SODIUM, 57 MG CHOLESTEROL.

TOTAL TIME
5 minutes

SERVINGS
4

MENU
Serve after Crostini with Olivada (see pages 262, 49) and Chilled Moroccan Tomato Soup (see page 26), or after Beans and Greens (see page 120) with Bruschetta (see page 262) and tomatoes.

We first encountered this dish being demonstrated in a local grocery store by the folks from Goat Folks Farm in Interlaken, New York. We were delighted by the surprising flavors and by how quick and easy it is to make. Use a locally produced cheese, if you can, for the freshest taste.

INSIDE-OUT MANGO

TOTAL TIME

5 minutes

SERVINGS

2

A luscious ripe mango makes a very agreeable dessert after any Indian curry or tropical, Mexican, or Southeast Asian dish. When we first heard about this exotic way to serve a mango, we didn't believe it would work. But if you're careful and gentle with the succulent fruit, you can turn it inside out with surprising, stunning results.

1 ripe mango
1 lime

Lay the mango on its flattest side on a cutting board. Press down with the palm of one hand on top of the mango, and with a long-bladed knife carefully slice off the top half of the mango with a horizontal cut about ½ inch above the center, which will clear the large fibrous pit. Turn the mango over and similarly slice off the other half. Score the juicy flesh of each half in a crisscross fashion, taking care not to pierce the skin. Gently turn each half of the mango inside out. Sprinkle with lime juice and serve immediately. Fresh mango cut this way may be eaten with a knife and fork, or by picking it up with your hands and biting the chunks of fruit from the skin.

PER SERVING: 42 CALORIES, 0.3 G PROTEIN, 0.2 G FAT, 11 G CARBOHYDRATE, 1 MG SODIUM, 0 MG CHOLESTEROL.

LEMON DATE BARS

2 cups chopped pitted dates
juice of 1 lemon
½ cup water

≈

½ cup margarine or butter, softened
¾ cup brown sugar, packed
1¾ cups unbleached white flour
1 teaspoon salt
½ teaspoon baking soda, sifted
1 cup rolled oats

Preheat the oven to 350°.

In a saucepan, combine the dates, lemon juice, and water. Cook, covered, on low heat for 10 minutes, stirring occasionally. Remove from the heat and set aside.

In a bowl, cream together the margarine or butter and brown sugar. Stir in the flour, salt, and baking soda. Add the oats and mix well, using your hands. The dough will be crumbly but will hold together when squeezed. Press two-thirds of the dough into an oiled 8- or 9-inch square baking pan. Stir the date mixture and spread it over the dough. Crumble the remaining dough on top. Bake for 30 minutes. Cool in the pan. Cut into 16 bars.

PER BAR: 192 CALORIES, 2.2 G PROTEIN, 6.2 G FAT, 33.6 G CARBOHYDRATE, 216 MG SODIUM, 16 MG CHOLESTEROL.

VARIATION

Use dried figs or dried apricots instead of the dates.

PREPARATION TIME
15 minutes

TOTAL TIME
45 minutes

SERVINGS
16 bars

MENU
Lemon Date Bars go with almost anything but are especially well suited to sunny cuisines. Serve them after Mediterranean Lentil Salad (see page 131), Eggplant Mykonos (see page 208), Chakchouka (see page 288), or California Dream Salad (see page 123), or take them on a picnic with Pan Bagnat (see page 266).

Lemon Date Bars are sweet, tangy, chewy, and crunchy, contain no eggs, and can be made without dairy products as well. These sturdy but delectable bars keep well and travel well.

MAPLE WALNUT SUNDAE

TOTAL TIME

5 minutes

SERVINGS

4 to 6

This sauce can be made well ahead of time and keeps almost indefinitely in the refrigerator. Although maple syrup is a product of the early spring, we make this sundae year-round. In fact, we like it best in autumn with New England harvest meals. Top a Maple Walnut Sundae with a dollop of whipped cream and a crisp apple slice to really do it up.

¾ cup toasted walnut pieces (see page 354)
½ cup maple syrup

≈

frozen yogurt or ice cream

Combine the toasted walnuts and the maple syrup. Heat if desired. Spoon over ice cream or frozen yogurt.

PER SERVING (1/4 CUP ICE CREAM WITH 1/4 CUP SAUCE): 340 CALORIES, 5.4 G PROTEIN, 19.1 G FAT, 40.1 G CARBOHYDRATE, 76 MG SODIUM, 38 MG CHOLESTEROL.

Moosewood Fudge Brownies

½ cup butter
3 squares (1 ounce each) unsweetened chocolate
1 cup lightly packed brown sugar
½ teaspoon pure vanilla extract
2 large eggs
½ cup unbleached white flour

Preheat the oven to 350°.

Butter an 8- or 9-inch square baking pan.

In a heavy large pot, melt the butter and chocolate together, stirring occasionally. While they melt, assemble the rest of the ingredients (if mixing by hand, beat the eggs with a fork in a separate bowl). When the butter and chocolate have melted, remove the pot from the heat. Add the brown sugar and vanilla and beat by hand or with an electric mixer. Add the eggs (just crack them directly into the pot if using an electric mixer). Stir in the flour, and mix until the batter is thoroughly blended and smooth.

Pour the batter into the pan and bake for about 20 minutes, until the brownies are just beginning to pull away from the sides of the pan and are fudgy in the center. For more cakelike brownies, bake an additional 5 minutes.

PER 2-INCH BROWNIE: 153 CALORIES, 1.8 G PROTEIN, 9.3 G FAT, 18 G CARBOHYDRATE, 71 MG SODIUM, 42 MG CHOLESTEROL.

N O T E : Any leftover brownies can be crumbled for a sundae topping. These crumbs freeze very well and can be eaten without defrosting.

PREPARATION TIME
10 minutes
TOTAL TIME
30 minutes
SERVINGS
16 brownies

Moosewood's fudge brownies were adapted from a recipe found twenty years ago on the back of a box of chocolate. We've been serving them at the restaurant almost every day since then, and the demand from our customers, our children, our friends, and casual passers-by has remained overwhelming. Some things never change.

To gild the lily, top with a scoop of your favorite ice cream.

PEACH PARFAIT WITH AMARETTO CREAM

TOTAL TIME

10 minutes

SERVINGS

4

MENU

A creamy indulgence and especially welcome after a light, piquant entrée, such as Antipasto Salad (see page 118) or Spaghetti with Zucchini and Lemon (see page 195).

*T*his dessert really glorifies fresh peaches in their prime. The cream can be whipped several hours ahead and chilled, covered, but assembly of the parfaits should be at the last minute.

1 cup heavy cream, well chilled
2 tablespoons amaretto (almond liqueur)
2 tablespoons confectioners' sugar

≈

4 ripe fresh peaches
8 amaretti (crisp Italian almond cookies)

Whip the cream, amaretto, and sugar until stiff. Peel and slice the peaches. Crumble the cookies. In individual dessert cups or parfait glasses, layer the peach slices, cookie crumbs, and whipped cream, layering everything twice. Serve immediately.

PER 4-OZ SERVING: 227 CALORIES, 1.7 G PROTEIN, 15.8 G FAT, 19.4 G CARBOHYDRATE, 39 MG SODIUM, 56 MG CHOLESTEROL.

VARIATION

Use about 2 cups of strawberries or pitted fresh sweet cherries instead of peaches. Crisp sugar cookies or ginger snaps can replace the amaretti, in which case you may wish to use 1 teaspoon of vanilla extract whipped into the cream rather than the amaretto.

PEARS WITH GORGONZOLA

¼ **pound Gorgonzola cheese**
¼ **pound low-fat cream cheese (Neufchâtel)**
¼ **cup finely chopped toasted hazelnuts (see page 354)**

≈

4 ripe pears, whole or sliced

In a small bowl, using a fork, mash together the cheeses and the chopped hazelnuts. If made in advance, the cheese mixture should be covered and refrigerated, but it will taste best served at room temperature.

Serve whole pears in a bowl and the cheese mixture in a crock on the side, and let everyone help themselves. Or core the pears, slice them into wedges, toss them with lemon juice to prevent discoloration, and serve on individual dessert plates beside a generous spoonful of the cheese mixture.

PER SERVING: 270 CALORIES, 13.8 G PROTEIN, 15 G FAT, 23.8 G CARBOHYDRATE, 206 MG SODIUM, 28 MG CHOLESTEROL.

VARIATIONS

• Use walnuts instead of hazelnuts.
• Use apples instead of pears.

TOTAL TIME
10 minutes

SERVINGS
4

This is a rich, filling, and sophisticated finale for fall and winter meals. The complex and interesting combination of flavors and textures is best enjoyed when pears are perfectly ripe, sweet, and luscious.

Try the cheese mixture with crackers, or on toast with roasted red pepper strips, or tossed with hot pasta.

SAUTÉED BANANAS

It takes only a moment to transform bananas into this fragrant, warm, delightful treat, which makes a nice addition to any meal with a tropical flavor. Serve Sautéed Bananas on frozen plain or vanilla yogurt or ice cream, or with whipped cream, sweetened sour cream, or yogurt.

If your bananas have ripened beyond firmness, you may prefer to use them in Creamy Banana Ice (see page 308).

2 firm ripe bananas

≈

1 tablespoon butter
½ teaspoon cinnamon
2 tablespoons frozen orange juice concentrate
1 tablespoon orange liqueur, such as Grand Marnier
    (optional)

≈

frozen yogurt or ice cream

Peel and slice the bananas into ½-inch-thick rounds. In a heavy saucepan or skillet on medium heat, melt the butter until it just begins to bubble. Stir in the cinnamon until it is evenly distributed in the foaming butter. Add the orange juice concentrate and the liqueur, if desired, stirring constantly. When the concentrate is melted and the sauce is smooth, add the banana slices, stirring gently but quickly to coat them evenly, about 30 seconds. Serve immediately on frozen yogurt or ice cream.

SAUCE PER SERVING: 83 CALORIES, 0.7 G PROTEIN, 3.1 G FAT, 14.4 G CARBOHYDRATE, 30 MG SODIUM, 8 MG CHOLESTEROL.

STRAWBERRIES THREE WAYS

HINT: Strawberries stay fresh longer when they are stored unwashed in the refrigerator.

1 quart strawberries, cleaned and stemmed
1 tablespoon sugar, or to taste
½ cup orange juice, ¼ cup Grand Marnier, or
      1 teaspoon balsamic vinegar

In a bowl, combine the strawberries with the sugar and orange juice, Grand Marnier, or balsamic vinegar. Cover and refrigerate for at least 30 minutes, but not much longer than half a day.

PER 4-OZ SERVING (USING ORANGE JUICE): 58 CALORIES, 0.9 G PROTEIN, 0.4 G FAT, 13.9 G CARBOHYDRATE, 1 MG SODIUM, 0 MG CHOLESTEROL.

TOTAL TIME

10 minutes

SERVINGS

4

This is a little trick to make fresh strawberries taste even better and more like themselves. If the strawberries will be used as a topping for ice cream or shortcake, purée about a quarter of them in a blender until smooth and pour the sauce back over the remaining whole berries.

Six-Minute Chocolate Cake

CAKE
PREPARATION TIME

6 minutes

GLAZE
PREPARATION TIME

15–20 minutes

TOTAL TIME

1 hour and 20 minutes

SERVINGS

one 9-inch round or
8-inch square cake

We first spotted this recipe in 1976 in House & Garden *magazine, attracted, obviously, by the title. We were pleasantly surprised by the truth of the advertising and discovered other charms of this cake as well. It is an economical, low-cholesterol, delicious dark cake that goes into the oven in 6 minutes with no mixing bowl to clean, because the batter is mixed directly in the baking pan.*

CAKE

1½ cups unbleached white flour

⅓ cup unsweetened cocoa powder

1 teaspoon baking soda

½ teaspoon salt

1 cup sugar

½ cup vegetable oil

1 cup cold water or brewed coffee

2 teaspoons pure vanilla extract

2 tablespoons vinegar

GLAZE

½ pound bittersweet chocolate

¾ cup hot water, milk, or half-and-half

½ teaspoon pure vanilla extract

To make the cake, preheat the oven to 375°.

Sift together the flour, cocoa, baking soda, salt, and sugar into an ungreased 8-inch square or a 9-inch round baking pan. In a 2-cup measuring cup, measure and mix together the oil, water or coffee, and vanilla. Pour the liquid ingredients into the baking pan and mix the batter with a fork or a small whisk. When the batter is smooth, add the vinegar and stir quickly. There will be pale swirls in the batter where the baking soda and the vinegar are reacting. Stir just until the vinegar is evenly distributed throughout the batter. Bake for 25 to 30 minutes. Set the cake aside to cool, and if you choose to make the glaze, reset the oven to 300°.

For the glaze, melt the chocolate in a small ovenproof bowl or heavy skillet in the oven for about 15 minutes. Stir the hot liquid and the vanilla into the chocolate until smooth. Spoon the glaze over the cooled cake. Refrigerate the glazed cake for at least 30 minutes before serving.

CAKE PER 2-INCH PIECE: 237 CALORIES, 3.3 G PROTEIN, 15.4 G FAT, 27.3 G CARBOHYDRATE, 100 MG SODIUM, 1 MG CHOLESTEROL.

GLAZE PER 2.35-OZ SERVING: 208 CALORIES, 5 G PROTEIN, 21 G FAT, 12.3 G CARBOHYDRATE, 15 MG SODIUM, 4 MG CHOLESTEROL.

VARIATION

To make a dozen cupcakes, follow the recipe directions, mixing the batter in a bowl. Pour the batter into a cupcake pan lined with paper baking cups, and bake at 375° for 20 minutes. While the cupcakes bake, prepare the glaze. When the cupcakes are ready, remove them from the oven and spoon on the glaze. Refrigerate for at least 30 minutes before serving.

Our favorite topping for this cake is the simple chocolate glaze, but be sure to use a good-quality chocolate, such as Caillebaut, for the best results. Or top with your favorite frosting, dust with confectioners' sugar or cinnamon sugar, or serve with whipped cream, ice cream, or sliced fruit. Fresh Orange Compote (see page 309) is another ideal topping.

TROPICAL FRUIT SALAD

TOTAL TIME

15 minutes

SERVINGS

4

MENU

Tropical Fruit Salad is the ideal accompaniment to every dish in this book that begins with the word "Caribbean" — Caribbean Black Beans (see page 168), Caribbean Fish in a Packet (see page 245), Caribbean Yellow Rice and Pigeon Peas (see page 154).

uantities are not critical in this healthful and appealing salad. Choose whatever fruit is ripe and colorful in the market. The ginger and lime dressing turns simple chopped fruits into an enticing dessert, side dish, or main dish for brunch.

DRESSING

½ **teaspoon ground ginger**
1 **tablespoon honey**
¼ **cup fresh lime juice (1 – 2 limes)**

PREPARE ABOUT 4 CUPS OF SOME OR ALL OF THESE FRUITS

bananas, peeled and sliced
pineapple, peeled and cut into bite-sized pieces
cantaloupe, peeled and cut into bite-sized pieces
mango, peeled and cubed
kiwi, peeled, halved, and sliced into half-circles
strawberries, stemmed and halved

In a small bowl, mix the ginger and honey together well and then stir in the lime juice. Set aside. As you cut the fruit, place it in a large serving bowl, pour the dressing over it, and stir. The lime juice will keep the fruit from discoloring.

This salad keeps well, covered, in the refrigerator for 2 or 3 hours. If you wish to make the salad several hours ahead of time, omit the bananas and store the salad in the refrigerator. Stir in the bananas a few minutes before serving.

Serve at room temperature or chilled.

SALAD WITH DRESSING PER 1-CUP SERVING: 101 CALORIES, 1.7 G PROTEIN, 0.6 G FAT, 25.2 G CARBOHYDRATE, 15 MG SODIUM, 0 MG CHOLESTEROL.

DRESSING PER SERVING: 12 CALORIES, 0 G PROTEIN, 0 G FAT, 3.3 G CARBOHYDRATE, 0 MG SODIUM, 0 MG CHOLESTEROL.

Yogurt Cheese Pie

1 quart low-fat yogurt (plain * or vanilla- or lemon-
    flavored, made without gelatin)

≈

1½ cups crushed graham crackers (about 5 ounces)
¼ cup melted margarine or butter
2 tablespoons brown sugar or maple syrup (optional)

≈

2–4 cups fresh berries or sliced fruit (strawberries,
    peaches, blueberries, raspberries, pitted cherries), or
    ½ cup fruit conserves or preserves

Add 1½ teaspoons pure vanilla extract and ⅓ cup maple syrup to plain yogurt.

TOTAL TIME

(after the Yogurt Cheese is
ready) 15 minutes

SERVINGS

6

*Once the Yogurt
Cheese has
been prepared,
this is a snap. Arrange
colorful pieces of fruit
on top to create an
attractive pattern.*

The night or morning before you will serve this pie, prepare Yogurt Cheese (see page 52).

Prepare the pie crust: In an 8- or 9-inch pie pan, mix the graham cracker crumbs with the melted margarine or butter and the brown sugar or maple syrup. Stir well and press into the pie pan evenly. Spread the Yogurt Cheese over the crust. Top with the fresh fruit or fruit conserves.

Serve right away, or chill until ready to serve. Yogurt Cheese Pie will keep, covered and refrigerated, for 3 days.

PER SERVING: 313 CALORIES, 10.2 G PROTEIN, 12.4 G FAT, 42.9 G CARBOHYDRATE, 343 MG SODIUM, 30 MG CHOLESTEROL.

Pantry List

A meal can be quickly prepared and still have variety and flair, if you have ready access to a range of basic ingredients. Whether you are a spur-of-the-moment cook or prefer to plan your meals in advance, a well-stocked pantry is essential and will be a blessing on those days when you meant to shop but couldn't, or when guests arrive unexpectedly.

Grains, pastas, and canned and dried beans all store well and form the basis for many different meals. Herbs, spices, condiments, and other seasonings enhance these basic ingredients. Keep a supply of family favorites on hand, but supplement them with some less familiar pantry items to add new interest to your menus.

Grains, beans, flours, nuts, spices, and dried fruits are available in bulk at well-stocked natural food stores and supermarkets. Bulk foods are usually less expensive; when you get home, transfer your purchases from the paper or plastic bags to glass jars, which are more attractive, make it easier to locate a particular item, and give greater protection from insect invasions.

The pantry list that follows contains many of the ingredients called for in the recipes in this book. We assume you have the really basic staples (flour, oil, salt, sugar, potatoes, onions, mayonnaise) on hand. Before you go shopping, glance over the list and make a note of the items that have been used up or that you would like add to your pantry.

BEANS (DRIED OR CANNED)

butter beans	field peas	lentils (red, brown)	pintos
black turtle beans	red kidney beans	limas	split peas
black-eyed peas	cannellini	navy or pea beans	(green, yellow)
chick peas	(white kidney beans)	pigeon peas	

GRAINS

bulghur	couscous	millet	rice (Arborio, basmati,
buckwheat groats	grits	quinoa	brown, white)
cornmeal			

NUTS AND SEEDS

almonds	hazelnuts	pine nuts	sesame seeds
cashews	peanuts	walnuts	tahini

PASTA

Asian-style:	Italian-style:		
rice, soba, and	long and thin	flavored	
udon noodles	short and chunky	whole-grain	

SPICES AND DRIED HERBS

allspice	coriander	five-spice powder	paprika
annatto	cinnamon	garam masala	rosemary
basil	cloves	marjoram	saffron
bay leaf	cumin	mint	sage
black pepper	curry powder	mustard seed	tarragon
cardamom	dill	nutmeg	thyme
cayenne	fennel	oregano	turmeric
Chesapeake Bay seasoning			

CANNED GOODS

artichoke hearts	olives (black,	roasted red peppers	tomato paste
capers	Calamata, Spanish)	salsa	whole tomatoes
coconut milk (unsweetened)	pimientos	tomato juice	

CONDIMENTS

chili paste or chili oil	fish sauce	soy sauce	vinegars
Chinese fermented	fruit spreads	Tabasco or other	wasabi
black beans	hoisin sauce	hot sauce	
curry paste			

MISCELLANEOUS

dried fruits (apricots,	dried mushrooms	seaweeds (hijiki, nori)	vegetable bouillon
dates, raisins)	(porcini, shiitake)	sun-dried tomatoes	(cubes or powder)
	fresh garlic		

WINES AND LIQUEURS

Chinese rice wine	liqueurs (amaretto,	Marsala	sherry
dry red and white wines	Grand Marnier)	mirin	

REFRIGERATED ITEMS

cheeses	miso	tofu	yogurt
fresh ginger root	seitan		

FROZEN FOODS

black-eyed peas	pizza crust	tortillas	tempeh
lima beans	puff pastry		

Guide to Ingredients

ALLSPICE. We find the clove-cinnamon-ginger flavor of allspice an asset to desserts, mulled cider, and savory bean dishes. Whole allspice berries should be freshly ground for the best aroma.

ANNATTO (achiote seed). The small red annatto seed imparts a vibrant yellow-orange color and delicate flavor to dishes of Latin America. We use annatto to create a brilliant cooking oil for coloring sauces and rice: In a very small pot or skillet (a stainless steel measuring cup works well), swirl 1 teaspoon of annato seeds in 1 tablespoon of oil on medium-low heat, watching to prevent scorching, until the oil becomes bright reddish orange; strain the oil and discard the seeds. Annatto is available in stores specializing in Latin American foods.

ARTICHOKE HEARTS. Cooked artichoke hearts can be purchased canned or frozen. At Moosewood we use canned artichoke hearts packed in brine. These plain artichoke hearts have more possible uses in recipes than the marinated kind packed in jars, and they're also less expensive. Available in well-stocked supermarkets.

BASIL. The spicy perfume of fresh basil enlivens foods as ethnically diverse as Pesto Genovese and Thai stir-fries. Dried basil lacks the full bouquet of the fresh herb but can be used in recipes in this book that do not specify fresh basil. Fresh sprigs of basil, loosely wrapped in plastic, can be kept refrigerated for several days.

BAY LEAF. Chowders, stews, sauces, stocks, and marinades are highlighted by the refreshing scent of bay leaves. Look for dried leaves that are green or gray-green but not brown and brittle. This strongly flavored herb should be used in moderation; 2 large bay leaves will season a whole pot of soup.

BEANS. Beans are an excellent source of protein, complex carbohydrates, vitamins, fiber, and other nutrients, as well as being an essential traditional element of meatless cuisines. Cooks with foresight (and time) can prepare dried beans ahead of time for quick addition to later meals (see pages 354–55), but canned and frozen beans are reasonable alternatives. We often use frozen lima beans and black-eyed peas. We look for canned beans with no additives beyond salt. Some brands we've used include THE ALLEN'S, AMERICAN PRAIRIE, EDEN, GOYA, PROGRESSO, and SAHADI.

Beano is a product for people who have trouble digesting beans. It's an enzyme that helps the body digest complex sugars in beans without breaking down the useful fiber. A few drops of the liquid are applied to each cooked serving. We haven't conducted any controlled studies of this product, but if you've had trouble in the past, this is a simple remedy worth trying. It is available in natural food stores and many supermarkets.

BLACK PEPPER. Ground black pepper gives a zest and warmth to so many savory dishes that it's earned a special place at the table, away from its colleagues on the spice rack. Freshly ground peppercorns are far superior to preground pepper; a pepper mill or grinder is a good investment to replace the traditional shakers.

BOUILLON POWDERS AND CUBES. Homemade vegetable stock (see page 359) is richer and more flavorful than broth made with bouillon powder or cubes; however, bouillon can be prepared in an instant. We have found that the following brands are a useful substitution for homemade stock: MORGA (salted or salt-free bouillon cube or vegetable broth powder), GAYELORD HAUSER (salt-free vegetable broth powder), FRONTIER HERBS AND SPICES (vegetable or vegetarian "chicken" or "beef" flavors, salted or salt-free broth powders). All are available at natural food stores and well-stocked supermarkets.

BUCKWHEAT. A staple of Eastern Europe, buckwheat groats, also called *kasha*, are a distinctively flavored, substantial, high-protein grain. This quick-cooking grain can be eaten as a side dish or breakfast cereal. For cooking directions, see page 356. Buckwheat is available in natural food stores or in the Jewish specialty foods section in the supermarket.

BUCKWHEAT NOODLES. Called *soba* in Japan, these are flat and thin, resembling linguini, and have a distinctive nutty flavor and heartiness. We use them in brothy soups and noodle salads.

BULGHUR. A quick-cooking form of whole wheat, bulghur has a nutty flavor and chewy, but light, texture. Bulghur is made of wheat berries that have been precooked, dried, and cracked. See page 356 for cooking directions. We use bulghur for tabouli and other grain salads and for stuffings for vegetables. Bulghur is available in natural food stores and in well-stocked supermarkets.

CAPERS. The pickled flower buds of a Mediterranean shrub, capers are a sharp, distinctively flavored addition to sauces, stews, fish dishes, and salads. Capers are packed in brine, so it is best to rinse and drain them before using. Opened jars should be kept refrigerated.

CARDAMOM. Sold as pods or seeds, this intensely aromatic spice is used in Indian, Northern European, and Middle Eastern cuisines. Cardamom is an expensive spice, but its strong flavor goes a long way: just ½ teaspoon for a whole loaf of Finnish sweet bread. Grind the seeds just before using.

CATSUP. While many people assume catsup to be as American as apple pie, the name actually comes from the Indonesian *kechap*. The Western version, a sweet-sour tomato-based sauce, differs substantially from the soy-based Southeast Asian sauces. We use catsup in Russian dressing, sweet-and-sour sauces, and of course on tofu burgers and tofu "meat" loaves. We choose brands that have no additives or preservatives and are low in sugar. Available in natural food stores and well-stocked supermarkets.

CAYENNE. Cayenne is finely ground dried hot red peppers. Commercial products vary in heat intensity, so start small, perhaps ⅛ teaspoon of cayenne for 4 servings. We've found there's no reason to limit hot pepper to obviously spicy dishes. You can add a lift to other savory foods with the addition of a pinch of cayenne; the flavors will be enhanced but not overwhelmed. For best results, add cayenne at the start of cooking a dish, sautéing it with other primary seasonings such as garlic or onions. Cayenne added later, without enough cooking, may taste harsh.

CHEESE. Parmesan, Romano, cheddar, mozzarella, feta, and Monterey Jack are cheeses we find very useful. Pasta, pizzas, quesadillas, and omelets are just some of the favorite cheese-enhanced dishes we automatically think of for fast meals.

Firm aged cheeses, like Parmesan and Romano, are long keepers. Buy them as wedges; grated cheeses may be convenient, but they're not worth the sacrifice in flavor. It doesn't take long to grate a small amount of these very flavorful cheeses with a hand grater, and it takes even less time if you use a food processor. Less commonly available, but with a sharp, distinctive flavor, is ricotta salata, a dry, salted, aged cheese found in many supermarkets and Italian specialty stores.

Soft cheeses such as brie, chèvre, and fresh mozzarella have a short shelf life once their packing has been opened, and so are best purchased right before use.

Smoked cheese, such as cheddar or mozzarella, provides a vegetarian alternative to the distinctive flavors of smoked meats. Look for genuinely smoked unprocessed cheeses for the best quality.

Many cheeses are available as reduced-fat, or "lite," cheeses, usually with a third less fat than conventional cheeses. Some low-fat cheeses are just fine, but others may not melt well, or may have textural or flavor problems, so experiment. Soft cheeses such as cottage and ricotta can be purchased in low- or no-fat varieties. Neufchâtel cheese, often labeled "lite" cream cheese, has approximately a third less fat than regular cream cheese and is almost indistinguishable in flavor and texture.

For people avoiding dairy products, soy cheeses may be an acceptable, though somewhat expensive, alternative. SOYA KAAS has two nicely flavored and meltable types of soy cheese: jalapeño pepper and mozzarella. SOYCO brand soy "parmesan cheese" is good.

CHESAPEAKE BAY SEASONING. Popular beyond the shores of the bay, this seasoning is a distinctive mix of spices and herbs used to flavor seafood dishes, chowders, and stews. Two brands to look for are OLD BAY and MCCORMICK.

CHILES.

Fresh chiles. Fresh chile peppers add more than just heat to food; their complex flavor contributes a full-bodied zestiness. It doesn't take long to mince a fresh hot pepper (see page 349), and 1 small pepper can adequately season a dish to feed 4.

In the last few years, we've noticed a marked increase in the variety of fresh chile peppers available in markets here in Ithaca. We've seen — in descending order of piquancy — habanero, serrano, Super Chile, cayenne, jalapeño, Mexi-bell, Anaheim, and poblano. Cooks who live in the West or Southwest will undoubtedly have a wider selection. In our experience, peppers of the same variety, picked from different parts of the plant or purchased at different times, can vary in hotness from fiery to mellow. To avoid overseasoning, taste a tiny piece before deciding how much to add during cooking, or use small amounts in the dish and serve a spicy salsa at the table for diners who can take the heat. Eat bland starchy foods, such as rice, bread, or tortillas, to still the fires of a particularly hot dish; liquids will spread the fire throughout the mouth and throat. Fresh chiles will keep in the vegetable drawer of a refrigerator for a few weeks.

Dried whole chiles. Garlands of whole dried chile peppers make decorative, useful kitchen ornaments. Dried chiles can be ground in a spice grinder to the desired consistency — fine or coarse. Use small dried chiles, whole or halved, to season cooking oil: heat them gently in the oil to avoid scorching, and then either remove the chiles for a mild flavor or leave them in to increase piquancy.

CHILI OIL. Asian specialty stores and well-stocked supermarkets are the source of hot pepper oils that are used as a last-minute addition to spice savory foods. Use the concentrated oil sparingly, a few drops at a time. Chili oil will keep indefinitely when stored at room temperature.

CHILI PASTE. Various chili pastes of Asian origin — Chinese, Thai, or Indonesian — are usually composed of chile peppers, oil, salt, and other spices such as garlic or curry. Chili pastes add piquant heat to savory foods. Usually packed in glass jars, they are available in Asian markets or well-stocked supermarkets. Refrigerate after opening.

CHINESE FERMENTED BLACK BEANS. These soy beans fermented with salt and spices contribute a rich, aromatic quality to Chinese-style dishes. Packed in jars or plastic bags, they are available at Asian markets and well-stocked supermarkets. Once opened, they should be refrigerated, and will keep almost indefinitely.

CHINESE WHEAT AND EGG NOODLES. Very similar to domestic pasta. Udon noodles, similar in shape to a wide linguini, are a Japanese type we especially like for flavor and texture.

CILANTRO (FRESH CORIANDER). Prized for its fresh, clean fragrance and unique flavor, cilantro has long been popular in the cuisines of Latin America, Africa, Asia, and India, although its widespread use in American kitchens is relatively new. Try adding cilantro to spicy salsas, bean dishes, soups, guacamole, marinades, sauces, and stews. The chopped fresh leaves are best included at the end of cooking time. Dried cilantro is flavorless and should be avoided.

For some people, cilantro is an acquired taste, but once it's acquired, many people act like new converts. Cilantro can be found in well-stocked supermarkets and in Asian or Hispanic groceries. Cilantro that is loosely wrapped in plastic will keep refrigerated for up to 1 week.

CINNAMON. Familiar, sweet, and evocative, cinnamon is a universally popular spice. We were once told by a real estate agent friend that heating a little cinnamon in the oven or microwave was a helpful device to create a "homey" ambience in a house for sale. No one needs to be told about its use in myriad desserts; however, in Asian and Latin American cooking, cinnamon is used as a fragrant spice for savory soups, sauces, curries, and stews.

CLOVES. Spicy with a rich, concentrated flavor, cloves are a valued addition to curry mixes, desserts, and beverages. Use with care, as a pinch or two of ground cloves may be a sufficient amount to season a dish without overpowering it.

COCONUT MILK. Tropical Asian, Caribbean, and African cuisines all use coconut milk with its unique smooth texture and rich flavor. We use an unsweetened coconut milk without preservatives from EPICUREAN INTERNATIONAL. Other brands may be available in your area. Avoid the heavily sweetened types that are used as beverage mixers. To make coconut milk at home, see page 360. Store leftover coconut milk in a tightly sealed jar in the refrigerator, or freeze it in ice cube trays and transfer it later to a closed container in the freezer.

CORIANDER SEEDS. The dried light brown, round seeds of the coriander plant have a distinctly different, sweeter taste and aroma than cilantro, the fresh herb of the same plant. We use freshly ground coriander in Indian curries, Mexican bean dishes and casseroles, soups, stews, and marinades.

COUSCOUS. A popular quick-cooking grain of North African origin, couscous is basically tiny pearls of pasta made from finely milled semolina wheat. For cooking directions, see page 356. We use couscous for grain salads, in stuffings for vegetables, and as a bed for saucy foods.

CRUSHED RED PEPPER FLAKES. Crushed red pepper is dried red chiles in the form of coarsely ground flakes. It can be added during cooking, but the flakes are also well suited for use as a condiment for prepared foods: soups, sauces, pasta dishes, pizzas, and stews.

CUMIN. We use freshly ground cumin seeds to impart a robust fragrance and flavor to curries, salsas, bean dishes, soups, and marinades. For heightened aroma, roast the whole seeds for a couple of minutes in a dry skillet or a toaster oven before grinding (see page 354).

CURRY PASTE. Prepared from a highly concentrated blend of spices and vegetable oils, curry pastes vary with the country of origin (typically India, Thailand, or Indonesia). All have a familiar multidimensional bouquet, and they range from mild to hot in spiciness. Curry paste added at the start of cooking will infuse the dish with its flavor; however, it can also be added as a quick final seasoning to soups, sauces, rice dishes, mayonnaise, and dressings. Available at Asian and well-stocked markets, an opened jar of curry paste will keep indefinitely in the refrigerator.

CURRY POWDER. There are dozens of mixtures of spices commercially available as curry powder. Enthusiasts of Indian food are more likely to purchase curry powder at an Indian food store or a spice shop, or to make their own mix, than to buy supermarket brands.

DILL. A popular herb in the cuisines of Northern and Eastern Europe and the Middle East. The mellow flavor of dill leaves, sometimes called dill weed, enriches potato dishes, cucumber salads or pickles, yogurt or sour cream dips, dressings, fall and winter stews, rice pilafs, green beans, and fish dishes. Dried dill is an acceptable substitute when the fresh herb is unavailable. Both fresh and dried are best added toward the end of the cooking time. Dill seed, with a caraway-like flavor, is often used in bread, soups, and stews.

DRIED FRUIT. A healthful snack at home and a good fellow traveler for long journeys. They are a handy addition to desserts, compotes, Neufchâtel or cream cheese spreads, and fruit chutneys. Look for untreated, unsulfured fruit at natural food stores or supermarkets. Store in a cool, dry pantry location. To plump and tenderize dried fruit, cover with an equal amount of boiling water and allow it to steep for 10 to 15 minutes, until softened.

FENNEL. The nutty, sweet, anise flavor of fennel seeds nicely complements breads, cookies, Italian biscuits, soups, marinades, and tomato sauces. Whole fennel seeds are effectively used in baked goods and marinades; freshly ground seeds are more often our choice for all other culinary uses. At the restaurant, one of our favorite salad toppings is chick peas marinated in olive oil, vinegar, fennel seeds, and dill.

FISH SAUCE. Made from fermented salted fish, fish sauce is a classic condiment in the cuisines of Southeast Asia and China. Cooking significantly reduces the "fishy" odor, leaving a unique rich taste to season stir-fries, sauces, soups, and dressings. Available in Asian food stores, this salty product requires no refrigeration.

FIVE-SPICE POWDER. A blend of star-anise, fennel, Szechuan peppercorns, cloves, and cumin, five-spice powder is a fragrant, spicy seasoning used in Chinese cooking. Cook with small amounts of this highly flavored spice (½ teaspoon will season four servings of a stir-fry).

FRUIT CONSERVES AND SPREADS. We prefer the rich, full flavor of all-fruit sugarless spreads to that of their sugared counterparts. Besides the obvious partnership with breads of all sorts, try them in dessert sauces, cake fillings, pancake toppings, or mixed with low-fat ricotta cheese as a spread or crêpe filling. SORREL RIDGE, POLANER'S ALL FRUIT, WOODSTOCK, JUST FRUIT, and KNUDSEN'S brands are available in supermarkets or natural food stores.

GARAM MASALA. A masala is a blend of spices used for seasoning Indian foods. Garam masala, unlike curry powder, is made with spices that are roasted before they are ground. This mellows the mix and allows for its addition to foods near the end of cooking time. Garam masala can be purchased in well-stocked supermarkets or specialty stores.

GARLIC. At Moosewood, garlic may be our most indispensable seasoning. It's best used in fresh form; dried and powdered garlic lack full fragrance and have an unpleasant aftertaste. An acceptable alternative is prechopped garlic packed in glass jars with no preservatives. POLANER and FLORA are two brands available in well-stocked supermarkets.

Look for fresh heads or bulbs of garlic that are firm and solid, with no brown or soft sections. Heads with large cloves are easier to peel and handle (see page 349) than those with small cloves. Store garlic in a cool, dry place but not in the refrigerator, where it might sprout or mold.

GINGER ROOT. The fresh, clean fragrance and spicy taste of ginger root are essential elements of Asian, African, and Caribbean cooking. Choose roots that are firm and not dry or shriveled. Whole ginger roots can be stored in the refrigerator, wrapped in plastic, for up to 2 weeks. For long-term refrigerated storage, peeled whole pieces of ginger can be covered with sherry in a closed jar. Use the sherry for cooking when the ginger has departed. Whole roots can also be stored in plastic bags in the freezer. Frozen roots are easy to grate; do as much as needed for a given recipe and return the remainder to the freezer. Fresh ginger root is available in produce markets and supermarkets, as well as in Asian food stores. Powdered dried ginger, which is often used to flavor baked goods, has a very different flavor and should not be used as a substitute.

HERBS AND SPICES. "Herb" most frequently refers to a plant's leafy parts, either fresh or dried. "Spices" are primarily of tropical origin and are usually derived from seeds, fruits, barks, and roots. The fragrance and flavor of herbs and spices contribute depth and dimension to foods.

Dried herbs and spices. Store dried herbs and spices in a cool part of your kitchen, away from direct sunlight or excessive heat, but not so far that they'll be inconvenient to use. We use an electric spice or coffee grinder to fresh-grind whole spices before cooking; the essential oils are dramatically more fragrant and powerful than in the preground versions. Most of us have found it well worth the expense to have a spices-only coffee grinder, so that our curries don't taste like coffee and our coffee doesn't taste like cumin. If your coffee grinder is doing double duty as a spice grinder, unwanted spice residue can be removed by grinding a couple of tablespoons of raw rice and then wiping the interior clean.

Fresh herbs. We prefer fresh herbs for much of our cooking. When substituting fresh herbs for dried in a recipe, the rule of thumb is to triple the amount and add the fresh herbs toward the end of cooking. In the summertime, when fresh herbs abound in our gardens and at the farmers' market, we freeze them and make pestos, herb butters, and herb vinegars (see Fresh Herbs, page 361) for use later in the year.

HIJIKI. With an assertive ocean flavor and nutty aroma, hijiki seaweed provides crisp texture and generous nutrients to soups, stir-fries, and simple vegetable dishes. Before serving or adding it to other foods, soak hijiki for 6 to 8 minutes in an equal volume of water. Available in Asian markets and natural food stores.

HOISIN SAUCE. Made of soybeans, sugar, vinegar, and spices, hoisin is a sweet Chinese condiment. It is traditionally used in *mu shu* dishes, where it is drizzled on delicate pancakes that are then filled with stir-fried ingredients and rolled. We sometimes add hoisin to other sauces for Chinese dishes.

HOT SAUCE. See Tabasco, page 342.

MARJORAM. The piquant taste of marjoram is reminiscent of its family member oregano, but with a sweeter flavor. As with most herbs, the fresh leaves have a more complex flavor than the dried, but either can be used in soups, stews, bean dishes, dressings, and sauces, and in marinades for vegetables or fish.

MAYONNAISE. We've visited friends with sad refrigerators, almost empty except for a jar of mayonnaise waiting patiently for a cheese sandwich to give its life meaning. This ubiquitous condiment has been overused at deli counters in sodden, gloppy potato, macaroni, and other salads. However, we find it a useful base for quick dressings or spreads. Because of the increase in salmonella-related food-borne illnesses, we decided it was unwise to serve foods containing uncooked eggs at Moosewood, and we began using commercial mayonnaise instead of making our own. We use mayonnaise made with fresh lemon juice and without onion and garlic powder (HELLMANN'S is the widely distributed national brand we use, but there are also good local brands). We jazz it up with fresh herbs, pesto, lemon or lime juice, chopped garlic, scallions, red onion, tomatoes, olives, curry powder and other spices, herbed vinegars, or flavorful oils such as extra-virgin olive oil.

MILLET. Millet is a small yellow highly nutritious grain that is used as a staple in the cuisines of much of Africa. For cooking directions, see page 356. Serve it with a saucy stew or "as is" with butter. Millet is available in natural food stores and well-stocked supermarkets. Be sure to get hulled millet, not birdseed! Store this perishable grain in a tightly capped container in the refrigerator.

MINT. Mints can refresh, cool, and enliven. When fresh mint is available, we use it for cooking and as an appealing garnish of vivid green, clean-scented leaves. Besides spearmint and peppermint, look for apple, orange, or pineapple mint. Mint dries well, retaining most of its essential oils. We use mint in tabouli, pilafs, dips, salads, simple vegetable sautés, preserves, and custards.

MIRIN. Also known as "hon-mirin." A sweet Japanese cooking wine with a distinctive flavor that resembles sweet sherry but is not quite the same. It is a colorless alcohol made from the glutinous short-grain rice called mochigome and has a median alcohol content of about 17 percent and a sugar content of about 26 percent. Mirin is often used in stocks, sauces, and marinades in combination with soy sauce, sesame oil or sesame paste, and ginger. It is traditionally included in teriyaki sauce, ponzu, and gomatare.

MISO. A thick purée used for flavoring many kinds of dishes, miso is a product of the fermentation of soy beans, salt, and various grains. This traditional Japanese food is high in protein and acts as an aid to digestive enzymes. In the U.S., the most commonly available types of miso are *white or rice miso,* mild and relatively sweet, *red or barley miso,* savory and versatile, and *dark soy miso,* thick and more strongly flavored. Miso adds a deep rich flavor and good complementary protein to dressings, soups, spreads, stews, and sauces. Refrigerated, it will keep indefinitely. Natural food stores are a good source of a variety of misos. Brands that we like include ONOZAKI, EDEN, MISO MASTER, and SOUTH RIVER.

MUSTARD. In the last few years, the addition of herbs, spices, wines, and sweeteners have transformed this once mundane condiment. The Dijon type is our most frequently used mustard. White wine, spices, and vinegar give Dijon its distinctive flavor. Dressings, sauces, sandwiches, soups, and stews are enlivened by the savory tang of mustard.

MUSTARD SEEDS.

Yellow mustard seeds. Ground yellow mustard seeds are the pungent basis for the familiar condiment; whole seeds are useful as a pickling spice. Freshly ground mustard seeds add zest to salad dressings, marinades, and sauces.

Black mustard seeds. Less pungent than their yellow relatives, black mustard seeds are used in Indian cooking. To release their nutty flavor, gently heat the whole seeds in oil, or other fats, until they "pop," then add other ingredients to the seasoned oil. Available in Indian groceries or specialty food stores.

NORI. A dark green or purplish seaweed, sheets of nori are the traditional wrappers for sushi rolls as well as being a highly nutritious seasoning for foods. The briny flavor of nori is enhanced if you toast it just before use by passing a sheet of the seaweed very briefly over a gas flame until it is crisp. Nori, available in Asian markets or natural food stores, is sold dried in thin sheets packed in cellophane, plastic, or cans.

NUT BUTTERS. Besides the ever-popular peanut butter, cashew, almond, and hazelnut butters can be an occasional treat. Natural food stores and supermarkets stock nut butters without sweeteners, added fats, preservatives, or stabilizers. Stir nut butters thoroughly to distribute the oil before storing in the refrigerator.

NUTMEG. We use nutmeg as a classic aromatic spice for spinach dishes, white sauces, desserts, fruit punches, and crêpe or French toast batters. This is yet another spice with a notably livelier fragrance when freshly ground rather than preground. It is quickly done by grating a whole nutmeg on the finest blade of a hand grater or with a specially designed nutmeg grater.

OLIVE OIL.

Pure olive oil is a fragrant cooking oil indispensable to the cuisines of the Mediterranean world. Olive oil is appealing to people trying to reduce cholesterol levels because it is a monosaturated fat. Store olive oil in a cool dark place.

Extra-virgin olive oil is made from the first pressing of the highest-quality olives. It has a low smoking point, so it isn't suitable for cooking; it is loved for its richly aromatic, fruity flavor and is used in dressings and marinades, to flavor cooked foods or salads, or merely to drizzle over a hunk of crusty bread. We make the simplest of dips for raw vegetables by adding a dash of salt and pepper to a flavorful extra-virgin olive oil.

OLIVES. The briny tang of olives enlivens salads, soups, salsa, spreads, sauces, and fillings. The three kinds that we use the most are:

Calamata. Rich and meaty, the Calamatas we use are unpitted Greek imports. We like their flavor so much, we'll take the time to slice the pit away to use the flesh for cooking.

California ripe olives. Canned varieties of black olives that are inexpensive and readily available, and although lacking in the richness of flavor of their Mediterranean kin, have an appeal of their own.

Spanish olives. The familiar green olives, with or without the pimiento stuffing, are a useful savory addition to rice dishes, cheese spreads, and bean dishes.

Look in delis and specialty stores for other kinds of olives to serve as appetizers or with salads. Black Gaeta, green Sicilian, and Ligurian are some Mediterranean types we enjoy.

OREGANO. The pronounced flavor of oregano is easily recognized as the dominant herb of many commercial pizza sauces. There's no reason to limit its use to tomato sauce, however; oregano combines well with other Mediterranean foods — eggplant, zucchini, garlic, olive oil, parsley, and fresh tomatoes.

PAPRIKA. We recommend sweet Hungarian paprika. Hot paprika can be used as a cayenne substitute. Paprikas should be cooked over gentle heat to avoid scorching.

PARSLEY. Fresh parsley is the most reliably available herb in American markets. It blends nicely with the flavors of other herbs as well as adding its own fresh, clean taste. Parsley is a time-honored breath sweetener. Immerse the stems in a container of water or loosely wrap bunches in plastic, and store in the refrigerator. Dried parsley is essentially worthless, lacking in both flavor and color. We never use it.

PASTA. Moosewood cooks eat a lot of pasta, both in the restaurant and at home. We recommend Italian imported pasta for higher quality in taste and texture. In Italy, where pasta is a national obsession, government standards limit ingredients, additives, and production processes to the extent that a finer product is more likely than with our domestic brands.

Recipes in this book call for an assortment of shapes and sizes of Italian pasta that engage the palate as well as the eye. The following guidelines may help in choosing pasta shapes:

• Long strands work well with tomato sauces and pestos: spaghetti, fusilli, linguini.
• Hollowed shapes are well paired with chunky vegetable sauces: shells, penne, ziti, orecchietti (little ears).
• Flat pastas are good with creamy, smooth, or cheese sauces: fettuccine, tagliatelle.
• Very short or small pastas are used in soups and bean dishes or as side dishes: pastina, tubetini, orzo (rice-shaped pasta, also called rosa marina).

Fresh pasta. Supermarkets now carry vacuum-packed fresh pasta, formerly available only if made at home or purchased in a specialty store. Fresh pasta has a softer texture and richer flavor than dried. Care should be taken to avoid overcooking, since it requires less cooking time.

Flavored pastas. Pastas flavored with tomatoes, herbs such as basil or cayenne, spinach, black beans, beets, and other diverse foods are available both fresh and dried. The flavors are usually subtle, but interesting visual effects can be achieved with variously colored pastas and sauces.

PEANUT OIL. Peanut oil is a pleasantly flavored oil that is a staple of African cuisines as well as Chinese and other Asian cuisines. It is especially good for deep-frying because it has a high smoking point.

PIMIENTOS. see Roasted red peppers.

PINE NUTS. Pine nuts, also called pignoli, are the edible seeds of certain pine trees. Pine nuts are expensive. Always store them in an airtight container or plastic bag in the refrigerator.

POLENTA. A versatile northern Italian dish, polenta is a simple cornmeal preparation. See page 357 for cooking directions. Coarsely ground cornmeal makes polenta with a substantial texture, but finely ground cornmeal cooks faster. Polenta can be topped with stew or with steamed or sautéed vegetables to make a hearty meal. Leftover polenta can be baked, broiled, grilled, or pan-fried and served plain or topped with vegetables, sauce, or cheese.

PORCINI MUSHROOMS. Imported dried Italian porcini mushrooms have a rich, woodsy flavor. Though they are expensive, a little goes a long way. Soak porcini in warm water for 20 to 30 minutes. Drain and use the mushrooms as needed, reserving the strained soaking liquid for use as a stock. Porcini are available in supermarkets, usually located with other Italian specialties.

PUFF PASTRY. Commercially prepared puff pastry makes an elegant presentation with little effort. It usually comes in 16-ounce packages containing two square or rectangular sheets. The frozen dough can be thawed in the refrigerator for several hours or overnight, or at room temperature in about 20 minutes. Puff pastry is available in supermarket freezer sections.

QUINOA. Touted as a "supergrain," quinoa (KEEN-wah) is an ancient Incan grain which contains more protein, vitamins, and minerals than most other vegetable or animal foods. It has a delicious mild, nutty flavor and a slightly crunchy texture. For basic cooking instructions, see page 357. Serve with Tomatican (see page 216) or steamed vegetables with Chimichurri Sauce (see page 108). Quinoa is available in natural food stores and well-stocked supermarkets.

RICE.

Arborio rice. An Italian short-grain rice of distinctive flavor and creamy texture. This rice can quickly absorb a large amount of liquid yet still remain firm. It is available in well-stocked supermarkets and in Italian specialty stores.

Brown rice. Our whole grain of choice at Moosewood. It's a perfect companion for so many of our dishes — the light, mild flavor complements without competing. In our history, brown rice was one of the keystones of vegetarian cooking associated with lifestyle changes of the early 1970s. There were stories of people living on nothing but brown rice, soy sauce, and steamed vegetables, with maybe a few crushed sesame seeds or a little seaweed thrown in on festive occasions. Be that as it may, brown rice does present the quick-cooking chef with the problem of a 45- to 50-minute cooking time. See page 357 for cooking instructions. Prepare more rice than needed for a given meal, then quickly steam the leftovers (see page 353) for subsequent meals. Cooked brown rice will keep up to 1 week in the refrigerator.

ARROWHEAD MILLS makes an instant brown rice that's ready in 12 minutes, but we think there is some sacrifice in flavor for the savings in time. It's available in natural food stores and well-stocked supermarkets.

Long-grain brown rice is dry and fluffy and is preferred in Chinese, Indian, Southeast Asian, and Middle Eastern cooking. Short-grain brown rice is moister and slightly sticky, with a somewhat sweeter flavor. It is extensively used in North America and Japan.

Basmati rice. Basmati rice has a fragrance reminiscent of popcorn, but with an almost floral quality. Basmati rice is available as a "white" or whole-grain brown.

White rice. Although not as nutritionally valuable nor as fully flavored as whole-grain rice, white rice will cook in a comparatively short time — about 20 minutes (see page 357). Long-grain is best for a side dish, since the grains are lighter and more separate than short or medium grains. Avoid using "instant" or "minute" types, since their flavor and texture are markedly inferior.

RICE NOODLES. Rice noodles are available in different thicknesses, from a thin vermicelli type (also called rice sticks) to a flat ¼-inch-wide noodle. Besides the usual method of cooking pasta in boiling water until tender (about 3 to 5 minutes), rice noodles can be soaked in warm water for 15 minutes. Drain in a colander and use in soups, stir-fries, and salads.

ROASTED RED PEPPERS AND PIMIENTOS. Sharing sweet flavor and lush, smooth texture, roasted red peppers and pimientos are surprisingly useful pantry staples that easily "dress up" simple foods such as salads, omelets, and stews. The pleasant smoky flavor of roasted peppers results from their being charred before peeling. Both products have better flavor when packed in glass jars than in cans. Look for them with Italian products or canned vegetables in supermarkets. Since the refrigerator shelf life of an opened jar of roasted peppers or pimientos is just a few days, we freeze the following purée to use as a flavor boost for soups and sauces: For ½ cup of roasted peppers or pimientos, use 2 tablespoons of olive oil and 1 garlic clove; blend in a processor or blender until smooth; freeze in ice cube trays and then pack the cubes in freezer bags.

ROSEMARY. Rosemary asserts its presence with the sharp scent of pine woods. Used with restraint, it's a wonderful herb for crusty breads, soups, marinades, roasted vegetables, fish, and stews. Fresh rosemary is increasingly available in markets. Dried rosemary is more brittle and somewhat woody; add it to dishes in a cheesecloth pouch for easy removal.

SAFFRON. The dried stamens of the saffron crocus provide an intriguing flavor and warm golden color to savory dishes. This expensive spice, always used in small quantities, should be purchased in strand, not powdered, form. It is a classic seasoning for risotto, pilafs, soups, breads, and bouillabaisse and other stews of the Mediterranean region.

SAGE. Sage is an unfairly ignored herb in the cooking repertoire of Americans, perhaps due to an over-association with holiday poultry stuffing. Used discreetly, sage enhances seasoned oils and herb butters, cheese spreads and sauces, grain pilafs, hearty soups, bean dishes, potatoes, and omelets. Use the fresh herb when it's available; the flavor is milder and sweeter than that of the dried leaves.

SALSA. Mexican-style spicy tomato-based sauces are essential pantry items for quick preparation of dips, bean dishes, burritos, tostadas, and quesadillas, or for use as a table sauce to add spark to any number of foods. Commercial brands, with no additives or preservatives, are available at natural food stores and well-stocked supermarkets.

SEITAN. A wheat product that contains the protein-rich gluten without the starch, seitan is a chewy meatlike food. It has been used as the basis of many Chinese vegetarian "mock meat" dishes in meals created in Buddhist monasteries. Mildly flavored, seitan picks up the seasonings of a given dish while adding a hearty, substantial quality. We use seitan in assertively seasoned dishes, spicy sautés, curries, and richly flavored stews. Seitan, also sold as *wheat gluten,* is available in natural food and Asian markets.

SESAME BUTTER. Made from roasted unhulled sesame seeds, sesame butter has a stronger taste and denser texture than tahini. Use it as you would any nut butter. Store it in the refrigerator. Sesame butter is available in natural food stores and well-stocked supermarkets.

SESAME OIL. Thick, amber-colored, and aromatic, dark sesame oil is made from roasted sesame seeds. Dark sesame oil burns easily and loses flavor when overheated, so it is not used for cooking, but rather as a condiment or flavoring for dressings, soups, sauces, and stir-fries. It is available at Asian groceries and well-stocked supermarkets.

SHIITAKE MUSHROOMS. The smoky flavor and chewy texture of shiitake mushrooms offer a nice contrast to more familiar vegetables in soups and stir-fries. To soften the dried mushrooms for cooking, submerge them in hot water for 20 minutes. Drain (reserve the liquid to use as a stock), trim off and discard the stems, and thinly slice the caps. Local markets may occasionally stock fresh shiitake, but the dried mushrooms are always available at Asian markets and well-stocked supermarkets.

SOY SAUCE. Essential for Asian cooking, soy sauce also adds flavor and salt to soups, stews, and sauces where its dark coloring will not detract from the appearance of a dish. Soy sauces vary in saltiness; use a conservative amount at first and add more later if you are not familiar with a given brand. American, Japanese, and Chinese products are available at natural food stores, Asian groceries, and supermarkets. Look for naturally brewed soy sauces that do not contain sugar, food coloring, or chemical additives.

Both *shoyu* and *tamari* are Japanese-type soy sauces. Shoyu sauces contain soybeans, wheat, water, and salt. Tamari, a by-product of the miso-making process, is saltier and more strongly flavored than shoyu and contains no wheat.

Light soy sauces work well with vegetarian and fish dishes. These should not be confused with "lite" or low-sodium soy sauces, which are reasonable choices for reduced-salt diets. SUPERIOR SOY is an imported light Chinese soy sauce.

SUN-DRIED TOMATOES. Savory dishes are enlivened by the tart-sweet taste of sun-dried tomatoes. Available packed dry or in oil, they're usually found with other Italian specialties in supermarkets. Dry-packed tomatoes are less expensive than oil-packed, but will need to be soaked in hot water for 15 to 30 minutes, then drained. Oil-packed tomatoes are ready to use. The salty but flavorful oil can be discreetly used to season savory dishes.

TABASCO AND OTHER HOT SAUCES. A splash or two of hot pepper sauce, such as Tabasco, adds a bright spark to many dishes. Look for hot sauces without preservatives, artificial colors, or other additives. Tabasco and related sauces can be kept indefinitely at room temperature.

TAHINI. Rich and creamy, with a nutty flavor, tahini is made from hulled toasted sesame seeds. Tahini enriches savory dishes, dressings, sauces, and desserts in the cuisines of Mediterranean Africa and the Middle East. Store refrigerated. Available in natural food stores and well-stocked supermarkets.

TARRAGON. One of the classic *fines herbes* of French cuisine, tarragon contributes an anise-like bouquet to the flavors of parsley, chives, and chervil. On its own, it makes an exceptional seasoning for vinaigrette dressings, mushroom sauces, fish, marinades, herb butters or seasoned oils, and stews. The dried herb needs to be used more sparingly than the fresh; the flavor has a haylike overtone.

TEMPEH. Tempeh, a cultured soybean product, is a relative newcomer to American cooking but is an age-old part of Indonesia's cuisine. The culturing process allows for easy digestion of the soybeans. Tempeh's chewy, hearty texture, high protein content, and nutty flavor encourage its use as a nutritious low-fat ingredient in vegetarian meals. It readily absorbs marinades and sauces and is dense enough to be grilled. Tempeh can be found in natural food stores, either fresh or, more commonly, frozen. Thaw frozen tempeh before using, but slice or cube it while it's still partially frozen to avoid crumbling.

THYME. The assertive flavor and scent of thyme benefit chowders and onion soups, stuffings, stews, croutons, bean dishes, and hearty casseroles. Thyme's flavor is strong; small amounts should suffice. Choose the dried leaf; avoid powdered thyme.

TOFU. Also known as *bean curd*, tofu is an extremely versatile, protein-rich, low-fat food whose history goes back more than 2,000 years to the Western Han Dynasty of China. Tofu has unfairly received a bad reputation as a "health" food completely lacking in appeal. Admittedly, plain, unprepared tofu is pretty boring; however this can be an asset for a product that can, chameleon-like, assume a multitude of roles.

Fresh tofu is available in well-stocked supermarkets, natural food stores, and Asian markets, either fresh-packed in water or vacuum-packed in dated containers. Fresh tofu should be used within 1 week of purchase, with a change of packing water every other day. "Silken" or soft tofu is a creamy product useful for soups, desserts, dressings, dips, beverages, and fillings. We use "firm" tofu for stir-fries, salads, broiling, and baking.

Seasoned tofu is a firm, dense tofu produced by extracting the water under pressure and subsequently cooking with soy sauce and seasonings. TOFU-KAN, processed by Ithaca Soy Foods, is a local product we use and recommend. It's available throughout the northeastern United States, from Maine to Maryland. Similar products may be regionally available in natural food stores or well-stocked supermarkets. Chinese markets sell *five-spice bean curd,* a seasoned tofu with a distinctive anise flavor. Variations in spicing and texture occur in the different regions of China, where pressed seasoned tofu is a widespread product. Conveniently used where the texture of softer tofu would be inappropriate, as in a sandwich, pressed tofu is equally versatile for savory dishes.

TOMATO PASTE. Sometimes just a tablespoon or two of tomato paste will add the right touch of acidity, color, and texture to a dish. Tomato paste in tubes has a fresher flavor than canned tomato paste, and the tubes can be kept in the refrigerator for occasional use. If you have difficulty finding the tubes (usually found with the Italian imports), canned tomato paste can be frozen in small 2- to 3-tablespoon packages.

TORTILLAS. If you live in a community where fresh tortillas are available, they should clearly be your first choice. If not, look for refrigerated or frozen wheat and corn tortillas that are free of preservatives. Frozen tortillas need to thaw, in their unopened package, for about 20 minutes at room temperature.

TURMERIC. Turmeric imparts a rich golden color and subtle taste to foods of the Middle East and India. We use it in curry spice mixes, soups, rice, and lentil and bean dishes.

VEGETABLE OIL. We find a bland vegetable oil without preservatives, such as soy or safflower oil, to be a good all-purpose cooking or salad oil.

VINEGARS. The sharp flavor of vinegar adds an important counterpoint to many dishes. Stock a variety of vinegars for a multitude of uses.

Apple cider vinegar. The most versatile vinegar in our kitchen, cider vinegar has a mild, unobtrusive flavor for dressings, marinades, and sauces.

Balsamic. Richly flavored, tart yet sweet, balsamic vinegar is the perfect companion to extra-virgin olive oil for a drizzle on a salad of mixed greens, fresh tomatoes, or steamed vegetables. Balsamic vinegar is, however, high in sulfites.

Distilled white. Especially useful for pickling or in Asian-style dressings and marinades, white vinegar is also fine for most cooking.

Fruit vinegars. Unusually flavored fruit vinegars add fragrance and taste to delicate salads. Buttercrunch or Boston lettuce and fresh tender vegetables are particularly well dressed with fruit vinegars and a light salad oil. Try a splash or two in a fruit salad.

Herbed vinegars. Salads, dressings, and marinades can be easily and richly flavored with herb vinegars (see page 362).

Rice vinegar. A versatile, mildly flavored vinegar whose signature dish is sushi. Use rice vinegar for Asian-style dressings, marinades, and sauces.

Wine vinegar. Red or white wine vinegars spark dressings with a hearty, full flavor. Red wine vinegar is the more assertive of the two and is good paired with Mediterranean herbs such as oregano, basil, rosemary, and thyme. We like to use white wine vinegar in sauces and marinades for cooked vegetable salads.

WASABI. Familiar to devotees of sushi, wasabi is a green Japanese radish with a pungent flavor and a sinus-clearing effect. Wasabi adds a lift to dipping sauces, soups, Asian noodle salads, and nori rolls. Wasabi powder is mixed with water to form a smooth paste, then set aside for a few minutes before using. Premixed wasabi paste and the dried powder are both available in Asian markets and well-stocked supermarkets.

WINES AND SPIRITS. Try to use organically grown wines to avoid the additives in many domestic and imported wines. For culinary purposes, we keep a supply of:

Red and white dry wines. Inexpensive table wines are adequate, as are leftover dinner wines.

Sherry. Both dry and the sweeter cream sherry.

Marsala. Richly flavored Italian wine; use sweet for desserts, dry for savory dishes.

Chinese rice wine and mirin. For Asian dishes. Rice wine is fairly dry; mirin is sweet.

Liqueurs. We frequently use amaretto and Grand Marnier in desserts.

WORCESTERSHIRE SAUCE. A commercially prepared condiment formulated by Victorian chemists Lea and Perrins, it is named after the Worcester shop where they accidentally discovered that aging their experimental concoction created a tasty sauce. The sauce contains molasses, anchovies or sardines, garlic, sugar, tamarind, soy sauce, vinegar, and spices. Vegetarian adaptations without additives or preservatives are now available — among them, LIFE brand, from Britain.

YOGURT. This cultured milk product is a familiar nutritious snack or light meal food; it is also a convenient base for or addition to dressings, sauces, soups, and desserts. For best quality, look for brands with no added thickeners or stabilizers. We like BROWN COW FARM yogurt, which is made with only yogurt cultures and milk (and natural flavorings, when flavored). Nonfat and low-fat yogurts are readily available in supermarkets. At Moosewood we serve low-fat yogurt and use it in cooking. Nonfat yogurt, although not as full-bodied, will also work in our recipes.

Preparation and Techniques

General Tips

• Before beginning any recipe, take the time to read the recipe through, and gather the ingredients and necessary equipment. Admittedly there are impatient, low-blood-sugar moments when we plunge, helter-skelter, into an unknown recipe — but we always regret it later.

• Purchase a timer if you don't already have one, to keep track of cooking time.

• Keep a measuring cup in often-used pantry items, such as flour or rice.

• Although preshredded cheeses, chopped nuts, and cut vegetables are more expensive than whole items, they may occasionally be a worthwhile expenditure when time is at a premium.

• Chop the same ingredients for multidish meals at one time; for example, if two dishes contain onions, cut and measure the amounts for both.

• Clean or soak dirty cooking pans or utensils as you go along. Have a sink filled with soapy water, or load the dishwasher. Pots that contained starches (rice, pasta, potatoes) or eggs and milk clean more easily if soaked in cold water.

Cutting Techniques

WE PREPARE MOST vegetables with a knife and cutting board. Although potentially fearsome to the novice, sharp knives easily pierce hard vegetables, whereas dull ones have a tendency to slip, possibly injuring fingers and hands. We use stainless steel knives that won't discolor food. Hold the food in place with one hand, curling the fingers down and under to protect the fingertips. Be attentive only to the task at hand.

Food processor shredding blades are extremely useful for cutting a relatively large quantity of vegetables for certain dishes — such as a cabbage-carrot slaw. Shredding and grating cheese is also efficiently handled with the processor shredding blade. Very hard, dense cheeses, such as Romano and Parmesan, are best cut into 1- to 2-inch cubes and processed in the work bowl with a steel blade to yield a finely grated product. This can also be achieved by very slowly pushing the hard cheese through the shredding blade.

The recipes in this book give specific instructions for how to prepare the ingredients (chopped onions, minced garlic, diced red pepper), often with an eye to the clock, because the way foods are cut is crucial to the speed with which they cook. Certain vegetable dishes (salad plates, stir-fries, stews) are enhanced by their visual appeal and look better when cut by hand. So, aside from timing considerations, aesthetic decisions determine how foods should be cut—large chunks for a rustic stew, elegant matchstick shapes for a salad plate, diagonally sliced vegetables for a stir-fry. We have tried to balance time and aesthetics. To avoid over- or undercooking, cut foods into relatively even pieces that will cook at the same rate.

CHOP. Cut foods into pieces ½-inch square or larger. Onions, however, should be cut no bigger than ½-inch square for quick cooking to a soft texture.

SLICE. Cuts are made ½ inch apart for thick slices, ¼ to ⅛ inch apart for thinner slices. Hold the knife blade at a 45° angle to food for diagonal slices.

DICE. Slices are further cut crosswise in each direction to create cubes ranging in size from ½ inch to ⅛ inch, or fine dice. To quicken this procedure, stack slices on top of each other and cut through the pile.

MINCE. Going one step smaller, minced foods—in this book commonly ginger root, garlic, and chile pepper—are achieved by chopping finely diced foods back and forth with a long-bladed knife. It's helpful to push the food back into a pile with the knife blade, since cut pieces tend to scatter about the chopping board.

Preparation Techniques

VEGETABLES

BEETS. We peel beets after they're cooked, because it is easier and more efficient than peeling raw beets. Scrub raw beets to remove any grit, trim the leaf stems to about an inch, and then boil or steam the beets until tender. Steaming is more appropriate for small beets up to 2 inches in diameter. Drain the hot beets and rinse them under or plunge them into cold water. When the beets have cooled enough for comfortable handling, the peels slide off easily just by squeezing the beets in your hands.

CARROTS. We usually peel carrots, because they have a more refined flavor when peeled, but there is a sacrifice in nutrition. When we have tender, young, sweet carrots, we don't peel them.

CHILES. The heat-producing substance is mainly concentrated in the white tissue and seeds within the pod, so when we want a milder "hot," we remove the ribs and seeds. To avoid a temporary but very unpleasant burning sensation, do not touch your eyes or face while handling chiles. Wash your hands thoroughly with soapy water after handling the peppers. Wearing rubber gloves if you're particularly sensitive is a good idea.

CUCUMBERS. When we have good, fresh summer cucumbers, the choice of whether or not to peel them depends on the flavor, appearance, and texture of the finished dish. We always peel cucumbers that have been waxed or oiled. When overly mature cucumbers have large seeds that might alter the texture of a dish, slice the cucumber lengthwise, scoop the seeds out with a spoon, and then slice or chop the cucumber.

EGGPLANT. We rarely peel eggplant, but we cut away any soft spots or blemishes. When slicing an eggplant crosswise, first cut off a strip of peel on each of two opposite sides of the eggplant from stem end to blossom end. Put one cut side down to keep the eggplant from rolling on the cutting board. On the other cut side, the knife is less likely to slip because it doesn't have to first puncture the peel.

GARLIC. To peel a clove of garlic, lay it on its side on a chopping board. Holding a broad-bladed, sturdy knife firmly with one hand, lay the flat side of the blade on the garlic clove and whack it with the base of your other palm. This loosens the skin for easy peeling. A garlic press is a useful tool; it produces a speedier and more intensely flavored result than minced garlic, because pressing releases more of the garlic's essential oils. Garlic can be either peeled or not before pressing; however, unpeeled garlic might clog up the press and require removing the peels from the press after each clove.

GINGER ROOT. Thin-skinned, young ginger root is fine unpeeled; use a paring knife to remove the tough, leathery skin of older ginger root. Ginger root can be minced, grated on the fine surface of a hand grater, or coarsely chopped and then pulverized in a food processor.

GREENS. To prepare kale, chard, collards, beet greens, or turnip greens, first discard any yellowed or damaged leaves. Strip the leaves from the large or tough stems and wash them thoroughly. Stack the leaves on a cutting surface and slice crosswise into 1-inch-thick slices, a good size for stews, stir-fries, and side dishes. Cut again in the opposite direction for smaller pieces for soups.

LEEKS. Cut off the root end and the tough dark green leaf ends, leaving the white bulb and tender parts of the green leaves. Discard any tough outer leaves or save them for stock. Cut the leeks in half lengthwise and carefully rinse them to remove any dirt lodged between the layers. Drain, and slice or chop as required.

ONIONS. For easiest peeling, cut off the root and stem ends, slice in half lengthwise, and then peel off the skin and outer layer of onion.

PARSNIPS. See Carrots.

POTATOES. Potato eyes, green spots, and damaged spots should be pared away. We usually don't peel potatoes, except for the occasional fluffy mashed-potato dish.

SWEET POTATOES. Baked whole sweet potatoes shouldn't be peeled, but sweet potatoes used in soup, stews, or other dishes will have a finer texture and flavor if peeled. Peeled sweet potatoes discolor rapidly. To prevent discoloration, immerse them in cool water until ready to cook them.

TOMATOES. We never bother to peel tomatoes; however, if you prefer peeled tomatoes and have the time, plunge them for 1 minute in boiling water, rinse under cold water, and slide off the loosened skin.

TURNIPS. Young roots up to 2 inches in diameter needn't be peeled. Older roots may have a tough skin that is best removed.

WINTER SQUASH. Squash that will be baked should not be peeled but simply cut in half and baked cut side down. Raw squash added to soups, casseroles, or stews, however, will require peeling. Although we struggle with peeling raw winter squash, here are a few tips that may make it easier. Butternut or other unridged varieties are easier to peel than acorn or delicata, which do not have a smoothly curved surface. For butternut, slice the squash in half crosswise where the larger, globelike section meets the thinner, cylindrical part, and slice off the top and bottom. Holding the squash cut side down, slice down the sides with wide strokes just deep enough to remove the peel. For ridged squash such as acorn, slice off the top and bottom, hold it cut side down, slice down the outer ridges, then cut the squash lengthwise into sections and remove any remaining peel with a paring knife or peeler.

FRUITS

• Fruits, particularly berries, should not be washed before storing, because it hastens their deterioration. Wash fruit immediately before serving. Tender berries should not be washed under the faucet; "bathe" them in a colander or strainer submerged in a larger container of cool water.

• To easily peel soft pitted fruits, such as peaches, nectarines, and apricots, drop them in boiling water for 1 minute, drain, cool for a minute, and then remove the skin.

• To avoid discoloration, toss sliced apples, peaches, and other non-citrus fruits with lemon juice. One teaspoon of lemon juice is enough for 3 or 4 apples.

• To more easily juice lemons, oranges, and limes, roll them on a counter, applying pressure with the heel of your hand. This helps to break the interior cells of the fruit.

• To section an orange quickly, cut both of the ends from the orange and place it cut side down on a cutting board. Slice down the sides of the orange with wide strokes, just deep enough to remove the peel and all of the white pith. Hold the peeled orange over the serving bowl to catch any dripping juice, and with a paring knife, carefully cut between the membrane and one side of each orange section and back out the other side to release it from the membrane. This can be done with one smooth in-and-out motion. When all of the sections are removed, squeeze any remaining juice from the membrane into the bowl.

• To safely peel and pit a mango (mango flesh is very slippery), lay the mango on its flattest side on a cutting board. Press down with the palm of one hand on the top of the mango, and with a long-bladed knife carefully slice off the top half of the mango with a horizontal cut about 1/2 inch above the center, clearing the large fibrous pit. Turn the mango over and similarly slice off the other half. Peel the skin from each sliced half and from the flesh still around the pit. Carefully cut the rest of the flesh away from the pit.

Cooking Techniques

BLANCHING

A METHOD OF boiling foods very briefly. Blanching takes the raw edge off vegetables intended for salads or crudités and is a preliminary step to freezing, roasting, or grilling vegetables. Foods such as bean sprouts, mushrooms, snow peas, and finely cut or julienned (matchstick) vegetables may be completely cooked by blanching. Blanching is an aid in peeling thin-skinned vegetables, such as tomatoes, and nuts, such as almonds. To blanch, submerge food in plenty of rapidly boiling water for a short time. Then plunge the food into cold water if you want to stop the cooking process.

BOILING/SIMMERING

A BOILING LIQUID is rapidly moving—churning and swirling with quickly moving bubbles that break on the surface. Simmering liquids are much quieter, cooking just below the boiling point.

To BRAISE, boil or simmer foods in a small amount of liquid so that they are not completely submerged. This is a low- or no-fat cooking technique if done without preliminary sautéing. The use of stock, wine, soy sauce, or juices as all or part of the cooking liquid will increase the flavor of the finished dish.

BROILING/GRILLING

BROILING AND GRILLING involve a direct heat source on one side of the food. Broiling is best done in a preheated oven, with the food approximately 3 inches from the heat. It's a good method for quickly cooking fish fillets, searing in the flavorful juices. This method requires close attention, and the food must be turned to cook evenly. Unattended foods can easily burn with high broiling temperatures. Meals using charcoal fires must be timed to allow the coals to progress to the gray-ash stage before grilling begins. Dense, hard vegetables—carrots or potatoes, for example—should be parboiled for 5 minutes before broiling or grilling.

MICROWAVES

HERE AT MOOSEWOOD, our surprisingly small kitchen has never included a microwave oven. Those of us who have microwave ovens at home use them mostly for warming up leftovers, and they are great for that. A quick survey showed that we also use them to soften or melt butter and chocolate, dry out lemon peel, heat water, and reheat coffee. That's about it, so if you want to adapt any of these recipes to microwave cooking, please consult a good microwave cookbook.

PRESSURE COOKING

MANY OF US HAVE HEARD OLD, scary family stories of pressure cooker accidents where Aunt So-and-so was cleaning beans off the ceiling and kitchen walls, thankful to have escaped bodily injury. Those days are gone now, thanks to a new generation of pressure cookers re-engineered to include mechanisms that don't allow opening until the pressure is reduced. Guidelines must still be followed, of course, and the large name-brand cookers cost around $200.

Pressure cooking is most effective for foods requiring long, moist heat—beans, stews, soups, and grains. Soaked beans can be cooked in 15 minutes or less, unsoaked in 30, compared to at least a couple of hours on the stovetop. Brown rice will be ready in only slightly more than half the time, reduced from 45 minutes to 25. Pressure cooking softens the fibers of food and blends the flavors. However, once the cover is locked down, there's no peeking or adding of seasonings until completion. Choose stainless steel, not aluminum, since aluminum reacts with acid foods, producing a metallic taste. Timers are essential for pressure cooking, as is following the manufacturer's advice on what not to cook (applesauce, cranberries, barley, split peas, and rhubarb, for example, tend to foam and clog the vent).

ROASTING/BAKING

WHEN ROASTING OR BAKING, it speeds things up to preheat the oven. However, preheating is crucial for quality only when baking cakes, breads, cookies, and soufflés. Roasting vegetables brings out the natural sugars and seals in juices while creating a crisp outer layer. We bake most of our fish entrées at the restaurant. It allows for a nice mingling of seasonings as well as requiring little or no attention, which frees you to prepare accompanying dishes.

SAUTÉING

TO SAUTÉ, cook vegetables and seasonings on top of the stove in a small amount of oil or butter, on medium-high heat, stirring occasionally. The oil should be hot when the food is added to the pan, so that the food will be sealed, preventing the release of juices. Usually sautéing is done without a cover, but sometimes we recommend covering sautéing food to speed up the cooking (then, strictly speaking, it's not sautéing but rather sauté-steaming). To sauté until just soft (translucent in the case of onions) means to cook until tender but not browned. To sauté until brown means to cook gently until golden brown on all sides. Vegetables retain their shapes better when they are sautéed before adding liquid and simmering.

STEAMING

STEAMED FOODS are cooked over boiling or simmering water or stock. Use a special two-piece steaming pot or a stainless steaming basket or rack that can be inserted into a pot with a tight-fitting lid. Keep the water level lower than the bottom of the steamer to avoid sogginess. Allow the water to come to a boil, and steam vegetables covered for heat efficiency and better color. Properly steamed vegetables are crisp and tender with good color and retained nutrients.

Steaming is an effective cooking method for most vegetables. Dense, hard vegetables should be cut into small pieces to steam, and are often more quickly and effectively cooked by boiling.

Steaming is a good method for reheating leftover noodles, rice, and other grains.

STIR-FRYING

STIR-FRYING IS A TIME-HONORED TECHNIQUE essential to many Asian cuisines. Foods are quickly stirred and tossed in a relatively small amount of fat on high heat. There are many advantages to this method: It requires only one pan—a wok or large skillet; the high temperatures seal in juices, resulting in crisp but tender vegetables; the quick cooking helps retain vitamins and minerals; and it can be done at the last minute in a relatively short time.

Since careful attention is required to avoid burning foods cooked on high heat, before you begin to stir-fry have all your ingredients chopped and assembled near the stove in the order in which they will be cooked. Cut each type of vegetable as uniformly as possible to ensure even cooking.

A vegetable's cooking time determines when it should be added to the stir-fry. Harder vegetables require longer cooking. Vegetables are listed below in categories, from long cooking time to short:

LONG: potatoes, sweet potatoes, winter squash, onions, carrots, eggplant, celery, leeks.

MEDIUM: cabbage, green beans, cauliflower, broccoli, mushrooms, peppers, summer squash, zucchini.

SHORT: greens (kale, Swiss chard, spinach, endive, escarole, bok choy), green peas, snow peas, tomatoes, tofu, bean sprouts.

TOASTING

Toasting heightens the aroma and flavor of seeds, such as sesame, cumin, and coriander. Toasted nuts are crisper and more flavorful than untoasted. Toast a single layer of raw nuts or seeds on an unoiled baking sheet in an oven or toaster oven at 350° (about 5 minutes for most nuts and just a couple of minutes for seeds) until they're fragrant and lightly browned.

How to Cook Dried Beans

IF YOU CAN adapt your routine to include preparing your own dried beans, you will find that it doesn't require much in the way of time and energy, and it brings the cost of the beans down from inexpensive to dirt cheap.

Dried beans must be soaked before they are cooked. If they aren't, the skins will burst before the beans themselves are tender. There are two ways to accomplish this. One method is much quicker than the other; however, the slower method guarantees a better, tenderer result. Note that although the quick-soaking technique takes less time, the longer presoaking method requires less attention.

First, spread out the dried beans on a baking sheet so that you can easily see and remove any shriveled beans, pebbles, and bits of dirt. Give the beans a quick rinse in a colander.

PLACE THE PICKED-OVER rinsed beans in a pot, add cold water to cover the beans plus at least 2 inches, and set aside to sit at room temperature. After 4 hours or more, drain off the soaking water. This will remove the hard-to-digest carbohydrates that are the source of beans' ill repute (a benefit not afforded by the quick-soaking method). Cover the beans with fresh water, and they are ready to cook.

THE QUICK-SOAKING METHOD

WHEN THE TEXTURE of the beans is not paramount, this is a much quicker alternative. After you've inspected and rinsed the beans, put them in a pot and cover them with water (2 inches deeper than the beans). Place the pot on high heat and bring the water to a boil. After the beans have boiled for 2 minutes, cover the pot and remove it from the heat. Allow the beans to sit for 1 hour (fava beans will be ready sooner; chick peas will take a bit longer). Now they are ready to cook!

STOVETOP COOKING

PUT THE COVERED pot of presoaked or quick-soaked beans (check to be sure that the water is 2 inches deeper than the beans) on high heat until the water comes to a rapid boil. Set the lid ajar and maintain a low boil, checking the water level occasionally, for 60 to 90 minutes, until tender (the exact time depends upon the type of bean).

OVEN COOKING

A SUREFIRE TECHNIQUE for the most fastidious cook. Preheat the oven to 350°. Place the picked-over, rinsed, soaked, and drained beans in a stovetop-safe casserole and cover them with fresh water (2 inches deeper than the beans). Place the beans on high heat and bring them to a rapid boil, then cover the casserole and place it in the oven. Bake for 1 hour (fava beans will be ready sooner; chick peas will take a bit longer). You've produced a show-quality bean.

NOTE: Adding salt or acidic ingredients such as vinegar, lemon juice, or mustard to beans before they are fully cooked will prevent the beans from becoming tender. Add these seasonings after the beans are fully cooked.

How to Cook Grains

BULGHUR

TO PREPARE BULGHUR as a side dish, measure 1 cup of bulghur into a bowl and cover with 1½ cups of boiling water and a dash of salt. Cover and set aside for 20 to 30 minutes. Alternatively, lightly sauté the dry grain in a small amount of oil, add boiling water or stock, and simmer over the lowest flame possible for 15 to 20 minutes or until the liquid is absorbed. Either way, when the bulghur is cooked, stir to fluff the grains. Bulghur that is used for tabouli, or in a casserole, should be prepared with equal amounts of water and dry grain for the best consistency. One cup of dry bulghur yields 2½ cups cooked.

BUCKWHEAT GROATS (KASHA)

TRADITIONAL PREPARATION OF kasha as a side dish: Heat a heavy saucepan with a tight-fitting lid. Mix 1 raw egg into each cup of buckwheat. Add the buckwheat to the pan and quickly stir on high heat until the egg has dried and the grains are mostly separate. For each cup of buckwheat, add 2 cups of boiling stock or water, 2 tablespoons of butter or oil, and a pinch of salt and pepper. Cover and simmer over the lowest possible heat for 15 minutes. Fluff the grains with a fork before serving.

Kasha can be prepared without the egg for a creamier consistency, or use 3 cups of water or milk to each ½ cup of grain for a breakfast cereal.

COUSCOUS

TRADITIONALLY, couscous is steamed over a simmering soup or stew. We use quick-cooking couscous and prepare it as follows: Place equal amounts of boiling water or stock and dry couscous in a heatproof bowl. Cover tightly and let sit for 5 minutes. Stir to fluff the grains; add a small amount of hot water if it's a little crunchy.

For whole wheat quick-cooking couscous: Stir the couscous into an equal amount of boiling water and simmer, covered, on low heat for 5 minutes. Remove from the heat, allow to sit for 5 minutes, and then stir to fluff.

Toss with a little butter or olive oil and add salt to taste.

MILLET

TO PREPARE MILLET, combine 1 cup of millet with a pinch or two of salt and 1¾ cups of water in a heavy saucepan. Cover and bring to a boil. Reduce the heat, stir, and gently simmer for 20 minutes. Then stir to fluff the grains, and taste. If it's still a little crunchy, add about ¼ cup of boiling water and steam, covered, for an additional 10 minutes.

To make 3 cups of polenta, bring 3 cups of water to a boil in a large heavy saucepan. Add 1 cup of cornmeal in a thin, steady stream while whisking briskly. Simmer on low heat for 10 to 20 minutes, stirring occasionally. Stir in salt, butter, and/or cheese to taste.

QUINOA

For 3 to 4 cups cooked quinoa, place 1 cup of raw quinoa in a fine strainer and rinse it well by running fresh water through it to remove the bitter saponin layer. In a covered saucepan, gently simmer the rinsed quinoa in 2 cups of water for 15 to 20 minutes, until the water is absorbed. When the white grains have become transparent and the spiral-like germ has separated, the quinoa is ready. For richer flavor, sauté the rinsed quinoa in 1 tablespoon of vegetable oil, stirring constantly for a minute, before adding the water and simmering as above.

RICE

BROWN RICE. One cup of raw brown rice yields 3 cups cooked. A heavy saucepan or pot with a tight-fitting lid is best for cooking rice, because it retains more moisture and is less apt to scorch the rice. Good rice can be made in a lighter pot with the use of a heat diffuser. Rinse the rice well and drain it. Briefly sauté the rice in a little oil, stirring briskly, for a minute or two. This helps to separate the cooked grains of rice, avoiding gumminess. Add cool water: For 1 cup of rice, add 2 cups of water, but for greater quantities of rice, lower the proportion of water to rice. For example, for 3 cups of rice, use about 4½ cups of water. Cover and bring to a boil over the highest heat. When steam escapes from below the lid, turn the heat off for 5 minutes. Return to very low heat and simmer for about 35 minutes, or until all of the water has been absorbed. Remove from the heat and let sit, covered, for a few minutes before serving.

BASMATI RICE. To cook brown basmati rice, follow the instructions for brown rice (above), using 2¼ cups of water for each cup of rice. To cook white basmati rice, rinse 1 cup of rice, drain. Bring 1¾ cups of water to a boil, add salt if desired, and add the rice and 1 tablespoon of butter or oil. Lower the heat, cover, and simmer until the liquid is absorbed, about 15 minutes. Fluff up the grains with a fork and let it sit for 5 minutes before serving.

WHITE RICE. Use 1¾ cups of water to each cup of rice and prepare as for brown rice, without the preliminary rinsing. The water should all be absorbed in 15 to 20 minutes of cooking.

How to Cook Pasta

Pasta is easily cooked well if you follow these five basic guidelines:

1

For 1 pound of pasta, bring 4 or 5 quarts of water to a rapid boil (use a large amount of water so that it will quickly return to a boil once the pasta is added, and so that the pasta will have room to float freely). Add salt if you wish, but there is no reason to add oil.

2

Estimate portions of about ¼ pound of pasta per person. Allow a larger portion of fresh pasta than dried, because it contains more water and so weighs more before cooking. Add the pasta to the boiling water, stir it with a wooden spoon to keep the pieces from sticking together, and cover the pot so that the water will quickly return to a boil. When the water boils again, remove the lid and stir again.

3

Because of all the variables, it is impossible to give an absolute cooking time. Don't count on the time suggested on the pasta box — it's usually too long. The only way to know when pasta is properly cooked is to taste it. Fresh pasta cooks almost immediately. Start to test dried pasta (by biting) after only a few minutes, and then test again every minute or so until it is *al dente* (tender but with a firm bite). Don't expect fresh pasta to be al dente. If you're not sure, it's better to slightly undercook pasta because it will continue to cook as long as it's hot.

4

As soon as the pasta is al dente, drain it in a colander; don't let it drain enough to dry. Never rinse with cold water (unless the pasta will be chilled and you're in a hurry). Transfer the dripping-wet hot pasta to a heated serving bowl and toss it with just enough sauce to coat the pasta. Pasta should be sparingly anointed with a sauce or vegetable or cheese, never drowned or overpowered by it. If your pasta seems undersauced and dry, a little reserved pasta cooking water may be the best thing to add.

5

Not every pasta dish is improved by adding cheese at the table. When cheese is served, it should be freshly grated. Use a cheese mill, a small Italian cheese grater, or the fine side of an all-purpose hand grater.

How to Make Vegetable Stock

2 large potatoes, thickly sliced
2 or 3 medium onions, quartered
3 or 4 medium carrots, thickly sliced
1 celery stalk, chopped
1 apple or pear, quartered
1 or 2 bay leaves
6 peppercorns
2½ quarts water

OPTIONAL VEGETABLES OR HERBS
garlic cloves
leeks, including tough green leaves
mushrooms, whole or stems (adds a distinctive flavor and
    dark color)
parsley, including stems
parsnips
scallions
sweet potatoes
tomatoes (in small amounts only, or stock may be too acid)
winter squash
zucchini or summer squash

FOR STOCK WITH AN ASIAN FLAVOR
sliced fresh ginger root
stock from soaking dried shiitake mushrooms

Scrub and cut the (unpeeled) vegetables and apple or pear. Place in a stockpot with the bay leaves, peppercorns, and water. Cover, bring to a boil, and simmer for 1 hour or more. Strain the stock through a colander or cloth, pressing out the liquid from the vegetables. (The remaining solid vegetables make good compost material or can be discarded.) Vegetable stock will keep refrigerated for 3 to 4 days; frozen, it will keep indefinitely.

How to Make Coconut Milk

I F YOU ARE USING a fresh coconut, cut the coconut meat into 1-inch pieces and place equal amounts of coconut and hot water in a blender. Purée at high speed for a couple of minutes. Let steep for 30 minutes. Pour the purée into a strainer set over a bowl. Press the pulp to squeeze out as much milk as possible. Squeeze by the handful to extract any remaining milk. Pour the milk through a fine-mesh strainer. One cup of coconut meat combined with 1 cup of hot water yields about 1 cup of coconut milk.

If you are using dried coconut, place 1 cup of unsweetened dried shredded coconut and 1½ cups of hot water in the blender. Let stand for 5 minutes. Purée for 1 minute and proceed as above. This yields a little more than a cup of coconut milk.

Covered and refrigerated, coconut milk will keep for up to 3 days. Frozen, it will keep indefinitely.

Fresh Herbs

In the summertime, when fresh herbs are plentiful, we freeze some to use in our winter stews. We make large batches of pesto, eat some right away, and freeze the rest. And then, some herb vinegar or herb butter might be in order.

For a complete guide to growing, harvesting, and using culinary herbs, we recommend *The Moosewood Restaurant Kitchen Garden*, by David Hirsch.

To Freeze Fresh Herbs

BASIL, CILANTRO, dill, mint, and tarragon freeze well and have a better flavor when frozen than when dried.

Rinse or soak the herbs in cool water to remove any grit. Drain, remove large stems, and chop. Pack in freezer containers or plastic bags; small amounts of frozen herb can be removed and used as desired. Or freeze the herbs in ice cube trays, a tablespoon of herbs covered with water in each space; when they're frozen, store the cubes in a plastic bag for convenient use later. Thawing is not necessary before adding to cooking foods.

How to Make Herb and Spice Oils

USE A MILD OIL that won't compete with the seasoning: corn, canola, light olive, soy, or safflower. For each cup of oil, use ½ cup of chopped fresh herb; or to make a spice oil, use ¼ cup of garam masala (see page 334) or curry powder (see page 334), or ⅛ cup each of ground cumin seed and ground coriander seed. Let stand at room temperature (a warm kitchen is fine) for 4 to 5 days to infuse the oil with the herb's essence. The herbs or spices will settle to the bottom. Carefully ladle or decant the clear oil into sterilized jars; discard the spent residue. Tightly cap, and store refrigerated for up to 6 months.

How to Make Herb Vinegars

USE FRESH HERBS that are clean, dry, and stripped of heavy stems. Appropriate herbs include basil, chervil, chives, cilantro, dill, marjoram, oregano, rosemary, sage, tarragon, and thyme. Cider vinegar and white wine vinegar are especially good for making herb vinegars, although any vinegar can be used.

Fill a clean glass jar with the herbs, pour in vinegar to cover, and cap the jar. Place the jar in a sunny spot outdoors or on your brightest windowsill for 4 to 6 weeks. Pour the steeped vinegar through a paper coffee filter into a nonreactive pot (stainless steel, enamel, or heatproof ceramic or glass) and discard the herbs. Gently heat the vinegar until it just begins to simmer. Do not boil. Pour the hot vinegar into sterilized jars and cap to seal. Herb vinegars stored in a cool, dark place will keep for about a year.

How to Make Pestos

PESTO WILL KEEP refrigerated for a week. Freeze pesto in ice cube trays, store the pesto cubes in plastic bags, and then pop a pesto cube into savory dishes for an immediate flavor boost. When preparing pesto specifically for freezing, omit the cheese, and add it to the thawed pesto before serving. If you have frozen leftover pesto with the cheese, whirl it briefly in a blender to improve its texture.

To make pesto, whirl all of the ingredients, except the oil, in a food processor or blender. When everything is well chopped, add the oil in a thin stream to form a smooth paste. If you are using a blender, it may be necessary to prechop the herbs and nuts by hand.

YIELDS

2 cups

PESTO GENOVESE

3 cups loosely packed fresh basil leaves
⅓ cup pine nuts or chopped almonds
½ cup grated Parmesan cheese
3 garlic cloves, coarsely chopped
½ cup olive oil
salt and ground black pepper to taste

PESTO PROVENÇAL

YIELDS

1 cup

1 cup loosely packed fresh parsley leaves
2 tablespoons fresh thyme leaves
2 tablespoons fresh rosemary leaves
1 tablespoon fresh oregano leaves
¼ cup coarsely chopped scallions
⅓ cup pine nuts or chopped almonds
¼ cup vegetable oil
salt and ground black pepper to taste

CILANTRO PESTO

YIELDS

1 cup

1 cup loosely packed fresh cilantro leaves
1 cup loosely packed fresh parsley leaves
⅓ cup whole almonds
1 small fresh chile, or ¼–½ teaspoon cayenne
2 garlic cloves, coarsely chopped
2 tablespoons fresh lime or lemon juice
¼ cup vegetable oil
salt and ground black pepper to taste

FINES HERBES PESTO

YIELDS

1 cup

1 cup loosely packed fresh parsley leaves
¼ cup loosely packed fresh tarragon leaves
2 tablespoons fresh thyme leaves
¼ cup coarsely chopped chives
⅓ cup pine nuts
½ cup grated Parmesan cheese
1½ teaspoons fresh lemon juice
¼ cup vegetable oil
salt and ground black pepper to taste

How to Make Herb Butters

U SE HERB BUTTERS as a spread on bread, as a topping for steamed vegetables or broiled fish, for sautéing, and for enriching grains or pasta.

Cream together all of the ingredients. Herb butters can be frozen for up to 6 months.

DILL-SCALLION BUTTER

¼ pound softened butter
2 tablespoons chopped fresh dill
2 tablespoons chopped scallions (green and white parts)
1 teaspoon prepared horseradish

LEMON-MINT BUTTER

¼ pound softened butter
2 tablespoons chopped fresh parsley
2 tablespoons chopped fresh spearmint
1 tablespoon fresh lemon juice
½ teaspoon grated lemon peel

SAVORY GARLIC BUTTER

¼ pound softened butter
2 tablespoons chopped fresh oregano
1 tablespoon chopped fresh marjoram
2 garlic cloves, minced or pressed

BASIL-DIJON BUTTER

¼ pound softened butter
2 tablespoons chopped fresh basil
1 tablespoon chopped fresh tarragon
1 tablespoon chopped fresh parsley
1 teaspoon Dijon mustard

SAGE-THYME BUTTER

¼ pound softened butter
2 tablespoons chopped fresh sage leaves
2 tablespoons chopped fresh parsley
1 teaspoon chopped fresh thyme

Menu Planning

Over the years spent cooking at the restaurant, we've adapted to the constraints of limited time and space. We've honed our skills and trained many new cooks to work in the "Moosewood style." In this chapter we share our insights, offer some serving suggestions, and talk you through a few sample menus. The Techniques chapter shows you how to streamline your cooking style, and the Pantry section shows you how maintaining a good basic larder makes quick meals possible.

We hope this book helps you use time wisely and efficiently to make a fast meal without sacrificing aesthetics, nutrition, or flavor. Even though there is an impressive and rapidly growing array of healthful prepared and/or frozen foods on the market, we still believe most strongly in cooking real whole foods from scratch. Working under time pressure in Moosewood's kitchen, each of us has learned to prepare several different menu items at the same time so that when the customers are served, all of the food is ready: neither undercooked nor overdone. At home the same principles can be applied, with the advantage that, with only yourself to please, you can deliberately plan for leftovers to incorporate into future meals.

Cooking Ahead and Using Leftovers

It's ALWAYS SMART to cook extra amounts of rice, beans, vegetables, and sauces to keep on hand to enhance the next few days' meals. It makes good sense economically to combine a little bit of this with a little bit of that. Small amounts of leftovers, which on their own seem hardly worth saving, may be just right for stretching and adding texture to a soup, or for serving with other small dishes for an interesting side-dish medley.

• If you hate to prepare onions but love to eat them, peel several at the same time and keep them, chopped, sliced, or whole, in a plastic bag in the refrigerator. Chilling reduces the fumes so that whole onions are easier to handle the next day. Prechopped or sliced onions will keep for several days in the refrigerator and make tomorrow's cooking quicker and more pleasant.

• If you often use fresh lemon juice, squeeze several lemons at once and keep the juice on hand, refrigerated, in a jar with an airtight lid.

• Double the amount of brown rice you need for one meal and save the rest for the next meal: make a quick rice salad or fried rice, serve it under a stew or with sautéed vegetables, toss it into a soup, or use it to make rice pudding.

• When you take the time to cook dried beans, make extra. They are a wonderful addition to soups and can be turned into dips, refritos, and salads.

• Leftover cooked vegetables, such as broccoli, asparagus, spinach, green beans, zucchini, tomatoes, mushrooms, and peppers, can be heated with a little oil and garlic to become fillings for omelets or frittatas.

• Leftover white sauce, cheese sauce, tomato sauce, or salsa can top steamed vegetables and toast, pasta, grains, or cornbread, turning a humble dish into a satisfying and beautiful meal.

• Two or three cold boiled potatoes, some quickly blanched carrot sticks and pepper strips, and a simple dressing served on fresh salad greens with crackers and hard-boiled eggs or slices of cheese create a colorful vegetable platter.

• Leftover plain pasta can be turned into a pasta salad or added to soup. Warm it in a skillet with olive oil, garlic, mushrooms, and broccoli or peppers and top it with freshly ground black pepper and grated cheese for a delicious, almost-instant meal.

Balance

• Bear in mind the aesthetics of the meals you plan. Think about color: steamed cauliflower on white pasta with a light cream sauce might taste great, but it looks pretty boring on the plate. Garnish the dish with chopped fresh tomatoes or sliced pimientos and sprinkle on a few walnuts and some parsley, and it becomes beautiful and tastes even better.

• Don't let the sensible desire to use up leftovers lead you to combine dishes that might either be poorly balanced or leave you with an upset stomach.

• Avoid serving several very highly spiced dishes at once. Unless you and your dinner companions are used to cuisines where many dishes contain hot pepper, fresh garlic, raw onions, and so on, you may want to balance and offset the impact of a peppery dish with a milder one. The same principle applies to acidic marinated dishes, which ought to be complemented with something savory or bland.

• Consider temperatures and textures as well as seasonings. Combine something smooth with something chunky, something rich and hot with a crisp, cool salad. Sometimes having a hot meal feels important to us emotionally, but often one hot dish plus one or two chilled or room-temperature dishes will suffice.

• Avoid serving two or more dishes containing dairy products and nuts at the same meal to reduce cholesterol and fat. Two or more starches can be costly in terms of calories.

Equipment and Strategy

WHETHER YOU'RE BEING CREATIVE with leftovers or starting from scratch, decide what will make meal preparation as smooth and efficient as possible. Look at the recipes and map out what needs to be cooked first. Think about space and equipment.

• If you're planning to bake more than one item, does your oven have the shelf space? Do the dishes need to bake at very different temperatures? If so, it's usually wise to put the dish that needs to bake for a longer time at a cooler temperature into the oven first. When it is finished, keep it covered in a warm spot while you broil or bake the second dish requiring a higher temperature in the now well-heated oven.

• If you are considering more than one dish requiring a skillet, using two skillets will save time and allow you to avoid having to wash the pan in the middle of preparing the meal.

• Do not plan complex meals in which one particular piece of equipment is needed for every dish.

• Cooking in the wrong size pots and pans can really slow you down. This may seem rather obvious, but we know from experience that the right equipment makes an enormous difference in how fast and how successful your meals will be. If you are trying to prepare a main dish that calls for the use of a large skillet, you will save yourself a lot of aggravation if you use a 12-inch skillet. If you're preparing crêpes, use a 7- or 8-inch pan or the crêpe will never be the right thickness and size.

• If you have the opportunity to prepare casseroles ahead of time and freeze them, it makes sense to use baking dishes that can travel from the freezer into the oven and out onto the table to serve. If you think you might use a microwave, don't use metal baking pans. (Of course, this strategy presumes that you have enough baking dishes so that you can leave one in the freezer.)

Time-Saving Tips for Preparation and Cooking

WHEN YOU PLAN a menu in which the dishes are to be served at different temperatures (cold, room-temperature, and hot), try this strategy. First, make the dish that will have to be chilled. Second, assemble the dish that has to bake or simmer for a while. While it cooks, prepare any other dishes: make the one to be served at room temperature, then cook any quick-cooking hot dish (such as a side vegetable) so that all the hot dishes are ready at nearly the same time. The chilled item will be cold by then, the baked item done, the room-temperature dish waiting to be served, and the hot vegetable ready but not overcooked. Of course, this assumes that you are not serving the meal in courses, but all at once. If you serve the meal in courses, you can enjoy a salad, soup, or appetizer while the main dish cooks.

• If you have time earlier in the day or the night before, prepare one or more dishes in advance.
• If needed, bring water to a boil while you gather and prepare ingredients.
• Remember to preheat your oven so that it will be the right temperature just as you're ready to bake.
• When you are preparing a meal using more than one recipe, check to see whether both call for some of the same ingredients. For example, prepare enough onions, garlic, and carrots for both dishes, and get them cooking in two separate pots.
• Try grating cheese or slicing fruit right at the table during the meal. It's faster, and it's fun!

Sample Menus

FOLLOWING ARE SOME sample menus using recipes from this book. We've chosen them to illustrate some of the time-saving strategies above. The procedures suggest a sequence of steps to follow to produce the meal as quickly as possible using conventional equipment. When you shop—the first step—please let the beautiful food available at the market inspire you. Somewhere in this or another of our books is just the right recipe to showcase that fresh produce in season or that exotic import. Great cooking doesn't have to be complicated, and quick and easy cooking need not be boring.

Eggplant Mykonos (see page 208) with feta cheese
Couscous (see page 356)
Carrot and Parsley Salad (see page 65)

Read the recipes and gather all of the ingredients.
Begin by preparing the Eggplant Mykonos according to the directions. While the stew is simmering, make the Carrot and Parsley Salad. Prepare the couscous last. The feta can be grated at the table. Serve the stew over the couscous, topped with feta, and the salad alongside.

≈

Cajun Skillet Beans (see page 167)
Cheese Grits (see page 147)
Fresh fruit

Read the recipes and gather all of the ingredients.
Put the water on the stove to boil for the Cheese Grits. Next, prepare the skillet beans. When

the water is boiling, stir in the grits and cook according to the directions (use a timer!). Go back and forth between the two dishes as necessary. The grits will be done first, but they can sit until the beans are done. Serve them together, and the fruit will be your dessert.

≈

Roasted Vegetable Salad with Garlic and Rosemary (see page 84)
Lemon Tomato Salad (see page 70)
French bread
Brie or other cheese

Read the recipes and gather all of the ingredients.

Begin to heat water for boiling the potatoes. If using brie, set it out to soften and come to room temperature. Preheat the broiler. Prepare the roasted vegetables and spread them on the broiler pan, following the recipe directions. While they broil, prepare the Lemon Tomato Salad. Finish by tossing the roasted vegetables with vinegar, salt, and pepper. Slice the French bread into rounds and spread with the brie. Serve with the Roasted Vegetable Salad and Lemon Tomato Salad.

≈

North African Cauliflower Soup (see page 33)
Corn Scones (see page 53)
Cheddar cheese

Read the recipes and gather all of the ingredients.

Preheat the oven and prepare the scones dough. Before shaping the dough into wedges, stop and chop the onions for the soup. Sauté the onions in a soup pot. While they are softening, shape the scones and put them into the oven. Set the timer for 15 minutes. Finish the soup while the scones bake. When they are done, turn off the oven and keep them warm. Garnish the soup, and serve with the scones and sliced cheese.

≈

Teriyaki Broiled or Grilled Fish (see page 256)
Brown rice
Broccoli and Carrots with Lime Dressing (see page 73)

Read the recipes and gather all of the ingredients.

Begin by cooking the brown rice (see page 357). While the rice cooks, rinse the fish and set it aside, prepare the teriyaki marinade according to the recipe, and marinate the fish. Heat the broiler (or grill). While the fish marinates, cook the broccoli and carrots. Prepare the dressing separately and set it aside. Broil the fish. When the fish is done, pour the Lime Dressing onto the vegetables and toss. The rice should be done, and all the food can be served at once.

≈

Caribbean Yellow Rice and Pigeon Peas (see page 154)
Cucumbers, tomatoes, and red onions with Creamy Garlic Dressing (see page 95)
Tropical Fruit Salad (see page 324)

Read the recipes and gather all of the ingredients.

Begin by making the fruit salad, and put it in the refrigerator to chill. Prepare the rice dish, following the recipe directions. When the rice and peas come to a boil, reduce the heat to low. While this simmers, make a simple salad by slicing a cucumber, 1 or 2 tomatoes and 2 slices of red onion separated into rings. Make the Creamy Garlic Dressing. Season the rice and peas to taste, and serve with the cucumber salad and dressing. The Tropical Fruit Salad can accompany the meal or be dessert.

≈

Broiled Polenta with Mushrooms and Cheese (see page 152)
Easiest Artichokes (see page 77)
Fresh Orange Compote (see page 309)

Read the recipes and gather all of the ingredients.

Put two pots of water on the stove to boil: one for the polenta and one for the artichokes. Prepare the artichokes first, and carefully drop them into the boiling water (seasoned if desired). Set the timer and then concentrate on the polenta. Cook it according to the directions, stirring as needed. Prepare and sauté the mushroom topping for the polenta, and grate the cheese. Oil the baking dish. When everything is ready, assemble the polenta with the mushrooms. At this point, check the artichokes. They might be done, depending on size. If not, continue to cook them.

Now prepare the compote and chill it (the assembled polenta can sit while you do this). Check the artichokes. If done (or close), heat the broiler and put in the polenta. Broil as directed. When the artichokes are done, drain and season them. Serve with the polenta. The compote is dessert.

≈

Barbecued Tempeh and Peppers (see page 260)
Savory Scallion Biscuits (see page 58)
Sweet Potato Salad (see page 135) and/or Vegetables in Mint Vinaigrette (see page 72)

Read the recipes and gather all of the ingredients.

Prepare the Sweet Potato Salad and/or the Vegetables in Mint Vinaigrette (when you dice the peppers for the salad or vegetables, chop the peppers for the tempeh dish as well), and chill. Preheat the oven to 400° and mix up the Savory Scallion Biscuits. Pop the biscuits into the oven and set the timer for 20 minutes. While they bake, make the Barbecued Tempeh and Peppers. The biscuits will probably be done about 5 minutes before the tempeh is finished. Turn off the oven and leave them in to keep warm. Serve the tempeh on top of the split biscuits, with the salad or vegetables alongside. This meal is colorful and the flavors are lively.

≈

Chèvre and Red Peppers Omelet (see page 289)
Mushrooms in Lemon Marinade (see page 81)
Multigrain Muffins (see page 56)

You will need two large skillets for this menu. The omelet serves 2 and the mushrooms serve 4 to 6, so consider how many people you're serving. The mushrooms keep well for 2 days and are nice to have on hand, but you might want to halve the recipe. Read the recipes and gather all of the ingredients.

Clean and cut all the vegetables.

Begin by preparing the muffins: Preheat the oven, mix the batter, set the timer, and bake. Now start the mushrooms: Sauté on medium heat for 4 minutes, add the lemon juice, salt, and pepper, and sauté for another minute. Remove to a serving bowl. Make the omelet in the second skillet. When the timer rings, turn off the heat but leave the muffins in the oven. Serve the omelet with the warm mushrooms alongside or spooned over the top. These muffins are sweet and taste especially good with unsalted sweet butter. This is a great menu for an elegant brunch, with cold juice and hot tea or coffee.

≈

Pasta with Greens and Ricotta (see page 188)
Dilly Beans (see page 66)
Baked Peaches with Marsala (see page 306)

Read the recipes and gather all of the ingredients.

Prepare the Baked Peaches with Marsala, but don't bake it—set it aside.

Put two pots of water on the stove to boil: one for pasta, one for the green beans. Prepare the green beans. Chop garlic for both dishes. Set aside the garlic for the beans. Begin sautéing the garlic and greens according to the recipe. While the greens are cooking, prepare the marinade for the beans and bring it to a simmer. Carefully drop the beans into the boiling water. Put the pasta in the other pot of boiling water and set the timer. Preheat the oven to 350°. Complete the pasta sauce according to the recipe. Chop the tomatoes for topping the pasta. Drain the beans and mix with the marinade as directed. Drain the pasta and proceed according to the recipe. The cheese is grated at the table.

Put dessert in the oven and set the timer.

Special Lists

Nondairy and Vegan Recipes

A LL THE RECIPES listed below are both nondairy and vegan, when made according to the notations, unless specified "nondairy only."

SOUPS

Black Bean Soup, made without the yogurt or sour cream
Cantonese Fish and Vegetable Soup (nondairy only)
Chilled Moroccan Tomato Soup
Green Jade Soup
Mexican Tomato Lime Soup, made without the cheese
Miso Soup
Noodles with Mirin
North African Cauliflower Soup
Portuguese White Bean Soup
Pumpkin and Porcini Soup, made without optional milk
Red Lentil Soup
Simple Garlic Broth
Spanish Potato Onion Soup

DIPS AND SPREADS

Black Bean Dip
Mockamole
Olivada
Spicy Peanut Dip
Tofu Tahini Spread

SALADS AND SIDES

Asian Cabbage Slaw
Carrot and Parsley Salad
Dilly Beans
Fennel and Orange Salad

Gigondes, served without optional creamy dressing
Lemon Tomato Salad
Marinated Zucchini
Vegetables in Mint Vinaigrette

Broccoli and Carrots with Tamari-Lime Dressing
Broiled Eggplant
Curried Cauliflower
Easiest Artichokes
Mushrooms in Lemon Marinade
Not Your Mother's Green Beans
Peperonata
Roasted Vegetable Salad with Garlic and Rosemary
Sesame Spinach
Shredded Zucchini
Spicy Kale
Stir-Fried Bok Choy and Hijiki

Easy Refritos
Mexican Seitan
Seasoned Tempeh

DRESSINGS, SALSAS, AND SAUCES

Honey Mustard Vinaigrette
Lemon Sesame Dressing
Roasted Garlic Dressing
Tofu-Basil Dressing
Tofu Mayonnaise

Brazilian Onion Salsa
Salsa Verde
Tomato-Orange Salsa

Asian Marinade
Chimichurri Sauce
Fennel-Mustard Sauce
Miso Sauce

Antipasto Salad, made without the cheese

Avocado Corn Salad

Beans and Greens

Black Beans and Rice Salad

California Dream Salad

    Tomato Herb Dressing

    Orange Mustard Dressing

    Japanese Carrot Dressing

Couscous with Artichoke Hearts and Walnuts

Diced Greek Vegetable Salad, without optional feta

Mediterranean Lentil Salad

Mediterranean Potato Salad

Soba Noodle Salad

Sweet Potato Salad

Udon Noodles and Vegetables

White Bean and Tomato Salad

GRAINS

Apricot Bulghur Pilaf

Bulghur Burgers

Couscous with Sun-Dried Tomatoes

North African Couscous Paella (nondairy only)

Kasha with Mushrooms

Coconut Basmati Rice

Golden Spanish Rice

Greek Rice Pilaf, without the feta

Herbed Lemon Pilaf with Almonds

Mediterranean Rice

BEANS

Black-Eyed Peas with Spinach

Cajun Skillet Beans

Caribbean Black Beans

Curried Chick Peas and Tofu

Field Peas with Kale and Sweet Potatoes

Greek-Style Cannellini and Vegetables

Honolulu Skillet Beans

Red, Gold, Black, and Green Chili

Orecchietti with Peas and Onions, without optional cheese
Pasta Valenzana, without optional cheese
Pasta with Beans and Endive
Pasta with Spicy Cauliflower
Pasta with Porcini Mushroom Sauce, without the cheese
Spaghetti with Zucchini and Lemon, without the cheese

STEWS

African Pineapple Peanut Stew
Caribbean Vegetable Stew
Chick Pea and Artichoke Heart Stew
Curried Vegetables with Dahl
Eggplant Mykonos, without optional feta
Green Beans and Fennel Ragout
Menestra
Sicilian Seafood Stew (nondairy only)
Tomatican
Tunisian Vegetable Stew, without optional feta
Vegetable Stifado, without optional feta
Winter Vegetable Stew

STIR-FRIES AND SAUTÉS

Broccoli-Tofu Stir-Fry
Curried Fried Rice
Fragrant Rice Noodles with Vegetables
Fried Rice
Gingered Greens and Tofu
Mushrooms with Chinese Black Bean Sauce
Pad Thai
Seitan – Green Bean Curry
Sweet and Sour Peppers

FISH (ALL NONDAIRY ONLY)

Asian Fish in a Packet
Caribbean Fish in a Packet
French Fish in a Packet
Greek Fish in a Packet, without optional feta
Braised Fish with Artichoke Hearts and Red Peppers

Fish Algiers
Fish with Tomato-Orange Salsa
Teriyaki Broiled or Grilled Fish

Barbecued Tempeh and Peppers
Broiled Tofu
Bruschetta
Crostini with avocado, beans, Black Bean Dip, Olivada, Peperonata,
    Salsa Verde, onions, roasted red peppers
Pan Bagnat, without optional cheese
Pissaladière on French Bread, without optional cheese
Tofu Burritos
Italian-Style Tofu Pizza, without optional cheese

Fresh Orange Compote
Inside-Out Mango
Lemon Date Bars
Six-Minute Chocolate Cake
Strawberries Three Ways
Tropical Fruit Salad

Company's Coming

THESE RECIPES, special enough for entertaining, will let you spend less time in the kitchen and more time with your guests.

Broccoli Egg-Lemon Soup
Green Jade Soup
North African Cauliflower Soup
Portuguese White Bean Soup

Olivada
Spicy Peanut Dip

SALADS AND SIDES

Apple-Celery en Bleu
Asian Cabbage Slaw
Fennel and Orange Salad
Mushrooms in Lemon Marinade
Roasted Vegetable Salad with Garlic and Rosemary

DRESSINGS, SALSAS, AND SAUCES

Caesar Salad Dressing
Roasted Garlic Dressing
Mango Salsa
Fennel-Mustard Sauce

MAIN DISH SALADS

Antipasto Salad
Green Bean Pesto Salad
White Bean and Tomato Salad

GRAINS

North African Couscous Paella
Broiled Polenta with Mushrooms and Cheese
Caribbean Yellow Rice and Pigeon Peas
Herbed Lemon Pilaf with Almonds
Risotto with Carrots and Feta

BEANS

Caribbean Black Beans
Greek-Style Cannellini and Vegetables
Red, Gold, Black, and Green Chili

PASTAS

Pasta Tutto Giardino
Pasta with Spicy Cauliflower
Penne with Sun-Dried Tomatoes and Capers

African Pineapple Peanut Stew
Cauliflower Paprikash
Chick Pea and Artichoke Heart Stew
Green Beans and Fennel Ragout
Sicilian Seafood Stew

STIR-FRIES AND SAUTÉS

Gingered Greens and Tofu
Pad Thai
Seitan – Green Bean Curry

FISH

Caribbean Fish in a Packet
Braised Fish with Artichoke Hearts and Red Peppers
Fish with Saffron and Garlic
Greek Scampi
Teriyaki Broiled or Grilled Fish

DESSERTS

Gingered Plum Sauce
Peach Parfait with Amaretto Cream
Six-Minute Chocolate Cake

Kid-Pleasers

EVEN YOUR PICKIEST eater will enjoy these!

SOUPS

Golden Cheddar Cheese Soup
Herbed Green Pea Soup
Miso Soup

DIPS, SPREADS, AND QUICK BREADS

Mockamole
Tofu Tahini Spread

Kid-Pleasers (continued)

Yogurt Cheese
Muffin Madness

Dilly Beans
Easiest Artichokes
Easy Refritos
Shredded Zucchini
Sugar Snaps in Lemon Butter

Honey Mustard Vinaigrette
Lemon Sesame Dressing
Queso Blanco Salsa

Bulghur Burgers
Cheese Grits
Saffron Orzo
Polenta

Spaghetti with Pecorino and Black Pepper

Winter Vegetable Stew

Broiled Tofu
Simple Quesadillas
Sweet Potato Quesadillas
Tofu Burritos

Simple Frittata
Cottage Cheese Apple Pancakes
Fruit-Filled French Toast

Creamy Banana Ice
Fruit Ricotta Mousse
Fruit Shakes
Lemon Date Bars
Maple Walnut Sundae
Moosewood Fudge Brownies

Buffets

THESE DISHES sit well and so are good choices for buffet-style meals or potluck suppers.

DIPS, SPREADS, AND QUICK BREADS

Black Bean Dip
Borani and French bread
Pesto Palmiers

SALADS AND SIDES

Fennel and Orange Salad
Fresh Mozzarella and Tomato Salad

MAIN DISH SALADS

Black Beans and Rice Salad
Greek Diced Vegetable Salad
Mediterranean Potato Salad
Sweet Potato Salad

GRAINS

Apricot Bulghur Pilaf
Mediterranean Rice

STEWS

Eggplant Mykonos

STIR-FRIES

Curried Fried Rice

SANDWICHES

Crostini

EGGS

Greek Spinach Frittata

DESSERTS

Coffee Ricotta Mousse
Fresh Orange Compote
Moosewood Fudge Brownies
Tropical Fruit Salad
Yogurt Cheese Pie

Home at 6, Dinner at 6:30

FOR THOSE NIGHTS when 30 minutes is all you have.

SOUPS

Cantonese Fish and Vegetable Soup
Tomato Garlic Soup with Tortellini

SALADS AND SIDES

Sesame Spinach
Lemon Tomato Salad
Easy Elegant Asparagus
Mushrooms in Lemon Marinade
Not Your Mother's Green Beans

DRESSINGS, SALSAS, AND SAUCES

Honey Mustard Vinaigrette
Fennel-Mustard Sauce
Miso Sauce

MAIN DISH SALADS

Beans and Greens
California Dream Salad
Couscous with Artichoke Hearts and Walnuts
Udon Noodles and Vegetables
White Bean and Tomato Salad

GRAINS

Saffron Orzo
Polenta
North African Couscous Paella
Coconut Basmati Rice

BEANS

Cajun Skillet Beans
Caribbean Black Beans
Curried Chick Peas and Tofu

PASTAS

Pasta Fresca
Spaghetti with Zucchini and Lemon

STEWS

Chick Pea and Artichoke Heart Stew
Tomatican

STIR-FRIES AND SAUTÉS

Fragrant Rice Noodles with Vegetables

FISH

Braised Fish with Artichoke Hearts and Red Peppers
Greek Scampi

SANDWICHES, FILLED TORTILLAS, AND PIZZAS

Simple Quesadillas
Chile and Bell Pepper Quesadillas
Spicy Corn Quesadillas

Sweet Potato Quesadillas
Herbed Chèvre and Tomato Pizza
Italian-Style Tofu Pizza

EGGS AND PANCAKES

Asparagus with Fried Eggs and Cheese
Chakchouka
Asian-Style Frittata
Light Broccoli Frittata

DESSERTS

Baked Peaches with Marsala
Goat Cheese with Honey and Walnuts
Pears with Gorgonzola
Sautéed Bananas
Strawberries Three Ways

Quantities

Recipes that we feel require specific amounts of vegetable or other ingredients have a measured or weight quantity listed, such as "1 cup chopped onions" or "10 ounces spinach." Other ingredients that needn't be as exactly measured are listed as, for example, "1 medium carrot" or "1 large eggplant."

Here's what we mean when we say "1 medium…":

Item	Amount Prepared	Approximate Weight
VEGETABLES AND FRUITS (RAW)		
Apple (1 medium)	1 cup, chopped	4 ounces
Avocado (1 medium)	1 cup, mashed	8 ounces
Banana (1 medium)	¾ cup, sliced	8 ounces
Broccoli (1 stalk)	2 cups florets	6 ounces
Cabbage (1 large)	10 cups, minced	1 pound, 12 ounces
Cantaloupe (1 medium)	4 cups, peeled and cubed	2½ pounds
Carrots (2 medium)	1 cup, diced	8 ounces
Cauliflower (1 medium)	2½ cups florets	1 pound
Celery (3 stalks)	1 cup, diced	8 ounces
Eggplant (1 medium)	4 cups, cubed	14 ounces
Green beans	1 cup	5 ounces
Green peas, shelled	1 cup	5 ounces
Green peas, unshelled	1 cup, shelled	1 pound
Green pepper (1 medium)	¾ cup, diced	4½ ounces
Leek (1 medium)	¾ cup, diced	3 ounces

Item	Amount Prepared	Approximate Weight
Lemon (1 medium)	2 tablespoons juice	
	1 tablespoon grated peel	
Mango (1 medium)	1 cup, peeled and cubed	1 pound
Mushrooms	1 cup, sliced	3–4 ounces
Onion (1 medium)	1 cup, diced	4 ounces
Orange (1 medium)	½ cup juice	
	2 tablespoons grated peel	
Parsley (1 bunch)	3½ cups, chopped	4 ounces
Pineapple (1 medium)	4 cups, peeled and cubed	3½ pounds (whole)
Potato (1 medium)	2 cups, diced	8 ounces
	1¼ cups, mashed	8 ounces
Spinach (fresh)	12 cups, loosely packed	10 ounces
Tomato (1 medium)	¾ cup, diced	4½ ounces
Canned tomatoes	3 cups with juice	28-ounce can
	1½ cups drained	28-ounce can
Winter squash (1 medium)	4 cups, cubed	1 pound, 4 ounces
Zucchini (1 medium)	2 cups, diced	10 ounces

CHEESES

Item	Amount Prepared	Approximate Weight
Bleu	1 cup	2 ounces
Cheddar	1 cup	3 ounces
Feta	1 cup	5 ounces
Gorgonzola	1 cup	2 ounces
Monterey Jack	1 cup	3 ounces
Mozzarella	1 cup	4 ounces
Muenster	1 cup	3 ounces
Parmesan	1 cup	3 ounces
Provolone	1 cup	4 ounces
Swiss or Jarlsberg	1 cup	3½–4 ounces

Item	Amount Prepared	Approximate Weight
	NUTS (WHOLE)	
Almonds	1 cup	8 ounces
Cashews	1 cup	6 ounces
Walnuts	1 cup	6 ounces
	SPROUTS	
Alfalfa	1 cup	¾ ounce
Mung bean	1 cup	2 ounces
	OTHER	
Currants (dried)	1 cup	5 ounces
Raisins	1 cup	6 ounces
Tofu (1 cake)	2 cups, ¼-inch cubes	12 ounces
	UTENSILS	
Skillets:		
small	6 inches	
medium	9 inches	
large	12 inches	
Saucepan:		
small – medium	2 quarts	
large	3 quarts	
Soup pot or kettle	4 quarts	
Dutch oven	6 quarts	

Liquid and Dry Measure Equivalencies

CUSTOMARY	METRIC
¼ teaspoon	1.25 milliliters
½ teaspoon	2.5 milliliters
1 teaspoon	5 milliliters
1 tablespoon	15 milliliters
1 fluid ounce	30 milliliters
¼ cup	60 milliliters

Liquid and Dry Measure Equivalencies (continued)

CUSTOMARY	METRIC
⅓ cup	80 milliliters
½ cup	120 milliliters
1 cup	240 milliliters
1 pint (2 cups)	480 milliliters
1 quart (4 cups; 32 ounces)	960 milliliters (.96 liter)
1 gallon (4 quarts)	3.84 liters
1 ounce (by weight)	28 grams
¼ pound (4 ounces)	114 grams
1 pound (16 ounces)	454 grams
2.2 pounds	1 kilogram (1,000 grams)

Oven Temperature Equivalents

DESCRIPTION	°FAHRENHEIT	°CELSIUS
Cool	200	90
Very slow	250	120
Slow	300 – 325	150 – 160
Moderately slow	325 – 350	160 – 180
Moderate	350 – 375	180 – 190
Moderately hot	375 – 400	190 – 200
Hot	400 – 450	200 – 230
Very hot	450 – 500	230 – 260

Index

avgolemono (egg-lemon soup)
   with broccoli, 24
avocado, 387
   corn salad, 119
   mockamole, 48
   ripening of, 119

baked peaches with Marsala,
   306
baking, 353
   more than one item, 369
balsamic vinegar, 344
banana(s), 387
   cornmeal pancakes, 298
   ice, creamy, 308
   muffins, 55
   sautéed, 320
   shake, 311
   tropical fruit salad, 324
barbecued tempeh and peppers,
   260
bars, lemon date, 315
basil, 329
   Dijon butter, 365
   freezing, 361
   pasta fresca, 184
   pesto, 130
   pesto Genovese, 362
   salsa verde, 105
   tofu dressing, 100
   vinegar, 362
basmati rice, 141, 340
   coconut, 155
   cooking, 357
   pilaf with dates and almonds,
      160
bay leaf, 329
bean(s), 165–76, 329–30
   black-eyed peas with spinach,
      166
   Cajun skillet, 167
   canned, 165
   Caribbean yellow rice and
      pigeon peas, 154

cooking extra amounts of,
   367, 368
curried vegetables with dahl,
   206
dried, cooking, 354–55
easy refritos, 79
field peas with kale and sweet
   potatoes, 170
gigondes, 69
Greek-style cannellini and
   vegetables, 172
and greens, 120
Honolulu skillet, 174
Mediterranean lentil salad,
   131
nondairy and vegan, 377
pantry list for, 326
pasta with endive and, 185
pressure cooking, 352
red, gold, black, and green
   chili, 175
red lentil soup, 36
soaking, 354, 355
suitable for entertaining,
   380
tangy limas with squash and
   tomatoes, 176
for 30-minute dinner
   preparation, 385
tomatican, 216
white, soup, Portuguese, 34
white, and tomato salad,
   137
see also black bean(s); chick-
   pea(s); green bean(s)
bean curd, see tofu
Beano, 330
bean sprouts:
   quantities of, 389
   stir-frying, 354
beet greens:
   preparing, 349
   spicy, 88
beets, preparing, 348

berries:
   preparing, 350
   see also specific berries
biscuits, savory scallion, 58
bisque, shrimp, 37
black bean(s):
   Caribbean, 168
   dip, 46
   easy refritos, 79
   red, gold, black, and green
      chili, 175
   and rice salad, 121
   soup, 23
black bean(s), Chinese
   fermented, 332
   sauce, mushrooms with, 234
black-eyed peas:
   Cajun skillet beans, 167
   with spinach, 166
black pepper, 330
   spaghetti with pecorino and,
      194
blanching, 351
blueberry:
   cornmeal pancakes, 298
   lemon muffins, 55
   multigrain muffins, 56
   ricotta mousse, 310
blue cheese, 388
   in apple-celery en bleu, 63
boiling, 351
bok choy:
   Asian fish in a packet, 244
   gingered greens and tofu, 232
   green jade soup, 28
   miso soup, 31
   stir-fried hijiki and, 89
   stir-frying, 354
borani, 47
bouillon powders and cubes, 330
braised fish with artichoke hearts
   and red peppers, 248
braising, 352
bran, in multigrain muffins, 56

cabbage (cont'd)
  Tunisian vegetable stew, 217
  see also bok choy
Caesar salad, 122
Caesar salad dressing, 94
Cajun-style dishes:
  skillet beans, 167
  spicy shrimp, 255
cake, six-minute chocolate, 322
Calamata olives, 338
California dream salad, 123
calories, 16
  percentage of, from fats, 17
canned goods, pantry list for, 327
cannellini:
  beans and greens, 120
  Greek-style vegetables and, 172
  pasta with endive and, 185
  and tomato salad, 137
cantaloupe, 387
  tropical fruit salad, 324
Cantonese fish and vegetable soup, 25
capers, 330
  penne with sun-dried tomatoes and, 190
carbohydrates, 16, 17
cardamom, 330
Caribbean-style dishes:
  black beans, 168
  fish in a packet, 245
  vegetable stew, 201
  yellow rice and pigeon peas, 154
carrot(s), 387
  Asian cabbage slaw, 64
  and broccoli with lime dressing, 73
  broiling or grilling, 352
  Cantonese fish and vegetable soup, 25
  dressing, Japanese, 125

Greek-style cannellini and vegetables, 172
green jade soup, 28
menestra, 210
pad Thai, 236
and parsley salad, 65
pasta tutto giardino, 186
Peruvian quinoa stew, 212
preparing, 349
risotto with feta and, 161
stir-frying, 354
winter vegetable stew, 220
cashews, 389
casseroles:
  dishes for, 369
  rice and beans with queso blanco salsa, 104
catfish, Chesapeake, 249
catsup, 330–31
cauliflower, 387
  curried, 75
  curried vegetables with dahl, 206
  paprikash, 202
  soup, North African, 33
  spicy, pasta with, 189
  stir-frying, 354
cavatelli with broccoli rabe, 181
cayenne, 331
celery, 387
  apple en bleu, 63
  mushroom Parmesan salad, 133
  stir-frying, 354
chakchouka, 288
chard:
  preparing, 349
  spicy, 88
  tomato garlic soup with, 42
  see also Swiss chard
cheddar cheese, 331, 388
  chile and bell pepper quesadillas, 270
  grits, 147

smoked, in broiled polenta with mushrooms and cheese, 152
soup, golden, 27
spicy corn quesadillas, 271
sweet potato quesadillas, 272
cheese, 331
  asparagus with fried eggs and, 287
  blue, in apple-celery en bleu, 63
  broiled polenta with mushrooms and, 152
  cheddar soup, golden, 27
  chèvre and red peppers omelet, 289
  chile and bell pepper quesadillas, 270
  cottage, apple pancakes, 299
  cottage, in garlic dressing, 124
  feta, in borani, 47
  feta, in Greek pasta salad, 128
  feta, in Greek pita, 265
  feta, in Greek rice pilaf, 157
  feta, in Greek spinach frittata, 291
  feta, risotto with carrots and, 161
  feta spinach pizza, 276
  Fontina zucchini pizza, 281
  garlic and greens pizza, 277
  goat, with honey and walnuts, 313
  Gorgonzola with pears, 319
  grating, 348
  grits, 147
  herbed chèvre and tomato pizza, 278
  mozzarella and tomato salad, 68
  nondairy substitutes for, 331
  pan bagnat, 266
  Parmesan mushroom celery salad, 133

herb(ed)(s) (*cont'd*)
oils, 361
pantry list for, 327
pestos, 362–63
tomato dressing, 124
vinegars, 344, 362
see also specific herbs
herb butters, 364–65
basil-Dijon, 365
dill-scallion, 364
lemon-mint, 364
sage-thyme, 365
savory garlic, 364
hijiki, 335
stir-fried bok choy and, 89
hoisin sauce, 174, 336
honey:
goat cheese with walnuts and, 313
mustard vinaigrette, 97
Honolulu skillet beans, 174
hot sauces, 342

ice, creamy banana, 308
ice cream, 304–5
with gingered plum sauce, 312
maple walnut sundae, 316
with sautéed bananas, 320
Indian-style dishes:
curried chick peas and tofu, 169
curried vegetables with dahl, 206
shredded zucchini, 87
ingredients, 329–45
quantities of, 387–90
inside-out mango, 314
Italian-style dishes:
antipasto salad, 118
asparagus with fried eggs and cheese, 287
baked peaches with Marsala, 306
beans and greens, 120

bruschetta and crostini, 262
peperonata, 83
polenta, 150
risotto with carrots and feta, 161
risotto with green beans and pesto, 162
seasoned tempeh, 85
shredded zucchini, 87
Sicilian seafood stew, 214
simple frittata, 292
see also pasta; pizzas

Japanese-style dishes:
carrot dressing, 125
miso sauce, 113
miso soup, 31
noodles with mirin, 32
Jarlsberg cheese, 388

kale:
African pineapple peanut stew, 200
field peas with sweet potatoes and, 170
garlic and greens pizza, 277
gingered greens and tofu, 232
green jade soup, 28
preparing, 349
spicy, 88
stir-frying, 354
tomato garlic soup with, 42
kasha (buckwheat groats), 141, 330
cooking, 356
with mushrooms, 148
kid-pleasers, 381–83
broiled tofu, 261
bulghur burgers, 144
cheese grits, 147
cottage cheese apple pancakes, 299
creamy banana ice, 308
dilly beans, 66

easiest artichokes, 77
easy refritos, 79
fruit-filled French toast, 297
fruit ricotta mousse, 310
fruit shakes, 311
golden cheddar cheese soup, 27
herbed green pea soup, 29
honey mustard vinaigrette, 97
lemon date bars, 315
lemon sesame dressing, 98
maple walnut sundae, 316
miso soup, 31
mockamole, 48
Moosewood fudge brownies, 317
muffin madness, 54
polenta, 150
queso blanco salsa, 104
saffron orzo, 149
shredded zucchini, 87
simple frittata, 292
simple quesadillas, 268
spaghetti with pecorino and black pepper, 194
sugar snaps in lemon butter, 90
sweet potato quesadillas, 272
tofu burritos, 273
tofu tahini spread, 51
winter vegetable stew, 220
yogurt cheese, 52
kiwi, in tropical fruit salad, 324
knives, 347

leek(s), 387
fragrant rice noodles with vegetables, 228
green jade soup, 28
preparing, 350
stir-frying, 354
leftovers, 367–68
grains, 141
with pasta, 180

Who or What Is the Moosewood Collective?

No one is quite sure what to say. When asked, most members just laugh with a kind of knowing chuckle and say, "Good question." Answering the question is a lot like taking a snapshot of a dancer: you capture an image but not the dance. Even so, a few accurate observations of the Moosewood Collective may be possible.

The Moosewood Collective is a group of eighteen people (four men and fourteen women) who own and operate Moosewood Restaurant, founded in 1973 in Ithaca, New York. They work together in all facets of the business and cooperate in recipe testing and writing the cookbooks that issue from their work at the restaurant and their personal experience. Regular meetings to discuss, inform, compare ideas, propose solutions to problems, and decide anything and everything form the backbone of their organization. Good food and flexible fair working conditions are their raison d'être. Together they work to foster a spirit of friendship and generosity, which helps to harmonize any differing opinions, personalities, and objectives. Honesty, using obstacles as challenges, and patiently awaiting moments of creative inspiration are everyday practices.

All the members of the Moosewood Collective are quite active in the community as well as in the restaurant. Among them are artists, calligraphers, architects, schoolteachers, dancers, musicians, dispute-resolution mediators, gardeners, martial artists, health care advocates, avid cyclists, and outreach volunteers. They are a busy bunch.

Here are a few of the vital statistics always required by investigators. The Moosewood Collective has a collective age of 786 years, weighs 2,527 pounds, is raising 16 children, and is caring for 19 cats, 8 dogs, and numerous goats, hamsters, and fish. They represent at least 5 different "spiritual" inclinations and share among them over a dozen ethnicities. Not one of them drives a 1993 car, although all of them do drive. Their collective IQ is still in question, since no one has determined how to verify a group's IQ yet. Still, they don't seem too worried to be without one.

By coincidence, 10 members have children, 10 members have worked together for more than 10 years, 10 members have worked extensively on this book, and no group of 10 mentioned is exactly the same. But just for the record, the 10 main contributors to this cookbook were Laura Branca, Linda Dickinson, Susan Harville, David Hirsch, Nancy Lazarus, Sara Robbins, Wynelle Stein, Maureen Vivino, Thomas Walls, and Kathleen Wilcox.